This High and Holy Moment
The First National Woman's Rights Convention, Worcester, 1850

This High and Holy Moment
The First National Woman's Rights Convention, Worcester, 1850

John F. McClymer
Assumption College

HARCOURT BRACE COLLEGE PUBLISHERS

Fort Worth   Philadephia   San Diego   New York   Orlando   Austin   San Antonio
Toronto   Montreal   London   Sydney   Tokyo

Publisher	Earl McPeek
Acquisitions Editor	David Tatom
Product Manager	Steve Drummond
Developmental Editor	Margaret McAndrew Beasley
Project Editor	Laura J. Hanna
Art Directors	Vicki Whistler and Susan Journey
Production Manager	Serena Barnett

Cover and p. 8 credit: Illustration from "We'll Show you when we come to Vote," sheet music: song and chorus by Frank Howard, published by W. W. Whitney's "Palace of Music," Toledo, Ohio (1869).

ISBN: 0-15-507941-7
Library of Congress Catalog Card Number: 98-89230

Photos 01–06 (p. 11) and Photos 08–12 (p. 185); Courtesy American Antiquarian Society.

Address for Domestic Orders
Harcourt Brace College Publishers, 6277 Sea Harbor Drive, Orlando, FL 32887-6777
800-782-4479

Address for International Orders
International Customer Service
Harcourt Brace & Company, 6277 Sea Harbor Drive, Orlando, FL 32887-6777
407-345-3800
(fax) 407-345-4060
(e-mail) hbintl@harcourtbrace.com

Address for Editorial Correspondence
Harcourt Brace College Publishers, 301 Commerce Street, Suite 3700, Fort Worth, TX 76102

Web Site Address
http://www.hbcollege.com

Harcourt Brace College Publishers will provide complimentary supplements or supplement packages to those adopters qualified under our adoption policy. Please contact your sales representative to learn how you qualify. If as an adopter or potential user you receive supplements you do not need, please return them to your sales representative or send them to: Attn: Returns Department, Troy Warehouse, 465 South Lincoln Drive, Troy, MO 63379.

Printed in the United States of America

8 9 0 1 2 3 4 5 6 7   039   9 8 7 6 5 4 3 2 1

Harcourt Brace College Publishers

To the members of the Worcester Women's History Project—
Colleagues and Friends

Preface

The Story Behind the Series

On April 2, 1911 a little-known industrial disaster, a fire, killed several workers at the Gypsy Grove mine near Scranton, Pennsylvania. A locomotive was hauling coal to the top of the breaker, the several-story structure where the coal was "broken" into baseball-sized lumps, when a spark from its smokestack leaped onto some paper. Within seconds the fire spread to the coal-dust-saturated wooden frame of the breaker which went up, in the words of the only survivor, "like a giant kitchen match." One of those killed was the checkweigh man, the union official who certified the tonnage credited to each miner. His name was John Earley. As the flames enveloped him, he cried out "Mary!"—the name of his five-year-old daughter.

More than three decades later, Mary McClymer, née Mary Earley, gave birth to a son whom she called John. What she sought in giving me her father's name—what we all seek when we inscribe births, deaths, and marriages so carefully into family Bibles or save photographs of our grandparents to show our grandchildren—was to affirm that our lives extend backward to people we have never seen and forward to people who will never see us but will know that we lived and that our living mattered. She sought what we all seek: meaning in the stories of history.

The American Stories Series

American Stories is a series of documentary readers, each devoted to some salient event in American history. Each brings together evidence about some of those whose lives mattered in the making of our common story. In each the goal is to enable students to use the evidence gathered to construct their own version of that story, to determine what happened, to decide who did what and why, and, most of all, to enable them to see for themselves why and how those lives mattered. The goal is to enable students to discover the fascination of "doing" history.

The Story behind This Volume

Lisa Connelly Cook had a question. She was, at the time (1995) taking courses at Clark University in Worcester, Massachusetts, including one on Women's History, and had run across a reference to the first national woman's rights convention which had met in Worcester in 1850. "This sounds like it might have been important. How come I never heard of it before?" It was important, and she was in good company in having never heard of it. All of the standard accounts jump from the Seneca Falls Convention of 1848 to Elizabeth Cady Stanton's and Susan B. Anthony's campaigns in New York for women's property and child custody rights in the latter half of the 1850s. Then they follow women's roles in the Civil War before recounting the split in the woman's movement in the immediate postwar years over the issue of enfranchising black *males*.

Lisa was not satisfied. "Where did the movement come from? I mean it had to *develop* before it could *split*, didn't it?" In point of fact, as she well knew, there was a growing scholarly literature on the roots of the movement in religious societies, moral uplift campaigns such as those against prostitution and for temperance, and other organizations of the 1830s. It was in these that women first began to claim a public role for themselves. By the end of the decade women like Angelina Grimké and Abby Kelley had achieved such prominence in the crusade against slavery that abolitionists divided over the propriety of women speaking in public before "promiscuous" audiences, i.e., those with both women and men. In 1840 the World Anti-Slavery Convention in London refused to permit female delegates from the United States to participate, a snub, according to Elizabeth Cady Stanton, that convinced her and Lucretia Mott that women needed a movement of their own.

"Well, didn't that movement *start* in Seneca Falls in 1848? And, if it did, why is the Worcester Convention of 1850 important?" It all depends upon what you mean by start. Certainly the 1848 Declaration of Sentiments adopted at Seneca Falls occasioned a lot of controversy. So did reports of other regional gatherings, including one in Ohio in 1850 at which only women were permitted to speak. But, was there a constituency out there ready to rally behind the banner of woman's rights? No one really knew. And that is why Abby Kelley, Lucy Stone, Paulina Wright Davis, and several others decided to find out by issuing an open "Call" to a convention in Worcester in the fall of 1850. If enough people answered the "Call," and if they could agree upon a series of practical steps, it would be possible to organize a woman's rights movement. If only a handful came, as abolitionist and woman's rights advocate William Lloyd Garrison and not a few others who signed the "Call" feared, then they would at least have the satisfaction of getting together with some old friends.

Because the Convention showed that there was a national, even an international, constituency for woman's rights and that the activists could agree upon a series of practical next steps, an organized movement grew out of it. This is why, in 1870, Elizabeth Cady Stanton and Lucretia Mott called a Twentieth Anniversary Convention in New York City. It is why Stanton nominated Paulina Wright Davis, who presided over the 1850 Convention, to preside over that of 1870.

"So," Lisa Cook said thoughtfully, "it is up to us to reclaim for the Worcester Convention its proper place." Now a Ph.D. candidate at Clark, she has more than done her part by founding the Worcester Women's History Project, a grassroots organization that is organizing a reenactment of the 1850 meeting on the occasion of its 150th anniversary in 2000 and a contemporary convention to assess where the women's movement stands on the brink of the new millennium. This book is my part.

Acknowledgments

Many people helped bring this project to fruition, starting with Drake Bush, then history acquisitions editor at Harcourt Brace College Publishers, whose patience, tact, and support helped launch "American Stories." This book would not exist, had Angela Dorenkamp, my long-time colleague and sometime collaborator, not introduced me to the small band who was starting the Worcester Women's History Project and, especially, to Lisa Connelly Cook, the real founder of the

WWHP. It was she who first sparked my interest in the 1850 Convention. Most of the research was carried out at the American Antiquarian Society. I would like to thank Joanne Chaison, chief librarian; Tom Knoles, curator of manuscripts; and Georgia Barnhill, curator of graphic materials. Laura Wasowicz's expertise on children's literature and songs proved essential.

Once again Carol Maksian, chief research librarian at Assumption College, and her staff, particularly Amanda Nelson and Larry Spongberg, went well beyond the call of duty to help. Many friends and colleagues shared their ideas and reactions. Among these Lisa Connelly Cook and Gerd Korman were especially helpful. Lucia Knoles gave generously of her time and friendship, even to the point of sharing her own research into mid-nineteenth-century American culture. I would also like to thank the following reviewers whose comments on the manuscript did so much to improve it: Stacy A. Cordery, Monmouth College; Eileen Eagan, University of Southern Maine; B. Jane England, North Central Texas College; Michael S. Mayer, University of Montana; Thomas Schoonover, University of Southwestern Louisiana. Thanks as well to David Tatom, senior acquisitions editor, and Margaret McAndrew Beasley, developmental editor at Harcourt Brace, for their many suggestions and support. With the assistance of a National Endowment for the Humanities Focus Grant, Assumption College, the American Antiquarian Society, the Worcester Women's History Project, and the Alliance for Education, a non-profit professional development agency for Central Massachusetts, sponsored a workshop for teachers, grades 5–12, on "Women's History and the Web" which I co-directed, with James Moran, director of outreach at the AAS. The participants' comments and criticisms of the materials collected here have been most valuable. I would also like to express my gratitude to my students in History 213: Women in the American Experience, upon whom I tested an early version of this book. One of them, Sabrina Zadrozny, received a grant from the Assumption College Student Government Association for the summer of 1998 to help me organize the final workshop presentations and post them to the Web. Her work has gone far beyond that. Finally, to all those who visited the Worcester Women's History Project Web site, asked questions, offered suggestions, and demonstrated through their interest the salience of this story, I want you to know how much I have benefited from your comments.

Contents

Prologue

A t half-past ten o'clock on Friday morning [October 19, 1870] the convention assembled at Apollo Hall. A large number of the long-tried friends were on the platform and a fine audience in attendance. Mrs. [Elizabeth Cady] Stanton called the meeting to order and read the call.

WOMAN SUFFRAGE CELEBRATION

The Twentieth Anniversary of the Inauguration of the Woman Suffrage Movement in this country will be celebrated in Apollo Hall, in the city of New York, on the 19th and 20th of October, 1870.

The movement in England, as in America, may be dated from the first National Convention, held at Worcester, Mass., October, 1850.

The July following that Convention, a favorable criticism of its proceedings and an able digest of the whole question appeared in the *Westminster Review*, written by Mrs. John Stuart Mill [Harriet Taylor], which awakened attention in both hemispheres. In the call for that convention, the following subjects for discussion were presented: Woman's Right to Education, *Literary*, *Scientific*, and *Artistic*; Her Avocations, *Industrial*, *Commercial* and *Professional*; Her Interests, *Pecuniary*, *Civil* and *Political*: In a word, Her Rights as an *Individual*, and her Functions as a *Citizen*.

. . . We specially invite the presence of those just awakening to an interest in this great movement, that from a knowledge of the past they may draw fresh inspiration for the work of the future and fraternize with a generation now rapidly passing away.

As those who inaugurated a reform, so momentous and far reaching in its consequences, held themselves above all party considerations and personal antagonisms, and as this gathering is to be in no way connected with either of our leading Woman Suffrage organizations,

we hope that the friends of real progress everywhere will come together and unitedly celebrate this twentieth anniversary of a great national movement for freedom.

Committee of Arrangements. Lucretia Mott, Sarah Pugh, Elizabeth C.
Stanton, Ernestine L. Rose, Samuel J. May, C. I. H. Nichols.
On behalf of the Committee,
PAULINA W. DAVIS, Chairman.*

** A History of the National Woman's Rights Movement, for Twenty Years, with the Proceedings of the
Decade Meeting Held at Apollo Hall, October 20, 1870, from 1850 to 1870. With an appendix containing
the history of the movement during the Winter of 1871, in the National Capitol.* Compiled by Paulina W.
Davis (New York: Journeymen Printers' Co-operative Association, 1871).

Introduction: "The Upward Tending Spirit of the Age"

In 1870, at the Twentieth Anniversary National Woman's Rights Convention, Paulina Wright Davis, who presided over the first two conventions in addition to the twentieth, said:

> Were I to go back of these [first] conventions, to see what had roused women thus to do and dare, I should be obliged to go into a long history of the despotism of repression, which German jurists call "soul murder," an unwritten code, universal and cruel as the laws of Draco,[1] and so subtle that, entering everywhere, they weigh most heavily where least seen.

Davis's words are worth pondering. Although largely unknown today, she did as much as any other individual to launch the woman's rights movement. As the *Call* to the 1870 gathering noted, "the movement in England, as in America, may be dated from the first National Convention, held at Worcester, Mass., October, 1850" which she had organized. Elizabeth Cady Stanton, one of the authors of the *Call*, observed in nominating Davis to chair the convention, "as Mrs. Davis had called the first National Convention twenty years ago, and presided over its deliberations, it was peculiarly fitting that she should preside over this also."

Stanton's motion was approved unanimously, and Davis opened the convention by reading a "History" of the National Woman's Suffrage Movement. After she finished, Stanton again took the podium.

---

[1] Athenian ruler whose code (c. 621 B.C.) made most crimes punishable by death. His successor, Solon, repealed all of the Draconian measures except those applying to murder.

She "thought Mrs. Davis, in her modesty, had not done justice to herself; her work commenced before any of the woman's rights conventions were held.

> Mrs. Davis took an active part . . . in the early movements for "Moral Reform," and was a contributor to *McDowall's Journal* and *Woman's Advocate*, which were published for many years. She established too the first woman's rights paper ever published in the country, *The Una*, in January, 1852. In looking over the pages of this paper it is surprising to see how perfectly the leaders of this movement understood all the bearings of this question, and with what boldness they followed the truth in all directions, in the consideration of woman's social as well as political wrongs. I state these facts in regard to Mrs. Davis, that our report, which is to be published, may do full justice to all.

Paulina Wright Davis, however unknown today, was with Lucretia Mott, Abby Kelley Foster, Lucy Stone, Susan B. Anthony, and Elizabeth Cady Stanton, one of the founding mothers of the woman's moment. Her views, in consequence, are to be reckoned with. And she insisted that a key to understanding why she and other pioneers were "roused" to "do and dare" was their frustration with that "unwritten code, universal and cruel as the laws of Draco, and so subtle that, entering everywhere, they weigh most heavily where least seen." Their quarrel was with a "repression" that amounted to "soul murder."

Some of what she had in mind we know. Wives could not own property, could not even dispose of their own earnings. All belonged to the husband, as did the children. "Mrs. C.I.H. Nichols, of Vermont," Davis recalled, "made a profound impression" at the 1851 Convention. "There was a touching, tender pathos in her stories" of women trapped by the law's insistence that in marriage man and wife are one and that one the husband "which went home to the heart; and many eyes, all unused to tears, were moistened as she described the agony of the mother robbed of her child by the law." A wife with an abusive husband, Nichols and other early activists protested, had no recourse but to submit or flee. Her situation, as Ernestine Rose pointed out at the 1850 Worcester Convention, exactly paralleled that of the fugitive slave: The law recognized the husband's "right" to use "moderate" force to discipline his wife and children as well as his slave, and he could enlist public authorities in tracking both down if they tried to escape.

Women's situation was no better when it came to religion, education, employment, or other public spheres. For many early woman's rights advocates the position taken by leading ministers rankled most. "We must turn," Davis observed in 1870, "to the discussions in the churches as to the right and propriety of [women] speaking and praying in public" in order to see one of the chief provocations to the new movement. "The controversy there waxed hot, churches were divided, presbyteries were disturbed, Paul and Christ were made to appear antagonistic." Davis and many of her cohorts felt they had reached a turning point, that "women must choose between the freedom which Christ gave to all, or accept the false interpretation of priestly arrogance." One can hear that "arrogance" in the words of the General Association of Congregational Ministers of Massachusetts in 1838:

> The appropriate duties and influence of women, are clearly stated in the New Testament. Those duties and that influence are unobtrusive and private. . . . The power of woman is in her dependence, flowing from the consciousness of that weakness which God has given her for her protection and which keeps her in those departments of life that form the character of individuals and of the nation.

The Association went on to criticize those women "who so far forget themselves as to itinerate in the character of public lecturers and teachers" such as Abby Kelley Foster, the antislavery activist, who would play a leading role in the 1850 Convention. Lecturing on behalf of abolition was not, for the Association, the worst of it:

> We especially deplore the intimate acquaintance and promiscuous conversation of females with regard to things "which ought not to be named"; by which that modesty and delicacy which is the charm of domestic life, and which constitute the true influence of women in society are consumed, and the way opened, as we apprehend, for degeneracy and ruin.

Historians have yet to appreciate just how central their concern over the so-called social evil was to the thinking of early woman's rights activists. Prostitution was not a new problem in mid-nineteenth-century America, but contemporaries were convinced it was becoming worse as thousands of young men and women streamed into the rapidly growing cities away from the traditional moral influences of family, church, and neighbors. What the Congregational Ministers of Massachusetts, and the many others who shared their views, objected to was that respectable women should even publicly acknowledge that they knew such things existed, much less that they should actively campaign to eliminate the "social evil."

Making matters even worse was the fact that the leaders of the Magdalen movement, as the women who sought to rescue prostitutes styled their crusade, saw prostitution as more a matter of economic duress and sexual exploitation than moral collapse. Caroline Wells Healey Dall, for example, wrote a public letter to Paulina Wright Davis in the wake of the 1850 Convention to commend the willingness of the delegates to speak openly on the subject. Wells summarized the reformers' views:

> In every large city, there is a class of women, whose existence is a terror and reproach to the land in which they are born; whose name no modest woman is supposed to know; whose very breath is thought to poison the air of the sanctuary. I pass over the fact, so generally ignored, that there is a class of men corresponding to these women, and far viler in the sight of God, I doubt not. . . . I know that many whom I love will blame me bitterly for speaking on this subject at all, but that blame I must bear as God permits, for I feel bound to draw your attention to a few facts. Whatever elevates woman will diminish this class; but proper remuneration for her labor would draw many from it at once, almost all, in fact, who had not reached the lowest deep.

"Most women," Dall continued, "suppose that these miserable creatures are always the victims of their own bad natures, or want of principle; that they find their life a life of pleasure, and that they would not forsake it if they could, unless under the influence of religious conviction." There were some, Dall conceded, "who are born to this life as naturally and inevitably as the robin is born to cleave the air. Of such are foundlings, orphans, and the children of the extremely poor, whose habits of lodging are fatal to modesty, in most instances." The large majority, however, "began life honestly, but were compelled to sell themselves for bread. Of such are young exposed persons afraid to die, widows with large families dependent upon them, and single women burdened with the care of the infirm or aged." Further, when given a chance "to earn what is called an *honest* livelihood," many "leave this wretched life for months together."

An *honest* livelihood would only be possible if women could enter the same professions as men and earn the same wages. This was as true for women who expected to marry as it was for the woman of the streets, activists maintained. Because marriage was an economic necessity for most women, their situation could easily resemble that of a "kept woman." As Horace Greeley put it in an editorial reprinted here, "Marriage is indeed 'honorable in all,' when it *is* marriage; but accepting a husband for the sake of a position, a home and a support, is not marriage. (We must be excused from stating what it *is*.)"

Yet, even as we enumerate the visible restrictions under which women struggled, Davis reminds us that more "subtle" and invisible limitations cut even more deeply. How does a historian, coming along a century and a half and more afterward, see that which weighs "most heavily where least seen"? How does she or he spell out an "unwritten code"? Only by casting one's net as widely as space permits.

Seeing clearly what is usually "least seen" merely suggests the challenges we face as we seek to understand the origins of the woman's rights movement. It takes more than "repression" to provoke either rebellion or reform. Otherwise, as Leon Trotsky pointed out in his *The Russian Revolution*, human history would be a virtually unbroken record of insurrection. It is not, Trotsky went on, because most of the time the oppressed accept their lot in life or, perhaps, trust that wrongs suffered in this life will be reversed in that to come. They only rebel when they perceive their sufferings to be unnecessary and, Trotsky added, when they perceive the institutions that support repression as weak.[2] Insurrections begin with hope as well as with outrage.

We can catch a glimpse of this sense of hope in the official *Call* to the convention: "The upward tending spirit of the age, busy in a hundred forms of effort for the world's redemption from the sins and sufferings which oppress it, has brought" the "great question of Woman's Rights, Duties, and Relations . . . into distinguished prominence." Historians have long struggled to define the "spirit of the age." We can identify most, if not all, of the "hundred forms" of effort to which the *Call* referred. These include especially the crusades for abolition and for temperance but also the campaigns for universal public schooling, for more "natural" ways of life, including such practices as vegetarianism, and for more "natural" forms of medicine like the "water cure." There were also a wide array of moral reforms ranging from ending the delivery of mail on Sundays to discouraging the use of profanity in public.

---

[2] Leon Trotsky, *The Russian Revolution: The Overthrow of Tzarism and The Triumph of the Soviets*, selected and edited by F. W. Dupree (New York, 1959), p. 249.

There was, as Alice Felt Tyler wrote, "a ferment for reform," a sense of possibility. The extraordinary optimism of the North in mid-century runs through the *Call:*

> The signs are encouraging; the time is opportune. Come, then, to this Convention. It is your duty, if you are worthy of your age and country. Give the help of your best thought to separate the light from the darkness. Wisely give the protection of your name and the benefit of your efforts to the great work of settling the principles, devising the method, and achieving the success of this high and holy moment.

Optimism on so grand a scale that an entire generation shares the conviction that it was "settling first principles" and dividing "the light from the darkness," this is the mindset that fuels revolutions. Where did it come from? Certainly from something more than the very limited successes of ongoing reform movements.

Abolition had gained adherents throughout the North since its inception twenty years before. It won a victory in the Compromise of 1850 which abolished the slave trade in the District of Columbia. On the other hand, the Compromise also included a new Fugitive Slave Law which required local law enforcement officials to cooperate actively in the apprehension and return of escaped slaves. Certainly outrage over the Fugitive Slave Law far outweighed any satisfaction arising from the ending of the slave trade in the nation's capital.[3]

Temperance too had gained strength, particularly among the educated and the middle classes generally. No longer was liquor an unquestioned part of business or social gatherings. Indeed, sobriety was rapidly becoming an essential mark of respectability. But the influence of "demon rum" was still great, and temperance advocates were starting to turn to the power of the state to enforce their reform.[4]

Other reforms had achieved similarly mixed results. Thousands joined the organizations that historians sometimes call the "benevolent empire," societies to make the Bible available to all, to support Protestant missionaries at home and abroad, to distribute religious tracts on city streets, to organize Sunday schools, to discourage the use of tobacco and of spitting in public, and hosts of other noble ends. Yet few believed that the forces of "light" were on the verge of

---

[3] Virtually all abolitionists denounced the Compromise. Most saw it as further evidence of the constantly expanding power of the slave states.

[4] This was the so-called Maine Law which prohibited the manufacture and sale of intoxicating liquors.

overthrowing those of "darkness." Clearly the optimism of those who launched the woman's rights movement drew upon more than a tallying up of these triumphs and setbacks.

Their optimism rested on the widely held sense that their generation was witnessing the overthrow of restraints on human achievement that were as old as humanity itself and that the most basic institutions of society were, in the process, being reshaped. The telegraph and the railroad had annihilated space. Steam power had transformed the very nature of work. The success of their own republic had demonstrated that ordinary people could decide the basic questions of statecraft, formerly the preserve of monarchs and their courtiers. As they looked about them, the reformers of the mid-century North saw a country adding new states, new towns and cities, new industries and products, all at a dizzying pace. They lived on the cusp of the future, a future certain to be far different from the past.

Worcester, Massachusetts, site of the first two national woman's rights conventions, epitomized this new optimism. It was the first industrial center not on a waterway. Unlike Lowell or other mill towns, no river ran through it. Instead, it was a railroad city, the place where all the lines in New England crossed. No matter where in the region a train was going, it passed through Worcester. As a result, the city could import all of the raw materials used in its wire factories and machine shops; it also imported all of the energy it used, in the form of coal. The plows that broke the plains in the 1850s were made in Worcester. So was the telegraph wire that connected more and more of the country and, with the laying of the Atlantic cable, the United States and Britain. It was the first American city to be shaped by the transportation revolution.

Worcester's leading citizens prided themselves on the inventiveness of its mechanics. More patents were issued to Worcester County inhabitants than to those of any other in the nineteenth century, a fact frequently trumpeted in the city's newspapers. The largest building, raised in the mid-1850s, was Mechanics Hall. And, as befit a city devoted to innovation, Worcester was a hotbed of reform. All of its candidates for office in the 1850s, Democrats, Whigs, Free-Soilers, Know-Nothings, Republicans, professed their devotion to the anti-slavery cause. Temperance lecturers filled the city's halls. In the week following Christmas in 1854 William Lloyd Garrison, editor of the abolitionist paper, *The Liberator,* Henry David Thoreau, and Wendell Phillips spoke on consecutive nights. Small wonder that Abby Kelley

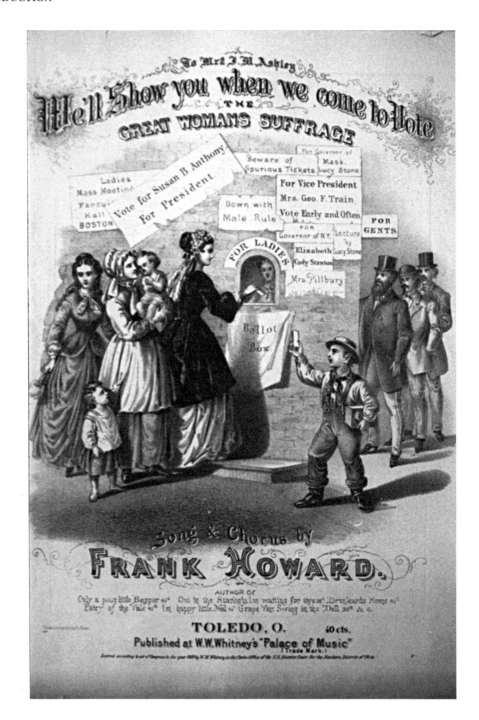

and husband Stephen S. Foster chose Worcester as their home base or that Thomas Wentworth Higginson, later to lead a black regiment in the Civil War, came to Worcester in 1852 to found his nondenominational Free Church.

Reformers such as these lived, they were sure, at a crucial historical juncture. Theirs was a society still plastic, still being molded. It was up to people of intelligence, courage, and high principle to seize the moment. The old necessities that had condemned the overwhelming majority of people to lives of unrelenting and unquestioning toil no longer applied. The old social structures of privilege that had annointed a few for lives of ease had been overthrown. The old superstitions that had chained people's imaginations had been shattered. So had old certitudes like the belief in the plenary inspiration of the Bible. The time was, as the *Call* had it, "opportune." It was the "duty" of those "worthy of your age and country" to aid in "the world's redemption from the sins and sufferings which oppress it."

Redemption was possible, but not inevitable. Good might triumph, but so might evil. It is this sense of the *radical* possibilities opening before them that we must recapture if we hope to grasp the "spirit" of this generation of reformers. And it is in this spirit quite as much as in centuries-old repression that we mush seek the origins of the woman's rights movement.

Woman's Nature and Proper Sphere

Thomas Nast (1840–1902) is often considered America's leading political cartoonist. He is especially known for his withering portraits of William Marcy ("Boss") Tweed and the members of his "Ring" of Tammany Hall politicians who ruled New York City in the late 1860s. Nast is also notorious for his anti-Catholic cartoons which contributed to a renewed wave of anti-immigrant sentiment in the 1870s. Nast's *Almanac* was very popular, and the 1871 volume contained humorist G. P. Webster's poem "A Dream of the Period" with Nast's illustrations.

Paulina Wright Davis insisted that a key to understanding why she and other pioneers of the woman's rights movement were "roused" to "do and dare" was their frustration with that "unwritten code, universal and cruel as the laws of Draco, and so subtle that, entering everywhere, they weigh most heavily where least seen." Their quarrel was with a "repression" that amounted to "soul murder." Together Webster's poem and Nast's drawings help us see a good deal about conventional notions of gender and gender roles, particularly those practices that "weigh most heavily where least seen."

THE PROPOSAL.

BEHIND THE SCENES.

KET-CAR POLITENESS.

THE NEW YORK ALDER-WOMAN.

THE COAL LADY.

MAN "I LEFT BEHIND ME."

A DREAM OF THE PERIOD

G. P. Webster

A dream I dreamt and 'twas not all a dream—
Disorder reigned, all things reversed did seem;
Women wore pantaloons, while men divine
Wore silks and ribbons, curls and crinoline.

I saw her proud, majestic, free from faults;
Nor cared she for ferocious man's assaults,
But sat her 'hobby' with defiant air
Which seemed to say, "Come on all, you that dare."

I saw men using powder lily white,
And "Bloom of Youth;" it was a jolly sight
To see them paint their eyebrows up with care,
Then load their heads with other people's hair.

I saw a cruel husband instigating
His wife to bloody deeds, she hesitating—
Just as that proud and bloody man, Macbeth,
Drove his poor wife to murder and to death.

Othello killed his wife! Oh, no good fellow!
'Twas cruel Desdemona killed Othello—
Married him first and took him from his mother,
And then her gentle husband she did smother.

A spirit whispered, "Let your heart rejoice
In man's soft melody." His tuneful voice
Yields sweeter strains and softer to the ear
Than blue birds' notes, when blooming spring is near.

My neighbor Jones seemed happy for his wife—
Called him her pet, the comfort of her life,
And passed the time in coaxing and carressing [sic];
Oh, happy Jones, his wife was such a blessing!

"A Dream of the Period," *Nast's Illustrated Almanac for 1871* (New York: McLoughlin Bros., 1870), pp. 56–63.

Alone and sorrowful, day after day,
At home, I passed my time, my wife away—
Made business all her care, while, weeping, I
Was left alone to suffer and to sigh.

I mildly said, "My dear come early home;
I fear, my love, you are inclined to roam.
What kept you out last night?" She answered, "Bah!"
I stopped a moment at the opera.

And Jewett, Wright, and Kennedy were there,
Worn down by toil; it is no more than fair
That we should have a little recreation!
Now, don't get mad and call it dissipation.

I saw a woman to her loved one kneeling,
Telling her love, and to his heart appealing;
He blushed, and answered "No," and then relenting,
Smiled, sighed, and answered Yes," at last consenting.

My wife went to the club, and took delight
In the "Sorosis" there, night after night;
She gave her time to feasting and to drinking,
Of her poor lonely husband never thinking.

And still I dreamed—imagine what my feeling,
When home, long after midnight, she came reeling,
And swore and grumbled while the door unlocking,
And roused the neighbors by her noisy knocking.

Roused by her rappings loud and furious ringing—
Bewildered, drowsy, sick, I heard her singing,
And cried, "Oh, stop!" and then she did upbraid me,
And said she only meant to serenade me.

Affairs of state seemed greatly to depress her;
The wrongs of women too did much distress her.
Said she, "You only have the grief you borrow,
While I must share a suffering people's sorrow."

I saw a man in garments light and airy,
With step fantastic, graceful as a fairy;
And wicked misses followed everywhere,
And pained and shocked him with their brazen stare.

Some women the wrongs of women did deplore,
Demanding equal rights for them, and more—
Made them the burden of their daily song,
But never dreamed that man could have a wrong.

And still my brain with fancies strange was teeming,
Not real—oh no! for I was only dreaming;
Man helpless seemed, while women played their pranks,
Rode, raced, talked politics, and set up banks.

I tried my very best my wife to please;
But still, a button gone from her chemise,
A garment torn, or hole in an old stocking,
And she would scold me in a manner shocking.

I told her how our little girl lay groaning
By fever parched, of our poor babe moaning
Upon my lap—how tired I was of nursing!
When she, excited, did some awful cursing.

She called me a tormentor, most provoking—
Fretful and discontented, always croaking;
Said cruel things to harass and to grieve me,
Then took her hat, and swore that she would leave me.

Michael, the cook, was impudent; while Terry,
The babe, neglected, passed his time with Jerry,
The chamberboy, and I was so tormented;
And yet my wife would bid me be contented.

A trotting horse she kept—could row a boat
In Oxford style, and had the right to vote;
Talked much of justice, law, and common sense,
And understood the art of self-defence.

My wife was always present at the races;
Gazed at the men, admired their pretty faces;
Bet freely on her nag, and always lost.
Drank, smoked, and never stayed to count the cost.

I thought I heard an earnest woman pleading
For a poor, weeping prisoner interceding—
Demanding, too, in tones loud and defiant,
Mercy for her poor, weak, and trembling client.

Guilty! Not so, she said, his face doth plead,
And in it simple innocence we read;
Pure loving thoughts are stamped in every feature—
Fie, woman, why pursue the gentle creature.

The bugle-call martial spirit rouses;
In padded coat and military trousers
She passed the day in drilling, marching, firing,
While men looked on half frightened, half admiring.

When drums and trumpets summoned her to duty,
She turned her back on home, and love, and beauty;
"Husband," she said, "now prove yourself a true man;"
Then she marched out to fight just like a woman.

Man stayed at home, in spite of all his cares
He still found time for sanitary fairs,
And sighed, "I'm lonely now! come back, my rover;"
Said Echo, "When this cruel war is over."

Man should be chaste, and quiet, and industrious;
Woman majestic, powerful, and illustrious.
Contentment is the gem that proves the true man,
While strength and dignity become a woman.

Men are not strong, and toil seems made for woman;
Man can not share it; no, 'tis deemed inhuman.
Charmed by his sweet angelic disposition,
They guard him from wrong and imposition.

Jane had a college chum, and loved her brother,
She wooed him, and he bade her ask his mother;
Jane had good sense, was free from all frivolity,
Besides, she had some gold—a shining quality.

Jane called, the mother stared, and then inquired
(As though she did not know) what she desired;
"I love your son," she answered, "and would marry."
"Go do it then," said she, "and do not tarry."

I dreamt that man had wrongs, that servants' vexing,
Annoyed him, were in many ways perplexing;
And when he sought a face that looked docility,
He found vile impudence and incivility.

"Woman," I said, "Leave off cigars and cursing;
Look at your gentle husbands, see them nursing
Your little babes, still uncomplaining, meek,
And they so fragile, and so weak."

The train had left; I saw a man belated,
And all alone the timid creature waited;
While well-dressed misses, impudent and daring,
Alarmed him by their naughty looks and staring.

A prophet then appeared (not one of old),
And strange reforms and fashions he foretold
These things shall come to pass—'twas thus he spoke
In tones so loud, and, wondering, I awoke.

THE LADY'S GUIDE TO PERFECT GENTILITY

Emily Thornwell

If Webster and Nast had fun with ideas of gender roles and separate "spheres," most took them very seriously indeed. One way of looking at roles is through the "how-to" manuals of the day. Guide books to correct behavior became very popular in the first half of the nineteenth century as tens of thousands of families, newly arrived in the city, and perhaps, in the middle class, sought to learn from books the forms of etiquette they had not learned on the farm from their parents. Those who assigned themselves the task of explaining the correct ways to behave saw their task as prescriptive rather than

The Lady's Guide to Perfect Gentility, in Manners, Dress, and Conversation, in the Family, in Company, at the Piano Forte, the Table, in the Street, and in Gentlemen's Society. Also a Useful Instructor in Letter Writing, Toilet Preparations, Fancy Needlework, Millinery, Dressmaking, Care of Wardrobe, the Hair, Teeth, Hands, Lips, Complexion, etc. By Emily Thornwell (New York: Derby and Jackson, 1856).

descriptive. So we should not read Thornwell's *Guide to Perfect Gentility* as an account of how people actually entered rooms or mounted horses. Instead we should pay attention to the cultural aspirations her work expressed. What was "gentility"? Why was it so much a matter of detail? And why was it so desirable in women? What sorts of "repression," to borrow Paulina Wright Davis's term, did these rules constitute?

THE TRUE FOUNDATION OF FEMALE LOVELINESS

Beauty Must Be Natural.   In order to have its full effect, beauty must be natural, and connected with perfect health. A fair skin and rosy cheeks are calculated to excite admiration; but if it be discovered that they are entirely produced by paint, that admiration becomes disgust; or if owing to disease, it is changed to pity.

• • •

Requisites to Female Beauty.   Exercise is unquestionably one of the very best means for the preservation of health; but its real importance is unknown, or but too lightly considered by the majority of females. Were they, however, to be made fully sensible of its extraordinary power in preserving the vigor of the body, in augmenting its capability to resist disease, in promoting its symmetrical development, in improving the freshness and brilliancy of the complexion, as well as its influence in prolonging the charms of beauty to an advanced age, they would shake off the prejudices by which they have been so long enthralled, and not voluntarily abandon means so completely within their power, and so simple, of enhancing all their physical perfections.

• • •

CHOICE COSMETICS FOR IMPROVING AND BEAUTIFYING THE SKIN

Cosmetic Juice.   Make a hole in a lemon, fill it with sugar-candy, and close it with a leaf gold, applied over the rind that was cut out; then roast the lemon in hot ashes. When desirous of using the juice, squeeze out a little through the hole already made, and with it wash the face with a napkin. This juice is said to cleanse the skin and brighten the complexion wonderfully.

• • •

Pomade for Removing Wrinkles.   Take two ounces of the juice of onions, the same quantity of the white lily, the same of honey, and one ounce of white wax; put the whole into a new tin pan, in a warm place, till the wax is melted; keep stirring the mixture with a wooden spoon, till it grows quite cold. You will then have an excellent ointment for removing wrinkles. It must be applied at night, on going to bed, and not wiped off till the morning.

• • •

Virgin Milk for the Complexion.   The virgin milk which is in most general use, and which is most salutary, is a tincture [of] benzoin [resin from trees] precipitated by water. To obtain the tincture of benzoin, take a certain quantity of that gum, pour spirits of wine upon it, and boil it till it becomes a rich tincture. Virgin milk is prepared by pouring a few drops of this tincture into a glass of water, which produces a milky mixture. This virgin milk, if the face be washed with it, will give a beautiful rosy color. To render the skin clear and brilliant, let it dry upon it without wiping.

• • •

THE HANDS

Means of Improving the Appearance of the Hands.   An elegant hand is regarded by many as betokening evident *prestige* in its possessor. Indeed, some persons, especially gentlemen, make the hand the test of beauty, calling a lady pretty, however ugly she may be otherwise, if she only can display a beautiful hand.

• • •

THE BREATH

Desireableness of a Pure Breath.   The purity of the breath is of the greatest consequence; what, indeed, could be so afflicting to one of the gentle sex as impurity in this respect? Yet it may occur without any neglect on her part, and it is not always that a remedy can be offered; in other words, there are cases where it is incurable.

Refreshing Draught for the Breath.   Take five to ten drops of hydrochloric acid in half a tumbler of spring water, a little lemon juice, and loaf sugar, rubbed on lemon peel to flavor it to suit the palate. Let this mixture be taken three times a day for a month or six weeks, and, if useful, then continue it occasionally. It is a pleasant refrigerant [i.e., tonic for reducing fever] and tonic draught.

• • •

GOOD TASTE

Naturalness.   The first great fundamental rule of good taste is *to be natural*; and it is from an infringement of this that many of our worst mistakes proceed. In manner or style, affectation is the source of the most flagrant offenses against taste.

• • •

Raising the Dress.   When tripping over the pavement [i.e., walking], a lady should gracefully raise her dress a little above her ankle. With the right hand, she should hold together the folds of her gown, and draw them towards the right side. To raise the dress on both sides, and with both hands, is vulgar. This ungraceful practice can only be tolerated for a moment, when the mud is very deep.

• • •

Propriety of Movement and General Demeanor in Company.   To look steadily at any one, especially if you are a lady and are speaking to a gentleman; to turn the head frequently on one side and the other during conversation; to balance yourself upon your chair; to bend forward; to strike your hands upon your knees; to hold one of your knees between your hands locked together; to cross your legs; to extend your feet on the andirons; to admire yourself with complacency in a glass; to adjust, in an affected manner, your cravat, hair, dress, or handkerchief; to remain without gloves; to fold carefully your shawl, instead of throwing it with graceful negligence upon a table; to fret about a hat which you have just left off; to laugh immoderately; to place your hand upon the person with whom you are conversing; to take him by the buttons, the collar of his cloak, the cuffs, the waist, and so forth; to seize any person by the waist or arm, or to touch their person; to roll the eyes or to raise them with affectation; to take snuff from the box of your neighbor, or to offer it to strangers, especially to ladies; to play continually with your chain or fan; to beat time with the feet and hands; to whirl round a chair with your hand; to shake with your feet the chair of your neighbor; to rub your face or your hands; wink your eyes; shrug up your shoulders; stamp with your feet, and so forth; —all these bad habits, of which we cannot speak to people, are in the highest degree displeasing.

• • •

Special Rules to Be Observed at the Table. . . . *Never use your knife* to convey your food to your mouth, under any circumstance; it is unnecessary and glaringly vulgar. Feed yourself with a *fork or spoon, nothing else;* a knife is only to be used for cutting.

• • •

Ladies should never dine with their gloves on; unless their hands are not fit to be seen.

In conversation at the table, be careful not to speak while eating a mouthful; it is indecorous in the extreme.

Bite not your bread, but break it with your fingers; be careful not to crumb it upon the table-cloth.

The knife and fork should not be held upright in the hands, but sloping; when done with them, lay them parallel to each other upon the plate. When you eat, bend the body a little toward your plate; do not gnaw bones at the table, always use your napkin before and after drinking.

• • •

The Lady on Horseback. In riding, the gentleman's first duty is to provide a gentle horse, properly caparisoned [a caparison is an ornamental covering for a horse's harness]. After seeing that the girths are tight, he leads the lady to the horse. With her back to the horse, she takes hold of the horn of the saddle, and the reins with her right hand, and places her left hand upon the shoulder of the gentleman, who stoops before her, making a stirrup of his clasped hands. Raising himself gently, the lady is placed in the saddle. The gentleman puts her foot in the stirrup, adjusts her dress, mounts his horse and takes his position, usually on the right, but authorities differ, and many prefer the left.

In dismounting, the lady, having lifted her foot from the stirrup, and her dress from the saddle, may be received in the gentleman's arms.

• • •

FEMALE DRESS; HOW TO COMBINE ELEGANCE, STYLE, AND ECONOMY

Points to Be Considered.   In the regulation of female dress too much is sacrificed to fashion and appearance. The whims of a French or English mantua-maker [dressmaker], or the depraved taste of some reigning beauty, are of infinitely more weight in determining the nature of clothing worn by females even of this country, than all the arguments drawn from the character of our climate, and the attention which experience teaches us should be paid to the season of the year, the state of the weather, and the amount of exposure.

Many of the diseases to which the delicate and youthful of the female sex are peculiarly liable, and by which so many of them are hurried into the grave in the spring-time of their existence, may be traced to impropriety of dress: either in preventing, by its unnatural tightness and inconvenient form, the proper growth of the body, and the natural and free play of its various parts and organs, or to a want of caution in accommodating it to the temperature of the season, and to the various and rapid vicissitudes of the weather.

. . .[I]n preparing for an evening ball or party, or even for a simple visit to a friend, it is too common for females, when the temperature of the external air is that of mid-winter, to retire from a warm parlor to a cold dressing-room, and there exchange a comfortable, warm gown, for one perhaps of thin silk or muslin (with wide sleeves of a still more flimsy material than the gown itself, which leave the arms almost entirely naked), and their worsted or cotton stockings and thick shoes, for flimsy silk stockings, and slippers of a scarcely more substantial material; and thus attired, with their neck and shoulders bare, or merely covered with thin lace, they sally forth into the damp and chilly air of the night, and arrive at the place of their destination shivering with cold. After several hours passed in a hot, close, often crowded apartment, and perhaps when the body has been heated by the exercise of dancing, they again brave the cold and dampness of the external air, and on arriving at their homes retire to their beds with cold feet and a shuddering frame.

Who can be surprised that the consequences of such imprudent exposure are affections of the throat and lungs, attended with cough and hoarseness, and too often terminating eventually in fatal consumptions [tuberculosis]? Motives of delicacy, as well as a proper regard for health, have been repeatedly urged in vain to enforce the strong necessity of relinquishing such destructive practices; the arguments of the moralist and of the physician have alike failed to induce conviction. And hundreds, who might have shone forth for years among the most estimable and lovely of the sex, have in early youth been dressed in the shroud, because, in an evil hour, they laid aside those parts of their apparel which their health as well as comfort rendered absolutely necessary.

• • •

CUT AND QUALITY OF DRESS ADAPTED TO THE MARRIED AND UNMARRIED, THE OLD AND THE YOUNG, AND TO DIFFERENT FIGURES

Young Ladies' Attire.   Situation in the world determines among ladies those differences which, though otherwise well-marked, are becoming less so every day. Every one knows that whatever be the fortune of a young lady, her dress ought always, in form as well as ornaments, to exhibit less of a *recherché* [fashionable] appearance, and should be less showy than that of married ladies. Costly cashmeres, very rich furs, and diamonds, as well as many other brilliant ornaments, are to be forbidden a young lady; and those who act in defiance of these rational marks of propriety make us believe that they are possessed of an unrestrained love of luxury, and deprive themselves of the pleasure of receiving those ornaments from the hand of the man of their choice at some future day.

. . . The Apparel of Older Ladies. The rules suitable to age resemble those which mediocrity of fortune imposes; for instance, old ladies should abstain from gaudy colors, *recherché* designs, too late [i.e., up-to-the-minute] fashions, and showy ornaments, as feathers, flowers, and jewels. A lady in decline, wearing her hair dressed, and having short sleeves, and adorned with necklaces, bracelets, etc., offends as much against propriety as against her interest and dignity.

• • •

EFFECTS OF DRESS UPON THE FEMALE FORM, ETC., ETC.

Lacing the Chest. When the chest is scientifically laced as tight as can be borne, it often causes the blood to rush to the face, neck, and arms, on taking exercise or remaining in a heated room. Young ladies at parties frequently become so suffused from this cause, that they present the appearance of a washerwoman actively engaged over a tub of hot suds. Tight lacing also causes an extreme heaving of the bosom, resembling the panting of a dying bird.

Effect of Tight Lacing on the Face, Neck, Arms, Shape, and Motion of the Body, etc. Those who wear very tight stays complain that they cannot sit upright without them; nay, are sometimes compelled to wear them in bed, and this strikingly proves to what an extent braces of any sort weaken the muscles of the trunk. It is this which disposes to lateral curvature of the spine. From these facts, as well as many others, it is evident that tight stays, far from preventing the deformities which an experienced eye might remark among ninety out of every hundred young girls, are, on the contrary, the cause of these deviations.

. . . In many persons, tight stays displace the breast, and produce an ineffaceable and frightful wrinkle between it and the shoulder; and in others, whom nature has not gifted with the plumpness requisite to beauty, such stays make the breasts still flatter and smaller. Generally speaking, tight stays also destroy the firmness of the breast, sometimes prevent the full development of the nipples, and give rise to those indurations [i.e., hardening] of the mammary glands, the cause of which is seldom understood, and which are followed by such dreadful consequences.

They also cause a reddish tinge of the skin, swelling of the neck, etc. A delicate and slender figure is full of beauty in a young person; but suppleness and ease confer an additional charm. Yet most women, eager to be in the extreme of fashion, lace themselves in their stays as tight as possible, and, undergoing innumerable tortures, appear stiff, ungraceful, and ill-tempered. Elegance of shape, dignity of movement, grace of manner, and softness of demeanor, are all sacrificed to foolish caprice.

• • •

THE ART OF CONVERSING WITH FLUENCY AND PROPRIETY

A Lady's Influence in Conversation.   Every woman whose heart and mind have been properly regulated, is capable of exerting a most salutary influence over the gentlemen with whom she associates; and this fact has been acknowledged by the best and wisest of men, and seldom disputed, except by those whose capacities for observation have been perverted by adverse circumstances.

Conversing with Modesty and Simplicity.   Always seek to converse with gentlemen into whose society you may be introduced, with a dignified modesty and simplicity, which will effectually check on their part any attempt at familiarity.

• • •

You may with propriety accept such delicate attentions as polished and refined men are desirous of paying, but never solicit them, or appear to be expecting them.

. . . How to Address Young Gentlemen.   Do not be tempted to indulge in another proof of feminine indecorum, which may be countenanced, but can never be sanctioned by example; that of addressing young gentlemen of your acquaintance, who are unconnected [i.e., unrelated] with you, by their christian names. It opens the way to unpleasant familiarities on their part, more effectually than you can well imagine, unless you have been taught the painful lesson by the imprudence of a friend.

• • •

Undue Pretensions to Learning.   . . . [W]hether your pretensions to learning are well founded or not; the simple fact that you aim to appear learned, that you deal much in allusion to the classics, or the various departments of science, with an evident intention to display your familiarity with them, will be more intolerable than absolute ignorance.

BROTHER JONATHAN'S WIFE

John Neal

As popular as her *Lady's Guide* proved to be, Emily Thornwell did not have the last word on how women ought to behave. Male writers frequently took up the subject. A prominent case in point is John Neal. He was one of the most celebrated novelists of the first half of the nineteenth century as well as publisher and editor of *Brother Jonathan,* a popular magazine of the 1840s which, he claimed, provided "the Cheapest Reading in the World." The name "Brother Jonathan" stood for the archetypical American in the same way that John Bull stood for his English equivalent. Sometime in the 1850s the figure of Uncle Sam appeared, soon to be

---

Brother Jonathan's Wife: A Lecture, by a retired editor [John Neal] (Philadelphia, 1842).

popularized by Thomas Nast. Uncle Sam dressed like Brother Jonathan in a red, white, and blue outfit but with a beard and without the feather in his cap which Brother Jonathan (himself a variant of Yankee Doodle) usually sported. Neal's prominence and literary reputation make his essay on the ideal American woman worth reading. Here one can find, in pristine form, some of the ideas about woman's nature and duties, her sphere, in a word, that woman's rights advocates most sought to discredit. One can also find ideas, such as the call for education for women, they most sought to advance. Of particular note is Neal's discussion of female sexuality, her capacity for what he calls "the highest pleasure." Many of the reformers of the age, from organizers of utopian communities to Sylvester Graham, focused upon marital relations as being in need of radical reform.

Neal's argument that the American woman already enjoyed her rights and was already the equal, if not the superior, of men may strike present-day readers as implausible on the face of it. His contemporaries read it differently. Indeed it was the conventional wisdom of the age. Tocqueville, who attributed the success of American society to the "superiority of its women," made the same argument as Neal in *Democracy in America*.

We hold up to the whole world, the faithful and loving helpmate of Brother Jonathan, as a model for every female to study, who seeks to attain to the position of wife. They may learn thereby, that to be qualified for so important and interesting a sphere of action, something more is necessary to be learned than to know how to make puddings and tea! Ignorance may decry female accomplishments, may prate about feminine retirement, about her sphere being limited to the household circle, and all that. But who will listen to such execrable nonsense? Is there any thing harsh or unfeeling, or unmatronly, or unfeminine, in being well-informed? The soul of woman is a bright emanation from the great fountain of spirit. Why then should she paper it up as carefully as if it were made of silver lace, and the breath of heaven would tarnish it? Nothing softens female delicacy so much as knowledge. Does knowledge make men indifferent husbands? Why then should it make women poor wives? Talk not to us of the blessings of ignorance. Feminine ignorance leads to scandal—to backbiting. If she knows nothing about things, she must talk about persons; if she cannot converse, she must gossip. If she is ignorant, she will thunder with her tongue, "and every one knows, and some by unhappy experience, what a dreadful plague a woman's scolding tongue is."

Cleanliness, neatness, frugality, and order, are also traits of character belonging to the subject we have chosen, and deserve special attention. It must be confessed, that these are all of great importance in the habits of a wife, mother and mistress of a family; and for the want of which, no literary attainments, however profound and extensive, can be a substitute. To mental improvement, the wife should unite a correct knowledge of household affairs. She who is to preside over a family should be most intimately acquainted with every thing that can preserve order or promote comfort.

She is the very personification of goodness and forgiveness, breathes the very atmosphere of love, and in her mouth is the law of kindness. She clings fondly for protection and support, to the man of her choice, and scatters sunshine in the pathway of his existence. Possessing a fine nervous system, and bright intellect, she is capacitated for the highest pleasure, which, if moderately enjoyed, is to woman what the sun is to the flowers: It beautifies, it refreshes and improves. But if immoderately enjoyed, it withers, desolates and destroys. Chastened pleasure calls forth all the sensibilities of her susceptible nature, and is as necessary to the full development of her charms, as the shade and the shower are to the lily; confirming its beauty and increasing its fragrance. It is her privilege to enjoy; it is the grand principle of her nature;—when the golden fruit is within reach, it is natural to pluck and eat. For the purpose of enjoyment, heaven has made her the most beautiful and susceptible being that exists. Her society charms—her person fascinates—to her we owe the sweetest enjoyments of life. Beauty woos to her embrace, and will find a ready response in every manly heart. She is indeed a creature to be adored—the most faithful of wives, and the fondest of mothers. She sweetens the charms of home, and is the pearl that enriches and adorns the social hearth. Religion is her panoply, and no one who wishes her happiness and who appreciates her virtue, would weaken their best security.

• • •

Unlike most of her sex, whether civilized or savage, throughout the globe, she is as free and independent as the wild winds of heaven. She is her own mistress—no body's slave. The periods of courtship and marriage, those blissful moments of existence, the sunniest and sweetest hours that shine upon the pathway of life, she can call her own. In herself is invested the *right* of disposing of herself.

• • •

The unalienable rights of woman are enjoyed by a very inconsiderable portion of the human race. Even among the polished and enlightened nations of Europe, she is greatly restricted in her just privileges. In no other country on the face of the globe, are her rights so well guarded by law, and so much respected by the unanimous voice of the people, as this. The customs of our country give to woman a freedom of communication with the opposite sex, by which she is enabled not only to become acquainted with their mental and moral qualifications in the main, but to study well their characters and dispositions in all their various ramifications. This is a desideratum of the utmost importance, a great privilege, especially before entering into the most interesting contract of human society [i.e., marriage]. It is important to woman in all the varied grades of association and relation, with which she may be connected with the other sex, in the minor as well as in the major points, that she know those well, with whom business or inclination, brings her in contact. Here she enjoys a community of rights and interests with man—she is his equal—she can do as she pleases, and every body knows that nothing can be more gratifying to the feelings of a woman, than to be able to do what she has a mind to! Here she is universally beloved and esteemed, and treated with the kindness due to her character and feelings as a woman, and the respect due to the interesting and exalted position she sustains, as the female representative of a powerful and independent nation. Here she is a *free woman!*

We may as well own to it as not—*she governs us!* Not indeed by physical force, but by the power of affection. She holds the empire of the heart, and throughout its extended and before untrodden dominions, ranges with queenly step, and reigns alone and peerless. The influence she exerts as wife, mother, daughter, sister, relative, friend, companion, and instructress, is immeasurably great. . . . When she chooses to step into the empire of letters, the sparkling scintillations of her vivid pen, fairly eclipse the sleepy, monotonous lucubrations of her sterner counterpart.

One of the recurrent themes in the woman's rights movement from the outset was opposition to what a later generation would call the "beauty trap," the indoctrinating of young women in the notion that they must devote all their energies to looking "pretty." As Ernestine Rose would put it at the Worcester Convention, women were expected to be either "a poppet [puppet] in the parlor" or a "drudge in the kitchen." One way of seeing this social pressure is by looking at popular jokes as in this piece from *Frank Leslie's Budget of Fun.* Historian Robert Darnton has remarked that one way of testing how well one understands an historical era is seeing if one understands the jokes. *Leslie's* was the leading humor magazine of the day. This mock praise for "homely girls" provides a striking counterpoint to John Neal's idealization of "Brother Jonathan's Wife."

HOMELY GIRLS

FRANK LESLIE'S BUDGET OF FUN (UNSIGNED)

The editor of the Cleveland *Herald,* having been tolerably profuse in his compliments to the pretty girls of Cleveland, has been requested to say a good thing in behalf of the homely ones, and he does it thus:

First—The homely girls of Cleveland are in a hopeless minority, but they mean well.

Second—They go to church every Sunday, and are fond of their meals. They had rather have their meals regularly than a new bonnet.

Third—They understand their business, and wear No. 16 gaiters.[1]

Fourth—They are bright, intelligent, devoid of low jealousy, fond of music, dance at Garrett's Hall as though it was the chief aim of life, and always go in when it rains.

Fifth—They always thank the gentlemen for giving them seats in the street cars; never flirt with the boys, because it's out of their line, and keep out of the fire.

"Homely Girls," *Frank Leslie's Budget of Fun,* January 1866.

[1] A style of ankle-high shoe. The joke is that pretty girls were always seeking opportunities to show off their well-turned ankles. Homely girls "knew their business" and thus covered up their ankles.

Sixth—They never have half a dozen young sprigs [i.e., lads] keeping company with them.

Seventh—They wash their own handkerchiefs, iron their own collars, and darn their own stockings.

Eighth—They never wear waterfalls that weigh over one hundred and fifty pounds, and have neither "rats" nor other animals in their hair.[2]

Ninth—They don't call the young bloods and other trash "perfectly splendid."

Tenth—They never eat between meals.

Eleventh—They are all going to get married.

Twelfth—They will all marry well.

Thirteenth—Their children will be bright and shining lights in the world.

Fourteenth—They won't keep hired girls till their husbands can afford them.

Fifteenth—They sleep under mosquito bars when convenient.

Sixteenth—They can make coffee and nutcakes, and can do chamberwork.

Seventeenth—They are O.K.

Eighteenth—They are homely, but oh, Jerusalem!

Nineteenth—They know they are homely.

Twentieth—They perspire when the thermometer is at ninety-four in the shade, and wear gored waists.[3]

Twenty-first—Young gentlemen don't squeeze them by the hand, and they like peanuts.

WOMAN'S WORK AND MAN'S SUPREMACY

Jane Grey Swisshelm

John Neal and others who proclaimed the "superiority" of American women nonetheless took for granted that men should have the final say. They were all afflicted with "masculine superiority fever" as Jane Grey

---

[2] The "waterfall" was a popular hairstyle in which the woman gathered her hair, naturally long enough to reach her waist, in a "fall" at the neck. Some women used wigs to make the "waterfall" bigger. A "rat" was another way of padding a woman's own hair to make it appear more puffed out.
[3] A [shirt]waist was a kind of blouse with full shoulders and a tapered waist. A gored waist was one with a triangular insert.

Jane G. Swisshelm, *Letters to Country Girls* (New York: J. C. Riker, 1853).

Cannon Swisshelm phrased it. And they were responsible in large measure, she charged, for the abuses many women had to silently endure. Swisshelm (1815–1884) was perhaps the most famous woman, Jenny Lind aside, in the United States at mid-century. She was born in Pittsburgh into the strict Covenanter branch of the Presbyterian Church. Her father died in 1823, and she helped support the family (mother, brother, and sister) by teaching lace-making; she also painted on velvet. At fourteen she became a schoolteacher. She married James Swisshelm in 1836; he was a farmer's son and a devout Methodist who insisted she give up painting. He also sought to turn her into a Methodist and insisted upon wifely obedience. In 1839 she left him to nurse her mother who died the following year. She then turned to journalism. In 1842 her husband returned to Pittsburgh, and they resumed living together on his family farm. In 1848 she launched the Pittsburgh *Visiter* [her spelling] as an anti-slavery and, later, woman's rights weekly. Within a few years national circulation topped 6,000 making it one of the most widely read reform papers. One of its most popular features was Swisshelm's weekly "letter to country girls" addressed to a fictional correspondent, Anniss, which she collected in book form in 1853. At the heart of Swisshelm's success was her ability to sound a new voice in public discussions about "woman's sphere." It was sharp, sometimes comic, often satiric, a voice men were not used to hearing from women in public. It was also a voice which mimicked the speech of others as when she has her "ignorant country boor" refer to his "darters" [daughters] and to "ingins" [Indians] and "niggers." Swisshelm's use of such language was accurate. It was how such people spoke. But it also echoed her opposition to the linking of woman's rights with those of black males, reprinted here, and her outspoken calls for the military suppression of the Native American tribes on the Great Plains.

It is hard not to read portions of the following "letter" as autobiographical or to see in her claim "I understand the disease [of the masculine superiority fever] very well" a thinly veiled reference to James Swisshelm.

I am puzzled this week. Anniss asks me to "say something about those rich old farmers who make their wives work out in the fields, and leave their babies in fence corners for the snakes to eat." She goes on to describe how the women, "after working in the fields until meal time, come home, cook, milk and churn, while the men lounge around and rest."

This is a very bad case, but a very common one, of the masculine superiority fever which has converted so many millions of men into ruffians. I understand the disease very well, and can cure it quite easily when I have access to the patient, and can get my prescriptions administered. One week of vigorous treatment will cure the complaint effectually; but it is hard to get the proper nurses and assistants!

These old fellows do not take the Visiter [Swisshelm's weekly paper]! I am too much out of "woman's sphere" to be tolerated in their august presence. No one has access to them but preachers and political stump speakers. They see no paper but a religious or political one. The former never speaks about woman, except to lecture her about her duties—her obligation to obey her husband—her vocation to forget herself and live only for the welfare of her liege lord and some particular church. The latter never speaks about woman or her interests a bit more than if such a creature never existed. The laws and policy they are discussing set her down midway between men and monkeys. She has no vote to solicit, no offices to confer, but is a kind of appendage to her master. Of course the ignorant boor gets a vast opinion of his own importance, as it is continually held up to view by church and state; and it cannot be wondered at that he practices what our divines, statesmen, philosophers, and poets teach. He is not able to comprehend the transcendent beauties of a system which places woman half-way between the rational and irrational creation—deprives her of the rights of self-government—the right to use her own faculties, because she is a superior being—an angel, too pure and precious to mix with sublunary things. He applies a common sense rule to the common principle, and argues "if Sallie has no right to hold office in church or state—if she is to submit to me in all things, to keep silence in churches, and learn from me at home, of course I must be wiser than she, and better too. The Constitution puts her down with 'niggers' and ingins, or a little below 'em. She is heaven's 'last best gift to man,' an' mighty useful one [I] can make her! She can make hay as well as I can—then cook the victuals while I'm restin', and raise some sons and darters in the meantime to take care uv me when I get old! Tell ye, there isn't a horse on the place I wouldn't rather lose nor Sallie!" So he puts his wife into "a woman's place," and keeps her there.

It is not the ignorant country boor, the pious old penurious farmer who acts out this philosophy, that is actually accountable for it. He is only living up to the spirit of the age—keeping pace with its authors, editors, poets, and divines! It is very well known that thousands, nay, millions of women in this country are condemned to the most menial drudgery, such as men would scorn to engage in, and that for one-fourth wages; that thousands of women toil at avocations which public opinion pretends to assign to men. They plough, harrow, reap, dig, make hay, rake, bind grain, thrash, chop wood, milk, churn, do anything that is hard work, physical labor, and who says any thing against it? But let one presume to use her mental powers—let her aspire to turn editor, public speaker, doctor, lawyer—take up any profession or avocation which is deemed honorable and requires talent, and O! bring the Cologne, get a cambric kerchief and a feather fan, unloose his corsets and take off his cravat! What a fainting fit Mr. Propriety has taken! Just to think that "one of the deah creathures," the heavenly angels, should forsake the spheres—woman's sphere—to mix with the wicked strife of this wicked world!

What rhapsodies we have from sentimental schoolchildren of both sexes, about soiled plumage on angels' wings; while stern, matter-of-fact tyrants crack their whips and shout, "Back to thy punishment, false slave!"

The evil of which Anniss complains is not a local affair, but a deeply rooted and unsightly cancer, which disfigures the entire face of the body politic. No permanent and general cure can be wrought in a day; but if she can get these old fellows, their wives and daughters, to read the Visiter [for] a year, we will undertake to mitigate the virulence of the disease in that neighborhood. So long as they read and hear nothing but squabbles between Whigs and Democrats about a Tariff, and sermons and homilies about the Scribes and Pharisees who lived long ago, the errors of Popery, and differences between John Calvin and John Wesley, you need never hope for a reformation in this matter.[1] They will have to hear, and learn, and know something about themselves, their own practices, opinion, duties, and errors, before they will mend their manners.

• • •

The efficient remedy for this class of evils is education, an equal education! If parents would give their daughters the same mental training they do their sons, they could not be converted into slaves so handily.

---

[1] Popery was a popular, if derogatory, term for Roman Catholicism; John Calvin was the sixteenth-century theologian and religious leader whose teachings inspired the Presbyterian church in which Swisshelm was raised. John Wesley was the eighteenth-century theologian and religious leader whose teachings inspired the Methodist church which her husband sought to make her join. Swisshelm's use of the term "reformation" in this context was a pun on the Protestant Reformation Calvin helped start and which Wesley saw himself as carrying on.

Every where there is a distinction between the education of boys and girls—if the boys get little, the girls get less; as they get more, the proportion is kept up. If you wish to maintain your proper position in society, to command the respect of your friends now, and husbands and children in future, you should read, read—think, study, try to be wise, to know your own places and keep them, your own duties and do them. You should try to understand every thing you see and hear; to act and judge for yourselves; to remember you each have a soul of your own to account for; —a mind of your own to improve. When you once get these ideas fixed, and learn to act upon them, no man or set of men, no laws, customs, or combinations of them can seriously oppress you. Ignorance, folly, and levity, are more or less essential to the character of a slave. If women knew their rights, and proper places, we would never hear of men "making their wives" do this, that, or the other.

THE SPHERE OF WOMAN

Johann Wolfgang von Goethe

This essay is a nearly perfect example of Jane Swisshelm's point about husbands and others infected with "masculine superiority fever" only putting into practice what "authors, editors, poets, and divines" preach. Johann Wolfgang von Goethe (1749–1832) was the most celebrated literary figure in the German language, author not only of *Faust* and *The Sorrows of Young Werther,* but of many works of science and philosophy. The Weimar edition of his complete works runs to 133 volumes. *Godey's Lady's Book* was one of the first, and by far the most successful, magazines for women. It printed poems, short stories, articles on fashion, education, family life, and scores of other subjects. The fact that Goethe's essay appeared in *Godey's,* which was edited by Sarah Josepha

---

"The Sphere of Woman," Godey's *Lady's Book*, March 1850 (Translated from the German of Goethe).

Hale, illustrates another of Swisshelm's points—that women as well as men proclaimed the glories of "the sphere of woman."

The accompanying illustration is not credited. It nicely captures the dream of the ideal woman, with her children gathered about her, with even the dog paying close attention as the woman's daughter reads aloud. Note the statue of Don Quixote in the background.

Women often complain that men are unjust towards their sex, in withholding from them higher mental culture, and in not allowing them full access to the sciences, thus keeping them down to mere household duties, and to the government of the domestic circle. It is, however, unjust that man, on this account, should be the subject of complaint. For has he not placed his wife in the highest and holiest position she can occupy when he places her at the head of his domestic relations, and intrusts to her the government of his household? When a man is harassed by external duties and relations, when anxiously employed in procuring the means of subsistence, and when he even takes part in the government of the state—in all these conditions of life he is dependent on circumstances, and can scarcely be said to govern anything, but is often reduced to the necessity of acting from motives of

policy, when he would gladly act from his own rational *convictions,* to conceal his real principles when he would delight to act frankly and openly; and even to act out the suggestions of fallacy and falsehood, when he would gladly act from sincerity and uprightness. To all this the man, in his external life in the world, is subject, and at the same time rarely attains the end for which he labors, but loses that harmony with himself, in which, nevertheless, the true ends and the true enjoyment of life consist. Whereas, the prudent woman reigns in her family circle, making happiness and every virtue possible, and spreading harmony and peace throughout her domain. What is the highest happiness of man, but to carry out what he knows to be right and good, and to have full control over the means to this end? And where are our dearest and inmost ends in life, but in the household? Where do we find our ever-returning and indispensable wants satisfied, but in the beloved spot where we rise up and lie down? What regular activity is required to carry out this ever-returning order of things? To how few men is it granted to return regularly like a star, and to preside both over the day and the night! But the woman who arranges her household, forms her domestic plans, watches over the economy of her house, and wisely dispenses her means, spreads harmony, love, and peace throughout the circle, makes her husband, whom she loves, a happy prince over that happiest domain. Her attention gathers all the knowledge she requires. . . . She is dependent on nothing, save the love and attachment of her husband, for whom she procures true independence—that which is internal and domestic. That which his labor has acquired, he sees properly secured and employed. Thus, in a spirit of true independence, he can devote his energies to great objects— and become to the state (by promoting its prosperity) what his wife is to the household over which she presides.

WOMAN'S POWER

Frank J. Walters

Part of the "spirit of the age" was an idealized notion of woman's nature, wonderfully exemplified in the following poem. It complemented the notion of a woman's sphere by ascribing to her inborn qualities which peculiarly fitted her for her "proper" roles. This idealization often served as an excuse, as any number of speakers at the Worcester convention pointed out, for restricting women's activities, lest their purity be sullied by contact with the tawdry worlds of business or politics. On the other hand, a close reading of the speeches will demonstrate that many woman's rights advocates sought to turn that argument on its head by claiming that women would, by virtue of their more spiritual nature, redeem these pursuits. Did rowdies infest the polls on election day? They would surely cease and desist, if women were voters. For some, this was simply a rhetorical ploy, a way of turning an opponent's arguments back against him. For other woman's rights activists, however, woman's higher spirituality, her "power" to redeem men, was a fundamental truth.

Oh! tell me not that woman's weak,
Inconstant, or unkind;
Though flippant writers often speak
As though dame Nature's master freak
Was molding woman's mind.
Around the sufferer's lowly bed,
When palls the heart of men;
When science falls and hope is fled,
And helpless lies the dying head,
Oh! who is constant then!
Who watches, with a tireless eye,
The faintly heaving breath?
Who hovers round, for ever nigh,
To catch the last expiring sigh,

"Woman's Power" by Frank J. Walters, *Godey's Lady's Book*, February 1850.

And soothe the pangs of death?
When disappointment sinks the soul,
And round us troubles throng;
When grief exerts its wild control,
And sorrow's stormy billows roll,
Then, then, oh! who is strong?
Man sinks beneath misfortune's blow
And hope forsakes his breast;
His boasted powers are all laid low,
His strength is swallowed up in woe,
When not by woman blest.
But she can cheer his drooping heart,
And rouse his soul again;
Can bid his cankering cares depart,
And, by her smiling, artless art,
Can soothe his keenest pain.
Is woman weak? Go as the sword,
The weapon of the brave,
Whose look, whose tone, whose lightest word,
Though e'en but in a whisper heard,
Commands it as her slave.
Go ask man's wild and restless heart
Who can its passions quell;
Who can withdraw hate's venomed dart,
Bid malice and revenge depart,
And virtue in it dwell.
If woman's weak, then what is strong?
For all things bow to her:
To her man's powers all belong;
For her the bard attunes his song,
Her truest worshiper.
Woman, a fearful power is thine:
The mission to thee given
Requires a strength almost divine,
A bosom that is virtue's shrine,
A soul allied to heaven.

STRANGE THINGS I HAVE SEEN AND HEARD

Minnie Myrtle

However much poets might proclaim woman's "power," the hard truth was that daughters were legally subject to their fathers, wives to their husbands. And, unlike the woman's power to solace or to save, a man's power was enforceable in the law courts. Like the slaveholder, as early woman's rights activists insistently pointed out, he could do virtually as he pleased. What this meant in too many cases was domestic abuse. Nancy Cummings Johnson (1815–1852) was one of the first to speak out against this.

The sketches and poems collected in *The Myrtle Wreath* first appeared in the *New York Daily Times,* (the book is dedicated to Henry Raymond, editor of the Times), and other papers. In carving out her literary career, Johnson was a contemporary and rival of Sarah Payson Willis Parton, who, under the pseudonym of Fanny Fern, published several best-selling collections of pointed, humorous sketches. The first, *Fern Leaves from Fanny's Port-Folio,* appeared the year before Johnson's posthumous *The Myrtle Wreath or Stray Leaves Recalled.*

Johnson wrote, in her introductory "Word to My Readers": "I have not written to instruct the wise, and have no ambition to write learnedly. I have hoped to impress the heart, and to amuse, believing this to be emphatically 'woman's mission'" (p. 10). This proclamation and her explicit refusal to advocate woman's rights disguise the radicalism of her work. In "Strange Things" and several other essays she leveled a scathing critique at those who sought to keep women in their "proper sphere." Especially striking is her insistence that the exercise of power is intensely pleasurable. Now forgotten, Johnson was a popular writer in the early 1850s, sufficiently famous to be included by her pen name in the political cartoons of the day. So her writing opens a window on how the debate about woman's "place" entered into the popular culture. She, Jane Grey Swisshelm, and Fanny Fern pioneered a new sort of public voice for women.

Minnie Myrtle [Nancy Cummings Johnson], "Strange Things I Have Seen and Heard," from *The Myrtle Wreath or Stray Leaves Recalled* (New York: Charles Scribner, 1854).

"Power is corrupting," says the politician—"Power is corrupting," says the foe to hierarchies. "Good men, the best men, should not be entrusted with absolute power." "Power is corrupting," says the enemy of slavery, "men should not be permitted the absolute control of human beings; however good the master may be, he will be tempted to indulge in tyranny, if there is nothing external to restrain him."

These are sentiments which I have often heard expressed by one who still exclaims, "I *will* be master in my own house; those who live with me shall *obey* me." And the obedience which is required of a wife is as servile as that which is rendered by any bond slave.

To his daughter he says, "Whilst you are in my house you will do as I say, if you are a hundred years old"; not because she would not obey willingly and happily, but because there is such pleasure in *exacting* obedience. All would gladly do right of their own accord; but that would not be sufficient; they must be compelled; they must feel in every nerve, and bone and muscle, that they are subject to the will of another. To order, thwart and torture, is a peculiar pleasure, and I am fully convinced, is not enjoyed by Princes, and Popes, and slave-owners alone.

I have seen the staunchest advocates of "Woman's rights" and "human freedom," exercise the most brutal tyranny over wives and daughters. I have seen a quiet Christian woman beaten, by a man who was ever railing against oppression. I have seen the marks of an *inch cable* on the shoulders of a grown up daughter, placed there by a man who was ever uttering anathemas against those, who, for any reason applied the lash to those over whom the law gave them power!

I have seen a little girl drop lifeless under the infliction of the rod, which was used not merely as an instrument of punishment, but to prove that he who wielded it had a right to do what he pleased with his own.

If those who rule with such authority lived where human beings are property, they would exult in its peculiar privileges, and triumph in the wrongs they could commit with impunity.

"Power is indeed corrupting." I have seen a young girl dragged from room to room by her hair, beaten and trodden upon, for only slight offence, by one whom she called mother, because *tyranny was sweet*—to inspire fear more pleasant than to inspire love.

I have seen in many families, wives and daughters and sisters, afraid with a fear not less slavish than that which inspires the most abject among those who are bought and sold, and all because those who held it delighted in swaying the iron sceptre and ruling with an iron rod. And those who are ruled are expected meekly to endure; their lips must be even wreathed in smiles and breathless gladness for those who have crushed all gladness from their hearts. "Power is corrupting," but it is not Kings and Politicians alone whom it corrupts.

SANCTITY OF MARRIAGE

Mrs. E. Oakes Smith

Marriage was dangerous for women. Their husbands could demand obedience from them, owned all the property, including that which wives earned or inherited, and automatically received custody of the children in case of separation or divorce. In addition to such legal disabilities were cultural ones. There was, Lucretia Mott pointed out during the 1850 Convention, what Susan Sontag would later dub a "double standard of aging" such that the expression "like an old woman" invariably meant ugly as well as foolish. Only young women could be attractive. And older men need not hesitate to court young women. Here surely was one aspect of what Paulina Wright Davis meant by "soul murder." The following analysis of the psychic cost of this standard is by Elizabeth Oakes Smith, of whom Davis wrote, "her graceful pen and fertile genius, came to the aid of our cause by defending the convention and the movers of it, through the columns of the *Tribune* and afterward published a series of essays entitled 'Woman and her Needs.'" Oakes Smith's piece is also interesting for the light it throws on what she referred to as "social and domestic evils, so secret, so petty and annoying, that they can neither be reached by public opinion nor legal enactment" especially to be found in marriage. "A right organization of society would aim at the relief of these, as being harder to be borne than others obvious to inspection and comment."

Mrs. E. Oakes Smith, "Sanctity of Marriage," reprinted in *Woman's Rights Tracts, . . . No. 5* (Syracuse, 1852 or 1853).

Oakes Smith typified one style of reform in mid-century America. Her view of a "true" marriage, one based upon the mature commitment of both partners, combines Christian ideas of love with Emersonian ideas about the value of the individual person. It is important to note that, grim as her portrait of many marriages as older men preying upon adolescent girls may be, she nonetheless holds out the prospect of a wholesale reform of marriage.

I have spoken of marriage as the Great Contract. In a true relation this holy and beautiful mystery of life would be a sacrament, whereas it now stands almost entirely as a civil or commercial co-partnership. In New England, even, where it might be supposed that marriage would be less adulterated, it has become very much a household arrangement for thrift or economy, where a woman is selected for her domestic points, in the same manner that a housekeeper is secured. Now, a slight salary for one in the latter capacity, would often times be in better taste than the taking of a wife. I even know of one woman, not by any means low in the scale of position, who proposed to do the labor of one of her servants, provided her penurious husband would pay her, a wife, the price of service, six dollars per month, which he was not ashamed to do. Now, will any one say that such a woman was a wife in the true sense—*one* with her lord and master, who paid her as he would pay a menial? Every married man, and every married woman, knows, either from experience or observation, that it is not an unfrequent [sic] thing for a man to refuse his wife the supply of money necessary to uphold her position in society, if she *fail to become in all things the subservient creature she is expected to be in the marriage relation.* "Surely we are bought with a price," a woman under such circumstances might quote, in the depths of her humiliation.[1] It requires but little penetration to see that a husband who puts the contract upon so coarse and external a basis, offers himself the strongest temptation for its violation.

She is to him a slave, a menial, an appendage, but not a wife; that is, not one with him in soul and life—his inmost self—the completion of his being—the one divine element linking him to the spiritual; the friend, companion, and comforter, with whom he is to take sweet counsel and walk to the house of God in company; yea, into

---

[1] First Corinthians 6: 20 [King James Version]: For ye are bought with a price: therefore glorify God in your body, and in your spirit, which are God's.

that divine tabernacle, that mansion into which no corrupt element finds a lodgement.

It may be that I claim too much of sanctity for marriage—that the common voice is against me, and therefore content to view it as a commercial relation, or one of social convenience only, and involving no questions of greater moment than those of legitimatizing offspring, and securing the transmission of property. Even in this point of view, it would be well that the *terms of contract should be such as to secure its inviolability, and therefore I claim that there should be equality of character in the contracting parties—legal equality, at the very least.*

There are social and domestic evils, so secret, so petty and annoying, that they can neither be reached by public opinion nor legal enactment; and a right organization of society would aim at the relief of these, as being harder to be borne than others obvious to inspection and comment. I would have the marriage relation so protected that as few of these evils should arise as possible. I would avoid the need of legislation, by securing the liberty of both parties equally, till each shall be fully competent to judge the nature of the proposed position [i.e., of wife]. I admit that a gentleman, in the true sense—a man of taste, of sentiment, genius, in other words, one capable of feeling a *great sense of human justice*—will not abuse the confidence of a "Childwife"; he will treat gently and most sacredly the trust of youth, inexperience, and beauty; but I do not write for these, but for those who discern the Truth "as through a glass darkly," who are blind leaders of the blind; wilfully [sic] ignorant, selfishly corrupt, or groping for Truth, and uncertain how to recognize her aspect.

• • •

To me there is something appalling, when I see a mere girl promising at the altar to love, honor, and obey, "till death." Ten to one she does not know or care whether he will deserve to be honored; and, as to obedience, her own stomach, as was said of Queen Bess, may or may not be too proud to bear any will but her own. Then, what does she know of human emotion, of the depths of her own soul or that of another?

When a man or a woman, however, has the courage to promise this, to love till death, they should be of years to realize the solemn import of the words, and willing to hazard the test. One should not be suffered to go forward and put his hand to the seal, clear in vision, cool in judgment, and responsible in law, while the other is blind, undiscerning, and irresponsible. I would say the contract is too momentous in its character to be lightly assumed; too sacred to be broken, and therefore should be well comprehended.

If my reader has followed me . . . , he will perceive that in claiming a woman's right to be [an] individual, and her right to the dignities of property, it was with the view that these might relieve her from the necessity of seeking in marriage that which society ought to award her as her right—that is, position, independent of her relation to one of the other sex; that she should be truly, nobly woman—marry or not marry, as her heart or her taste may dictate, and yet be honorable; she should *live* the truth in her own soul, even although that truth may indispose her to the hackneyed lives of her neighbors, and yet be honorable; that she should relieve the sick, whether as medical advisor or nurse; visit the afflicted, whether as a messenger of the Prince of Peace or a Sister of Charity—and yet be honorable; in all things she should so comport herself that her best and truest womanhood should be developed, and she be honorable, and honored in it; and finally, that if in the maturity of her beauty and the clearness of her intellect she be disposed to carry all this affluence of nature into this divine relation of marriage, she should be still honorable, not as a reflex of another's glory, but as of herself, lending and receiving.

● ● ●

I am aware that the large class of the other sex . . . fit only to admire "bread and butter girls," will oppose this theory of Marriage. It is the style to prate of "sweet sixteen," and to talk of the loveliness of girlhood—and most lovely is it, and sacred should it be held; and therefore the woman should not be defrauded of the period; she should not be allowed to step from the baby-house to the marriage altar. It should be considered not only unwise to do so, but absolutely indelicate. It should affix odium to parents and guardians, if done by their instrumentality; or if by the will of the girl, be regarded as an *evidence of precocious development, as unchaste as it is unwise.*

It is a popular error, that our sex are earlier developed than the other, and therefore sooner adapted to marriage. This, however, is physiological ground, upon which I do not wish to digress; but the assertion that women decay earlier, especially in this country, where early marriages so much prevail, is unfortunately true, and a truth that ought not to apply to us, where the intellect is active, at least, if not profound. And this decay is unquestionably to be imputed to this source. Girls are married and perplexed with the cares of housekeeping, when the pretty ordering of the "wee things" of the play-house would be in better keeping; they suffer the anxieties and sorrows of maternity at an age pitiful to comtemplate, when they should be singing like the lark to Heaven's gate, in the very exuberance—of youthful life and the joyousness of innocent emotion. Even admitting that some slight stirrings of the heart should remind her that she was a well-spring of happy affection, it does not follow that she should be put into bondage for the rest of her life to one whom the undeveloped girl may affect, but whom the woman may perhaps despise. A boy has, it may be, a dozen of "undying," "never to be forgotten" experiences of the kind, between the ages of fourteen and twenty-five, and yet shakes them like "dew from the lion's mane," and looks up, after each trial, if there is to be any manhood in him, with a better and stronger humanity; but if a lovely, susceptible girl, always kept in ignorance of her own nature, responds in the slightest degree to the promptings of her heart, she must be married, as if her heart were an effervescing wine, good for nothing if a sparkle escape, and not rather a deep and holy fountain of calm waters and healthful springs, making glad the wilderness of life, refreshing the arid desert of hearts worn and hackneyed by the toil and heat of the day in the wayfaring of the world.

That a woman should be past all joy, and beauty, and hopefulness, at a period when the other sex are in the perfection of their powers, is a most lamentable fact, and one utterly at variance with the designs of nature, who did not create her for the one purpose of the family relation, but to share in that freedom of being and joyfulness of life which is his [sic] gift to all, and doubly so to one created with such exquisite perfection and affluence of susceptibility as her own organization involves. It is not unusual for girls to be married and become mothers at sixteen, at the expense of health, happiness, and all the appropriateness and dignity of life; and men seem quite proud of these baby-wives, when in truth they should blush at their selfishness, as they too often will repent over their lack of forecast [i.e., foresight]. It is these early marriages that have produced so many crimes and outrages in society.

• • •

The protracted and wearying grief resulting from uncongenial relations is a fruitful source of insanity; and these ungenial relations will be found, in almost all cases, to have been those formed when *one* of the parties was too young to fully comprehend the magnitude of interest involved. I remember, when a child, having a confused idea that to be murdered was one of the possible contingencies of marriage; and this impression was created solely by reading in the public prints the many atrocious catalogues of the kind.

• • •

Miss [Dorothea] Dix[2] must have a mass of material on this ground, and God bless her for her noble mission, one peculiarly adapted to the instinctive and beautiful perceptions of womanhood.

THE BLOOMER

Elizabeth Smith Miller

Reform could take many forms. One of the most controversial dealt with dress. In mid-century, a woman of means wore five or six petticoats under her dress. Her skirt was long so that writers of etiquette books like Emily Thornwell had to provide instructions of how to lift it in a "genteel" way when climbing stairs or walking on a muddy street. A woman of the time often wore a corset since it was considered fashionable to have a "wasp" waist. Day dresses had long sleeves and high necks. Evening dresses were typically sleeveless and cut low in the bodice. Corsets not only cinched in the waist but also pushed up the breasts. "French-heeled" shoes—the heels were typically three or more inches high—completed an evening costume. No one ever accused women's clothes of being comfortable or practical. And many sought change. Some, like Thornwell, campaigned against the corset on the grounds that it imperiled women's health. This also was her reason, morality aside, for criticizing low-cut evening gowns. Others lamented the impossibility of keeping their skirts clean. The popular writer Fanny Fern once quipped that women should be paid by New York City for sweeping its streets every time they took a walk. Still others saw in women's dress the implements as well as the symbols of their subjection to men.

Despite all of this dissatisfaction, dress reform was a dangerous topic. In a culture as intent upon distinguishing masculine from feminine as the

---

[2] Dix led a crusade to improve conditions for the mentally ill.

United States in the nineteenth century, any change in a woman's appearance was sure to provoke ridicule. Indeed, Paulina Wright Davis, who was determined to build the broadest possible coalition in support of woman's rights, effectively banned discussion of dress from the 1850 Convention. "We think the subject an all important one," she wrote in the Proceedings, but "there is neither time nor room to treat it fitly now; no doubt future Conventions will devote to it the thorough consideration which it merits."[1] Despite this silence, opponents like James Gordon Bennett, editor of the New York *Herald,* lost no opportunity to charge that woman's rights activists sought to wear the "pantaloons" [pants]. The most famous dress reform of the day was the "bloomer." Following is a description of its invention, and of its abandonment by its inventor, taken from the Elizabeth Smith Miller collection of the New York Public Library.

I am asked to give a statement of my experience in adopting wearing, and abandoning the short skirt. In the spring of 1851, while spending many hours at work in the garden, I became so thoroughly disgusted with the long skirt, that the dissatisfaction—the growth of years—suddenly ripened into the decision that this shackle should no longer be endured. The resolution was at once put into practice. Turkish trousers to the ankle with a skirt reaching some four inches below the knee, were substituted for the heavy, untidy and exasperating old garment.

Soon after making this change, I went to Seneca Falls to visit my cousin Mrs. [Elizabeth Cady] Stanton. She had so long deplored with me our common misery in the toils of this crippling fashion, that this means of escape was hailed with joy and she at once joined me in wearing the new costume. Mrs. [Amelia Jenk] Bloomer, a friend and neighbor of Mrs. Stanton, then adopted the dress, and as she was editing a paper in which which she advocated it *[The Lily]*, the dress was christened with her name. Mrs. Stanton and I often exchanged visits and sometimes travelled together. We endured, in various places, much gaping curiosity and the harmless jeering of street boys. In the

---

[1] "For ourselves," Davis continued, "we will simply express the hope, that in discarding the inconvenient, unhealthy, untidy, graceless attire now conventionally appropriated to women by the fashions of civilized States, reformers will not feel driven to adopt the stiff, awkward, heavy, ill-shaped costumes in which men are encased. We are well convinced, that a Style of Dress can be invented, far more convenient for use, more easily modified to meet changes in circumstances, climate, or duties, and every way more appropriate and beautiful than any now worn by either sex.

winter of 1852 and 1853, when my father [Gerritt Smith, a wealthy advocate of abolition, woman's rights, and other reforms] was in congress [sic], I was also in the cosmopolitan city of Washington, where I found my peculiar costume much less conspicuous. My street dress was a dark brown corded silk, short skirt and straight trousers, a short but graceful and richly trimmed French cloak of black velvet with drooping sleeves, called a "cantatrice,"—a sable tippet [stole] and a low-crowned beaver hat with a long plume.

I wore the short dress and trousers for many years, my husband, being at all times and in all places, my staunch supporter. My father, also gave the dress his full approval, and I was also blessed by the tonic of Mrs. Stanton's inspiring words: "The question is no longer how do you look, but woman, how do you feel?"

The dress looked tolerably well in standing and walking, but in sitting, a more awkward, uncouth effect, could hardly be produced [or] imagined—it was a perpetual violation of my love of the beautiful. So, by degrees, as my aesthetic senses gained the ascendancy, I lost sight of the great advantages of my dress—its lightness and cleanliness on the streets, its allowing me to carry my babies up and down stairs with perfect ease and safety, and its beautiful harmony with sanitary laws—consequently the skirt was lengthened several inches and the trousers abandoned. As months passed, I proceeded in this retrograde movement, until, after a period of some seven years, I quite "fell from grace" and found myself again in the bonds of the old swaddling clothes—a victim to my love of beauty.

In consideration of what I have previously said in regard to fashion, I feel at liberty to add that I do not wear a heavy, trailing skirt, nor have I ever worn a corset; my bonnet shades my face; my spine was preserved from the bustle, my feet from high heels; my shoulders are not turreted [padded], nor has fashion clasped my neck with her choking collar.

All hail to the day when we shall have a reasonable and beautiful dress that shall encourage exercises on the road and in the field—that shall leave us the free use of our limbs—that shall help and not hinder, our perfect development.

Caroline Wells Healey Dall

There was, as Alice Felt Tyler maintained, "a ferment for reform" at mid-century. There was also strong resistance to calls for change. One can get a feeling for the intensity, the sense of righteousness, reformers brought to their crusades, in this essay by Caroline Wells Healey Dall.

Within a year Dall, from whose best-selling *Essays and Sketches* (1849) the following defense of "reforms" comes, would become an ardent proponent of woman's rights. It would be her interest in rescuing prostitutes and her conviction that only greatly expanded educational and economic opportunities would make that possible which would lead her into the movement. At the time of this essay, however, she discounted talk of woman's rights. Her initial dismissal of the movement, no less than her subsequent espousal of it, makes her an important witness to the elusive "spirit of the age."

... [T]he strength of the impulses which have led to recent philanthropic action cannot be estimated from a better premise than the fact that they have swollen and burst forth rather in despite of those to whom they looked for aid, than from any encouragement thence received. Slaves groan in their chains, drunkards quarrel in their cups, the strong men of rival nations go forth to rob one another, the miserable woman of the crowded city, cheated out of the just worth of her womanly craft, sells her virtue to buy bread for her children; society pets and honors him who buys it, and crushes her like a worm beneath its foot; and still the mass of men look on and say, "We cannot free the slave, we dare not close the grog-shop, we *will* vote for the defenders of the war, we *will* buy cheap clothing, and hold out no hand to help the sinking seamstress—nay we will keep ourselves in good fellowship with the seducer; for all you who have interested yourselves in these matters of reform, have gone too far. You are fanatics, all of you, as pestilential as

Caroline Wells Healey Dall, *Essays and Sketches* (Boston: Samuel G. Simkins, 1849), pp. 76, 82–84.

the very curses you undertake to remove. Beside, abolition is not a gospel; peace is not a gospel; temperance is not a gospel; but these 'three are one' in the Gospel of Christ. We believe *that;* we teach *that;* it includes all these. Have but a little patience, and moral reform itself will be the natural and beautiful fruit of its wide diffusion."

Patience, indeed! we have listened long enough to this. . . .

• • •

A false reproach has been many times thrown upon the advocates of modern reform. It has been said that in their fanaticism they have become men of *one* idea, devoured by their own zeal in behalf of a hobby [horse] well-nigh ridden to death, and that such is not the true spirit in which to undertake a reform. . . .

There is no modern reform that we take so little interest in as the movement in regard to the rights of women. It is true that there have been moments in our life when we would have given worlds to have sat for an instant on the bench, to have thrown one vote in the national assembly, to have spoken one hour at a caucus, or have held a governor's commission just long enough to freely resign it. But while the hot torrent of our blood asked for this, we never for a moment supposed that the court-room, the council-hall, or the caucus was a proper place for us. We only felt that if the *men* of our country had dwindled into caitiffs [cowards], it had the more need of her *women.* The business of our country and our age, it has been most truly said, is to organize the rights of man. One of the holiest of his rights is to find woman her proper place. It is *he* who is robbed by a wrong condition of things. We doubt very much whether Providence ever intended that women should personally share the duties of the commonwealth. We feel that this is utterly incompatible with the more precious and positive duties of the nursery and the fireside. But we long for the time to come when a finished education shall be every woman's birthright; when the respect of the other sex shall be her legitimate inheritance; when the woman of any rank will be able to obtain a livelihood for herself or her children without overtasking the generosity of man; when she shall no longer find herself, even for a moment, a tool or a plaything. We would willingly listen to her voice in the religious assembly.

OUGHT WOMEN TO LEARN THE ALPHABET?

Thomas Wentworth Higginson

Reformers thought they lived on the cusp of the future. Necessities which had bound the vast mass of humanity to lives of ceaseless toil seemed about to relax their grip. The equal tyranny of custom collapsed before their eyes. No longer must the ordinary man and woman live lives essentially like those of their parents and grandparents. The railroad conquered distance. So did the telegraph. Other machines replaced brute labor. Free schools made it possible for everyone who wished to have an education. Republican government meant ordinary citizens could participate in making the public decisions of the day. Constitutional protections guaranteed that individuals could say what they thought, worship or not as they chose, follow any career, seek any office. For the first time in human history, a large number of people felt they could be, in Charles Dickens's phrase, "heroes of their own lives." No one gave fuller or clearer expression to this sense of the radical possibilities of the age than Thomas Wentworth Higginson.

Higginson (1823–1911) was one of the most noteworthy reformers of the mid-nineteenth century. A crusader for woman's rights as well as for the abolition of slavery, his "Ought Women to Learn the Alphabet?," originally published in 1859, was one of the most influential contributions to the debate over women's roles in the public sphere. Higginson's memoir of his service during the Civil War, *Army Life in a Black Regiment,* became a minor classic. His chief claim to literary fame, however, is as Emily Dickinson's confidant and literary advisor.[1]

PREFATORY NOTE

The first essay in this volume, "Ought Women to Learn the Alphabet?," appeared originally in the *Atlantic Monthly* of

---

Thomas Wentworth Higginson, *Women and the Alphabet: A Series of Essays* (Boston and New York: Houghton Mifflin Company, 1881).

[1] Higginson made so many allusions to historical and literary figures in the following essay that to annotate them all would simply make the piece unreadable. So I have limited myself to providing brief explanations of those references whose general import is not clear in context.

February 1859, and has since been reprinted in various forms, bearing its share, I trust, in the great development of more liberal views in respect to the training and duties of women which has made itself manifest within forty years. There was, for instance, a report that it was the perusal of this essay which led the late Miss Sophia Smith to the founding of the women's college bearing her name at Northampton, Massachusetts.

The remaining papers in the volume formed originally a part of a book entitled *Common Sense About Women* which was made up largely of papers from the *Woman's Journal*. This book was first published in 1881 and was reprinted in somewhat abridged form some years later in London (Sonnenschein). It must have attained a considerable circulation there, as the fourth (stereotyped) edition appeared in 1897. From this London reprint a German translation was made by Fräulein Eugenie Jacobi, under the title *Die Frauenfrage und der gesunde Menschenverstand* (Schupp: Neuwied and Leipzig, 1895).

T. W. H.
Cambridge, Mass.

Paris smiled, for an hour or two, in the year 1801, when, amidst Napoleon's mighty projects for remodeling the religion and government of his empire, the ironical satirist, Sylvain Marchal, thrust in his "Plan for a Law prohibiting the Alphabet to Women."[1] Daring, keen, sarcastic, learned, the little tract retains to-day so much of its pungency, that we can hardly wonder at the honest simplicity of the author's friend and biographer, Madame Gacon Dufour, who declared that he must be insane. . . .

• • •

His proposed statute consists of eighty-two clauses, and is fortified by a "whereas" of a hundred and thirteen weighty reasons. He exhausts the range of history to show the frightful results which have followed this taste of fruit of the tree of knowledge; quotes from the *Encyclopædie*, to prove that the woman who knows the alphabet has already lost a portion of her innocence; cites the opinion of Molière, that any female who has unhappily learned anything in this line should affect ignorance, when possible; asserts that knowledge rarely makes men attractive, and females never; opines that women have no occasion to

---

[1] *Projet d'une loi portant defense d'apprendre lire aux femmes.*

peruse Ovid's "Art of Love," since they know it all in advance; remarks that three quarters of female authors are no better than they should be; maintains that Madame Guion would have been far more useful had she been merely pretty and [an] ignoramus, such as Nature made her, —that Ruth and Naomi could not read, and Boaz probably would never have married into the family had they possessed that accomplishment, —that the Spartan women did not know the alphabet, nor the Amazons, nor Penelope, nor Andromache, nor Lucretia, nor Joan of Arc, nor Petrarch's Laura, nor the daughters of Charlemagne, nor the three hundred and sixty-five wives of Mohammed; but that Sappho and Madame de Maintenon could read altogether too well; while the case of Saint Brigitta, who brought forth twelve children and twelve books, was clearly exceptional, and afforded no safe precedent.

It would seem that the brilliant Frenchman touched the root of the matter. Ought women to learn the alphabet? There the whole question lies. Concede this little fulcrum, and Archimedea[2] will move the world before she has done with it: it becomes merely a question of time. Resistance must be made here or nowhere. *Obsta principiis.* Woman must be a subject or an equal: there is no middle ground.

• • •

No doubt, the progress of events is slow, like the working of the laws of gravitation generally. Certainly there has been but little change in the legal position of women since China was in its prime, until within the last half century. Lawyers admit that the fundamental theory of English and Oriental law is the same on this point: Man and wife are one, and that one is the husband. It is the oldest of legal traditions. . . . the dogma of the Gentoo [i.e., Hindu] code, four thousand years old and more: "A man, both day and night, must keep his wife so much in subjection that she by no means be mistress of her own actions. If the wife have her own free will, notwithstanding she be of a superior caste, she will behave amiss."

Yet behind these unchanging institutions, a pressure has been for centuries becoming concentrated, which, now that it has begun to act, is threatening to overthrow them all. It has not yet operated very visibly in the Old World, where, even in England, the majority of women have not till lately mastered the alphabet sufficiently to sign their own name in the marriage register. But in this country the vast changes of

---

[2] A reference to the Greek mathematician Archimedes who proclaimed that, given a fixed point and a lever, he could move the world. Higginson feminized the name.

the last few years[3] are already a matter of history. No trumpet has been sounded, no earthquake has been felt, while State has ushered into legal existence one half of the population within its borders. Surely, here and now, might poor M. Marchal exclaim, the bitter fruits of the original seed appear. The sad question recurs, Whether women ought ever to have tasted of the alphabet.

• • •

Evidently, then the advocates of woman's claims—those who hold that . . . "the talent of the man and the woman is the same," with Socrates in Xenophon's "Banquet"—must be cautious lest they attempt to prove too much. Of course, if women know as much as the men, without schools and colleges, there is no need of admitting them to those institutions. If they work as well on half pay, it diminishes the inducement to give them the other half. The safer position is, to claim that they have done just enough to show what they might have done under circumstances less discouraging. . . . it may be shown that the departments in which women have equalled men have been the departments in which they have had equal training, equal encouragement, and equal compensation; as, for instance, the theatre. Madame Lagrange, the prima donna, after years of costly musical instruction, wins the zenith of professional success; she receives, the newspapers affirm, sixty thousand dollars a year, travelling expenses for ten persons, country-houses, stables, and liveries, besides an uncounted revenue of bracelets, bouquets, and *billets-doux*. . . . On the stage there is no deduction for sex, and, therefore, woman has shown in that sphere an equal genius. But every female common-school teacher in the United States finds the enjoyment of her four hundred dollars a year to be secretly embittered by the knowledge that the young college stripling in the next schoolroom is paid twice that sum for work no harder or more responsible than her own, and that, too, after the whole pathway of education has been obstructed for her, and smoothed for him. These may be gross and carnal considerations; but Faith asks her daily bread, and fancy must be fed. We deny woman her fair share of training, of encouragement, of remuneration, and then talk fine nonsense about her instincts and intuitions. We say sentimentally with the Oriental proverbialist, "Every book of knowledge is implanted by nature in the heart of woman," —and make the compliment a substitute for the alphabet.

---

[3] A reference to the creation of free public schools for both boys and girls in the North in the 1840s and 1850s.

Nothing can be more absurd than to impose entirely distinct standards, in this respect, on the two sexes, or to expect that woman, any more than man, will accomplish anything great without due preparation and adequate stimulus.

● ● ●

To disregard this truth is unreasonable in the abstract, and cruel in its consequences. If an extraordinary male gymnast can clear a height of ten feet with the aid of a springboard, it would be considered slightly absurd to ask a woman to leap eleven feet without one; yet this [is] precisely what society and the critics have always done. Training and wages and social approbation are very elastic springboards; and the whole course of history has seen these offered bounteously to one sex, and as sedulously withheld from the other. Let woman consent to be a doll, and there was no finery so gorgeous, no baby-house so costly, but she might aspire to share its lavish delights; let her ask simply for an equal chance to learn, to labor, and to live, and it was as if that same doll should open its lips, and propound Euclid's forty-seventh proposition. While we have all deplored the helpless position of indigent women, and lamented that they had no alternative beyond the needle, the wash-tub, the schoolroom, and the street, we have usually resisted their admission into every new occupation, denied them training, and cut their compensation down. Like Charles Lamb, who atoned for coming late to the office in the morning by going away early in the afternoon, we have, first, half educated women, and then, to restore the balance, only half paid them. What innumerable obstacles have been placed in their way as female physicians; what a complication of difficulties has been encountered by them, even as printers, engravers, and designers! . . .

We find, on investigation, what these considerations would lead us to expect, that eminent women have commonly been exceptional in training and position, as well as in their genius. They have excelled the average of their own sex because they have shared the ordinary advantages of the other sex. . . . who knows how many mute, inglorious Minervas[4] may have perished unenlightened, while Margaret Fuller

---

[4]A paraphrase of Thomas Gray's "Elegy in a Country Churchyard," stanza 15:
Some village Hampden, that with dauntless breast
The little tyrant of his fields withstood,
Some mute inglorious Milton here may rest,
Some Cromwell guiltless of his country's blood.

Ossoli[5] and Elizabeth Barrett Browning[6] were being educated "like boys."

This expression simply means that they had the most solid training which the times afforded. Most persons would instantly take alarm at the very words; that is, they have so little faith in the distinctions which Nature has established, that they think, if you teach the alphabet, or anything else, indiscriminately to both sexes, you annull [sic] all difference between them. The common reasoning is thus: "Boys and girls are acknowledged to be very unlike. Now, boys study Greek and algebra, medicine and bookkeeping. Therefore girls should not." As if one should say: "Boys and girls are very unlike. Now, boys eat beef and potatoes. Therefore, obviously, girls should not."

The analogy between physical and spiritual food is precisely in point. The simple truth is, that, amid the vast range of human powers and properties, the fact of sex is but one item. Vital and momentous in itself, it does not constitute the whole organism, but only a part. The distinction of male and female is special, aimed at a certain end; and, apart from that end, it is, throughout all the kingdoms of Nature, of minor importance. With but trifling exceptions, from infusoria [microcospic organisms] up to man, the female animal moves, breathes, looks, listens, runs, flies, swims, pursues its food, eats it, digests it, in precisely the same manner as the male: all instincts, all characteristics, are the same, except as to the one solitary fact of parentage. . . . The eagle is not checked in soaring by any consciousness of sex, nor asks the sex of the timid hare, its quarry. Nature, for high purposes, creates and guards the sexual distinction, but keeps it subordinate to those still more important.

• • •

Thus far, my whole course of argument has been defensive and explanatory. I have shown that woman's inferiority in special achievements, so far as it exists, is a fact of small importance, because it is merely a corollary from her historic position of degradation. She has not excelled, because she has had no fair chance to excel. Man, placing his foot upon her shoulder, has taunted her with not rising. But the ulterior question remains behind. How came she into this attitude originally? Explain the explanation, the logician fairly demands. . . .

---

[5] Author of *Woman in the Nineteenth Century*. Paulina Wright Davis, president of the first two national woman's rights conventions, wrote in her history of the movement that she had hoped Fuller would preside over the Worcester Convention.

[6] English poet, author of the wildly popular *Sonnets from the Portuguese*.

I venture to assert, then, that woman's social inferiority has been, to a great extent, in the past a legitimate thing. To all appearance, history would have been impossible without it, just as it would have been impossible without an epoch of war and slavery. It is simply a matter of social progress, —a part of the succession of civilizations. The past has been inevitably a period of ignorance, of engrossing physical necessities, and of brute force, —not of freedom, of philanthropy, and of culture. During that lower epoch, woman was necessarily an inferior, degraded by abject labor, even in time of peace, —degraded uniformly by war, chivalry to the contrary notwithstanding. Behind all the courtesies of Amadis and the Cid lay the stern fact, —woman [was] a child or a toy. The flattering troubadours chanted her into a poet's paradise; but alas! that kingdom of heaven suffered violence, and the violent took it by force. The truth simply was, that her time had not come. Physical strength must rule for a time, and she was the weaker. . . . From this reign of force, woman never freed herself by force. She could not fight, or would not. . . .

The reason, then, for the long subjection of woman has been simply that humanity was passing through its first epoch, and her full career was to be reserved for the second. As the different races of man have appeared successively upon the stage of history, so there has been an order of succession of the sexes. Woman's appointed era, like that of the Teutonic races, was delayed, but not omitted. It is not merely true that the empire of the past has belonged to man, but that it has properly belonged to him; for it was an empire of the muscles, enlisting, at best, but the lower powers of the understanding. There can be no question that the present epoch is initiating an empire of the higher reason, of arts, affections, aspirations; and for that epoch the genius of woman has been reserved. The spirit of the age has always kept pace with the facts, and outstripped the statutes. Till the fullness of time came, woman was necessarily kept a slave to the spinning-wheel and the needle; now higher work is ready; peace has brought invention to her aid, and the mechanical means for her emancipation are ready also. No use in releasing her till man, with his strong arm, had worked out his preliminary share in civilization.

• • •

Everybody sees that the times are altering the whole material position of woman; but most people do not appear to see the inevitable social and moral changes which are also involved. . . .

. . . But with us Americans, and in this age, when . . . Rochester grinds the flour and Lowell weaves the cloth, and the fire on the hearth has gone into black retirement and mourning; when the wiser a virgin is, the less she has to do with oil in her lamp; when the needle has made its last dying speech and confession in the "Song of the Shirt,"[7] and the sewing-machine has changed those doleful marches to delightful measures, —how is it possible for the blindest to help seeing that a new era is begun, and that the time has come for woman to learn the alphabet?

Nobody asks for any abolition of domestic labor for women, any more than of outdoor labor for men. Of course, most women will still continue to be mainly occupied with the indoor care of their families, and most men with their external support. All that is desirable for either sex is such an economy of labor, in this respect, as shall leave some spare time to be appropriated in other directions. The argument against each new emancipation of woman is precisely that always made against the liberation of serfs and the enfranchisement of plebeians, — that the new position will take them from their legitimate business. "How can he [or she] get wisdom that holdeth the plough [or the broom], —whose talk is of bullocks [or of babies]?"[8] Yet the American farmer has already emancipated himself from these fancied incompatibilities; and so will the farmer's wife. In a nation where there is no leisure class and no peasantry, this whole theory of exclusion is an absurdity. We all have a little leisure, and we must all make the most of it. If we will confine large interests and duties to those who have nothing else to do, we must go back to monarchy at once. If otherwise, then the alphabet, and its consequences, must be open to woman as to man. . . .

There are duties devolving on every human being, —duties not small nor few, but vast and varied, —which spring from home and private life, and all their sweet relations. The support or care of the humblest household is a function worthy of men, women, and angels, so far as it goes. From these duties none must shrink, neither man nor woman; the loftiest genius cannot ignore them; the sublimest charity

---

[7] Reference to the poem by Thomas Hood (1798–1845):

> With fingers weary and worn,
> With eyelids heavy and red,
> A woman sat in unwomanly rags
> Plying her needle and thread, —
> Stitch! stitch! stitch!

[8] A reference to one of the apocryphal books of the Bible [King James Version]: Eccl. 38:24–25: The wisdom of a learned man cometh by opportunity of leisure: and he that hath little business shall become wise. / How can he get wisdom that holdeth the plough, and that glorieth in the goad, that driveth oxen, and is occupied in their labours, and whose talk is of bullocks?

must begin with them. They are their own exceeding great reward; their self-sacrifice is infinite joy; and the selfishness which discards them is repaid by loneliness and a desolate old age. Yet these, though the most tender and intimate portion of human life, do not form its whole. It is given to noble souls to crave other interests also, added spheres, not necessarily alien from these; larger knowledge, larger action also; duties, responsibilities, anxieties, dangers, all the aliment that history has given to its heroes. Not home less, but humanity more. When . . . the stainless soul of Joan of Arc met God, like Moses, in a burning flame, —these things were as they should be. Man must not monopolize these privileges of peril, the birthright of great souls. Serenades and compliments must not replace the nobler hospitality which shares with woman the opportunity of martyrdom. Great administrative duties also, cares of state, for which one should be born gray-headed, how nobly do these sit upon a woman's brow! Each year adds to the storied renown of Elizabeth of England, greatest sovereign of the greatest of historic nations. Christina of Sweden, alone among the crowned heads of Europe (so says Voltaire), sustained the dignity of the throne against Richelieu and Mazarin. And these queens most assuredly did not sacrifice their womanhood in the process; for her Britannic Majesty's wardrobe included four thousand gowns; and Mlle. de Montpensier declares that when Christina had put on a wig of the latest fashion, "she really looked extremely pretty."

Les races se feminisent, said Buffon, —"The world is growing more feminine." It is a compliment, whether the naturalist intended it or not. Time has brought peace; peace, invention; and the poorest woman of to-day is born to an inheritance of which her ancestors never dreamed. Previous attempts to confer on women social and political equality . . . were premature, and valuable only as recognitions of a principle. But in view of the rapid changes now going on, he is a rash man who asserts the "Woman Question" to be anything but a mere question of time. The fulcrum has been already given in the alphabet, and we must simply watch, and see whether the earth does not move.

There is the plain fact: woman must be either a subject or an equal; there is no middle ground. Every concession to a supposed principle only involves the necessity of the next concession for which that principle calls. Once yield the alphabet, and we abandon the whole long theory of subjection and coverture: tradition is set aside, and we have nothing but reason to fall back upon. Reasoning abstractly, it must be admitted that the argument has been, thus far, entirely on the women's side, inasmuch as no man has yet seriously tried to meet them with argument. It is an alarming feature of this discussion, that it has reversed, very generally, the traditional positions of the sexes: the women have had all the logic; and the most intelligent men, when they have attempted the other side, have limited themselves to satire and gossip. What rational woman can be really convinced by the nonsense which is talked in ordinary society around her, —as, that it is right to admit girls to common schools, and equally right to exclude them from colleges; that it is proper for a woman to sing in public, but indelicate for her to speak in public; that a post-office box is an unexceptionable place to drop a bit of paper into, but a ballot-box terribly dangerous? No cause in the world can keep above water, sustained by such contradictions as these, too feeble and slight to be dignified by the name of fallacies. Some persons profess to think it impossible to reason with a woman, and such critics certainly show no disposition to try the experiment.

But we must remember that all our American institutions are based on consistency, or on nothing: all claim to be founded on the principles of natural right; and when they quit those, they are lost. In all European monarchies it is the theory that the mass of the people are children to be governed, not mature beings to govern themselves; this is clearly stated and consistently applied. In the United States we have formally abandoned this theory for one half of the human race, while for the other half it flourishes with little change. The moment the claims of woman are broached, the democrat becomes a monarchist. What Americans commonly criticize in English statesmen, namely, that they habitually evade all arguments based on natural right, and defend every legal wrong on the ground that it works well in practice, is the precise defect in our habitual view of woman. The perplexity must be resolved somehow. Most men admit that a strict adherence to our own principles would place both sexes in precisely equal positions before law and constitution, as well as in school and society. But each has his special quibble to apply, showing that in this case we must abandon all the general maxims to which we have pledged ourselves, and hold only by precedent. Nay, he construes even precedent with the most ingenious rigor; since the exclusion of women from all direct contact with affairs can be made far more perfect in a republic than is possible in a monarchy, where even sex is merged in rank, and the female patrician may have far more power than the male plebeian. But, as matters now stand among us, there is no aristocracy but of sex: all men are born patrician, all women are legally plebeian; all men are equal in having political power, and all women in having none. This is a paradox so evident, and such an anomaly in human progress, that it cannot last forever, without new discoveries in logic, or else a deliberate return to M. Marchal's theory concerning the alphabet.

Meanwhile, as the newspapers say, we anxiously await further developments. According to present appearances, the final adjustment lies mainly in the hands of women themselves. Men can hardly be expected to concede either rights or privileges more rapidly than they are claimed, or to be truer to women than women are to each other. In fact, the worst effect of a condition of inferiority is the weakness it leaves behind; even when we say, "Hands off!" the sufferer does not rise. In such a case, there is but one counsel worth giving. More depends on determination than even on ability. Will, not talent, governs the world. . . . In how many towns was the current of popular prejudice against female orators reversed by one winning speech from Lucy Stone! Where no logic can prevail, success silences. First give woman, if you dare, the alphabet, then summon her to her career: and though men, ignorant and prejudiced, may oppose its beginnings, they will at last fling around her conquering footsteps more lavish praises than ever greeted the opera's idol, —more perfumed flowers than ever wooed, with intoxicating fragrance, the fairest butterfly of the ball-room.

MANY MATTERS

Jane Grey Swisshelm

It is tempting to put mid-nineteenth-century reformers into a single, neat category. The only difficulty is that they won't all fit. Reformers not only argued with those who defended slavery or the use of alcohol or feared that granting women civil rights would overturn the family, they also argued endlessly with each other. One of the most vigorous participants in their debates was Jane Grey Swisshelm.

Jane Grey Swisshelm, *Half a Century,* 2nd ed. (Chicago: Jansen, McClurg and Company, 1880), pp. 145, 146–147.

Although an early and earnest advocate of woman's rights, Swiss-helm, as her controversy with Parker Pillsbury over the adoption at the Worcester convention of a resolution linking woman's rights with those of people of color, excerpted here, shows, soon became a bitter critic of the movement. Long after the dust had settled in her dispute with Pills-bury, Swisshelm's contempt for "universal" reform had not abated. The following excerpt from her autobiography makes that clear. It also suggests the bitterness she continued to feel toward those who ignored her advice about how to advance the cause of woman's rights. However, as a journalist, editor of the popular newspaper, the *Saturday Visiter* [sic], and long-time abolitionist, Swisshelm was herself an important reform voice. Her characterization of the "spirit of the age," as a result, demands serious attention. So does her "go easy" prescription for the woman's movement, if only because her proposed sequence of steps fairly accurately foretold the actual progress of women toward legal equality.

The period of the *Visiter* [1848–57] was one of great mental activity— a period of hobbies—and it, having assumed the reform roll [sic], was expected to assume all the reforms. Turkish trowsers [trousers, aka the Bloomer costume], Fourierism,[1] Spiritualism,[2] Vegetarianism, Phonetics,[3] Pneumonics,[4] the Eight hour [of labor per day] law, Criminal Caudling,[5] Magdalenism,[6] and other devices for teaching

---

[1] The social philosophy named after Charles Fourier (1772–1837). He was a well-known proponent of utopian socialist ideas (so-called after Marx's distinction between his own "scientific" socialism and the ideas of his predecessors); he was born in Besançon, France, and worked as a clerk before publishing his first work, *The Social Destiny of Man, or, Theory of the Four Movements* (1808). After inheriting his mother's estate in 1812, he devoted himself to developing the details of his ideas in such works as *The New Industrial World* (1829). He advocated a reorganization of society into self-sufficient units (*phalanstères* or phalanxes) which would offer a maximum of both cooperation and choice to members. A number of so-called utopian communities in the United States adopted Fourier's principles. Perhaps the best known of these was Brook Farm.

[2] In 1848, Kate and Margaret Fox, two sisters aged twelve and fifteen, who lived outside Rochester, New York, began their careers as mediums to the spirit world by deciphering the meaning of mysterious rapping sounds. Within a few years popular mediums were giving well-attended lectures, sometimes in a trance state, throughout the northern states in which they described the afterlife. Others held séances at which believers communicated with loved ones who had died or recovered memories of previous lives.

[3] A campaign for simplified spelling, based on phonetic principles.

[4] A system of breathing exercises for which proponents claimed health values.

[5] A caudle is a warm beverage, usually a mixture of wine or ale and eggs, sugar, and spices, given to the sick.

[6] A campaign to rescue prostitutes by providing shelter, occupational training, and religious counseling. Mrs. Sarah Tyndale led such a crusade in Philadelphia. Lucretia Mott's speech extolling her friend's success was one of the emotional high points of the 1850 convention.

pyramids to stand on their apex were pressed upon the *Visiter*, and it was held by the disciples of each as "false to all its professions," when declining to devote itself to its advocacy. There were a thousand men and women, who knew exactly what it ought to do; but seldom two of them agreed, and none ever thought of furnishing funds for the doing of it. Reformers insisted that it should advocate their plan of hurrying up the millennium, furnish the white paper and pay the printers.

• • •

The policy of the *Visiter* in regard to Woman's Rights, was to "go easy," except in the case of those slave-women, who had no rights. For others, gain an advance when you could. Educate girls with boys, develop their brains, and take away legal disabilities little by little, as experience should show was wise; but never dream of their doing the world's hard work, either mental or physical; and Heaven defend them from going into all the trades.

The human teeth proved that we should eat flesh, and the human form proved that men should take the ore out of the mines, subdue the inertia of matter and the ferocity of animals; that they should raise the grain, build the houses, roads and heavy machinery; and that women should do the lighter work. As this work was as important as the heavier, and as it fell principally on wives and mothers, they in these relations should receive equal compensation with the husband and father. By this plan, the estate acquired by a matrimonial firm, would belong equally to both parties, and each could devise his or her share, so that a woman would know that her accumulations would go to her heirs, not to her successor. Consequently, every wife would have an incentive to industry and economy, instead of being stimulated to idleness and extravagance as by existing laws.

Women should not weaken their cause by impracticable demands. Make no claim which could not be won in a reasonable time. Take one step at a time, get a good foothold in it and advance carefully. Suffrage in municipal elections for property holders who could read, and had never been connected with crime, was the place to strike for the ballot. Say nothing about suffrage elsewhere until it proved successful here.

2

The Convention

In 1870 Paulina Wright Davis wrote a history of the woman's rights movement on the occasion of the twentieth anniversary of the Worcester Convention which she had organized. In it she detailed some of the events leading up to that meeting. It is noteworthy that she devoted far more attention to the 1850 Salem, Ohio, convention than to the 1848 Seneca Falls gathering to which historians routinely point as the beginning of the woman's rights movement. Davis had no intention of slighting the work of the women who met at Seneca Falls. Both Elizabeth Cady Stanton and Lucretia Mott, who played leading roles in that convention, were friends. Both were on the podium when Wright Davis read her *History*. And Stanton had just nominated her to preside over the anniversary convention. Instead her relative inattention to Seneca Falls, her failure even to mention the "Declaration of Sentiments" adopted there, reflected the conventional views of the first generation of woman's rights activists.

Wright Davis joked about the Salem convention's decision not to permit men to participate. At the time, however, she regarded it as a major mistake. As she would make clear in her keynote speech at the Worcester Convention, she thought that women had to reach out for the support of men if they were to have any chance of success.

A History of the National Woman's Rights Movement, for Twenty Years, with the Proceedings of the Decade Meeting Held at Apollo Hall, October 20, 1870, From 1850 to 1870. With an appendix containing the history of the movement during the Winter of 1871, in the National Capitol. Compiled by Paulina W. Davis (New York: Journeymen Printers' Co-operative Association, 1871).

A HISTORY OF THE NATIONAL WOMAN'S
RIGHTS MOVEMENT

Paulina Wright Davis

Two years previous to the issue of the call of 1850, there had been three conventions held, one in Seneca Falls, one in Rochester, N.Y., and one in Ohio.

. . . The Ohio convention had some peculiar characteristics; it was held in the Friends' Meeting-House in Salem. It was officered entirely by women; not a man was allowed to sit on the platform, to speak or to vote. *Never did men so suffer.* They implored just to say a word; but no, the President was inflexible—no man should be heard. If one meekly rose to make a suggestion he was at once ruled out of order. For the first time in the world's history men learned how it felt to sit in silence when great questions were pending. It would have been an admirable closing, if a rich banquet had been provided to which the men should have had the *privilege* of purchasing tickets to the gallery, there to enjoy the savory odors and listen to the after-dinner speeches. A little pity, mingled with justice, prevented this *finale.* And at the close, after the adjournment, the men organized and indorsed [sic] all the women had said and done.

. . . In May, 1850, a few women in Boston, attending the Anti-Slavery meeting, proposed that all who felt interested in a plan for a National Woman's Rights Convention should consult in the ante-room. Out of the nine who went out into that dingy, dark room, a committee of seven were chosen to do the work. Worcester was the place selected, and the 18th and 19th of October [sic] the time appointed. The work soon devolved upon one person [Paulina Wright Davis]. Illness hindered one, duty to a brother another, duty to the slave a third [Abby Kelley Foster], professional engagements a fourth, the fear of bringing the gray hairs of a father to the grave prevented another serving; and thus the work was left to one, but the pledge was made and could not be withdrawn.

The call was prepared, an argument in itself, and sent forth with earnest private letters in all directions. This call covered the entire question, as it now stands before the public.

...This call, though moderate in tone, carefully guarding the idea of the absolute unity of interests and of the destiny of the two sexes which nature has established, still gave the alarm to conservatism.

Letters curt, reproachful and sometimes almost insulting, came with absolute refusals to have the names of the writers used or added to the swelling list already in hand. There was astonishment at the temerity of the writer in presenting such a request.

• • •

The convention came together on the bright October days, a solemn, earnest crowd of workers.

One great disappointment fell upon us. Margaret Fuller,[1] toward whom many eyes were turned as the future leader in this movement, was not with us. The "hungry, ravening sea," had swallowed her up, and we were left to mourn her guiding hand—her royal presence. To her, I, at least, had hoped to confide the leadership of this movement. It can never be known if she would have accepted this leadership; the desire had been expressed to her by letter; but be that as it may, she was, and still is, a leader of thought—a position far more desirable than of numbers.

THE "CALL" TO THE WORCESTER CONVENTION

Paulina Wright Davis

As she noted in her *History,* Paulina Wright Davis wrote the "Call" to the Worcester Convention. It clearly expressed her view not only of woman's rights, and wrongs, but of the proper strategy to adopt to achieve the first and redress the second. She would continue to help shape the public agenda of the woman's movement. She presided over the first two national conventions, created the first permanent woman's rights organizations—the standing committees formed at the conclusion of the 1850 meeting—and founded the first woman's rights

---

[1] Author of *Woman in the Nineteenth Century.* Fuller, with Ralph Waldo Emerson, was one of the founders of Transcendentalism.

newspaper, *The Una.* To say that scholars have underestimated her importance is an understatement.

A convention will be held at Worcester, Mass., on the twenty-third and twenty-fourth of October next, (agreeably to appointment by a preliminary meeting held at Boston, on the thirtieth of May last) to consider the great question of Woman's Rights, Duties, and Relations; and the Men and Women of our country who feel sufficient interest in the subject, to give an earnest thought and effective effort to its rightful adjustment, are invited to meet each other in free conference, at the time and place appointed.

The upward tending spirit of the age, busy in a hundred forms of effort for the world's redemption from the sins and sufferings which oppress it, has brought this one, which yields to none in importance and urgency, into distinguished prominence. One half of the race are its immediate objects, and the other half are as deeply involved, by that absolute unity of interest and destiny which nature has established between them.

The neighbor is near enough to involve every human being in a general equality of rights and community of interests; but, Men and Women, in their reciprocities of love and duty are one flesh and one blood—mother, wife, sister, and daughter come so near the heart and mind of every man that they must be either his blessing or his bane. Where there is such mutuality of interests, such an interlinking of life, there can be no real antagonism of position and action. The sexes should not, for any reason or by any chance, take hostile attitudes towards each other, either in the apprehension or amendment of the wrongs which exist in their necessary relations; but they should harmonize in opinion and cooperate in effort, for the reason that they must unite in the ultimate achievement of the desired reformation.

Of the many points now under discussion and demanding a just settlement, the general question of Woman's Rights and Relations comprehends these:

- Her Education, Literary, Scientific, and Artistic;
- Her Avocations, Industrial, Commercial, and Professional;
- Her Interests, Pecuniary, Civil, and Political; in a word
- Her Rights as an Individual, and her Functions as a Citizen.

No one will pretend that all these interests, embracing, as they do, all that is not merely animal in a human life, are rightly understood or justly provided for in the existing social order. Nor is it any more true that the constitutional differences of the sexes, which should determine, define, and limit the resulting differences of office and duty, are adequately comprehended and practically observed.

Woman has been condemned for her greater delicacy of physical organization to inferiority of intellectual and moral culture, and to the forfeiture of great social, civil, and religious privileges. In the relation of marriage she has been ideally annihilated, and actually enslaved in all that concerns her personal and pecuniary rights; and even in widowhood and single life, she is oppressed with such limitation and degradation of labor and avocation as clearly and cruelly mark the condition of a disabled caste. But, by the inspiration of the Almighty, the beneficent spirit of reform is roused to the redress of these wrongs. The tyranny which degrades and crushes wives and mothers, sits no longer lightly on the world's conscience; the heart's home-worship feels the stain of stooping at a dishonored altar; Manhood begins to feel the shame of muddying the springs from which it draws its highest life; and Womanhood is everywhere awakening to assert its divinely chartered rights, and to fulfil its noblest duties. It is the spirit of reviving truth and righteousness which has moved upon the great deep of the public heart and aroused its redressing justice; and, through it, the Providence of God is vindicating the order and appointments of his creation.

The signs are encouraging; the time is opportune. Come, then, to this Convention. It is your duty, if you are worthy of your age and country. Give the help of your best thought to separate the light from the darkness. Wisely give the protection of your name and the benefit of your efforts to the great work of settling the principles, devising the method, and achieving the success of this high and holy movement.

• • •

Editorial Note: Eighty-nine individuals signed "the Call," according to Harriet H. Robinson, *Massachusetts in the Woman Suffrage Movement*, 2nd ed., Boston: Roberts Brothers, 1883, Appendix D. They were:

Massachusetts: Lucy Stone, William H. Channing, Harriet K. Hunt, A. Bronson Alcott, Nathaniel Barney, Eliza Barney, Wendell Phillips, Ann Greene Phillips, Adin Ballou, Anna Q.T. Parsons, Mary H.L. Cabot, B.S. Treanor, Mary M. Brooks, T.W. Higginson, Mary E. Higginson, Emily Winslow, R. Waldo Emerson, William Lloyd Garrison, Charles F. Hovey, Sarah Earle, Abby Kelley Foster, Dr. Seth Rogers, Eliza F. Taft, Dr. A.C. Taft, Charles K. Whipple, Mary Bullard, Emma

C. Goodwin, Abby H. Price, Thankful Southwick, Eliza J. Kenney, Louisa M. Sewall, Sarah Southwick.

Rhode Island: Sarah H. Whitman, Thomas Davis, Paulina Wright Davis, Joseph A. Barker, Sarah Brown, Elzabeth B. Chace, Mary Clarke, John L. Clarke, George Clarke, Mary Adams, George Adams.

New York: Gerrit Smith, Nancy Smith, Elizabeth Cady Stanton, Catharine Wilkinson, Samuel J. May, Charlotte C. May, Charlotte G. Coffin, Mary G. Taber, Elizabeth S. Miller, Elizabeth Russell, Stephen S. Smith, Rosa Smith, Joseph Savage, L.N. Fowler, Lydia Fowler, Sarah Smith, Charles D. Miller.

Pennsylvania: William Elder, Sarah Elder, Sarah Tyndale, Warner Justice, Jane G. Swisshelm, Charlotte Darlington, Simon Barnard, Lucretia Mott, Myra Townsend, Mary Grew, Sarah Lewis, Sarah Pugh, Huldah Justice, William Swisshelm, James Mott, W.S. Pierce, Hannah Darlington, Sarah D. Bernard.

Maryland: Eliza Stewart.

Ohio: Elizabeth Wilson, Mary A. Johnson, Oliver Johnson, Mary Cowles, Maria L. Giddings, Jane Elizabeth Jones, Benjamin S. Jones, Lucius A. Hine, Sylvia Cornell.

RECREATING THE CONVENTION

This recreation of the convention brings together the published *Proceedings* and contemporary newspaper coverage. The *Proceedings* contains the texts of the resolutions proposed and adopted, lists committee memberships, prints several—but by no means all—speeches, and letters from supporters, such as Elizabeth Cady Stanton, unable to attend. It does not contain transcriptions or even summaries of the debates which those speeches and resolutions provoked. Fortunately, several newspapers published detailed accounts of each day's sessions which go a long way toward filling this gap. The papers were unabashedly partisan and did not scruple about allowing their editorial loyalties to influence their accounts. The official *Proceedings* was also a partisan account, it needs emphasizing, one which omitted any hint of disagreement or controversy among those attending the convention. All of the accounts, therefore, must be used with caution, but this does not necessarily lessen their value as historical sources. Woman's rights aroused passion in almost everyone, and the ensuing debates generated at least as much heat as they did light. As a result, one can use these sometimes conflicting and sometimes complementary versions of what happened in Worcester in 1850 to gain insight into the emotional furor the whole question of woman's "proper sphere" provoked. In addition, one can see reflected in them some of the strategies proponents and opponents of woman's rights adopted.

Some of the most thorough reportage of the 1850 Worcester Convention appeared in the New York *Daily Tribune*, edited by Horace Greeley. Greeley was one of the most influential editors/publishers of the middle third of the nineteenth century and a longtime crusader for a variety of reforms, including the abolition of slavery. The *Tribune*'s correspondent was the Rev. J. G. Forman of West Bridgewater, Massachusetts. He took an active part in the convention and was named to one of the committees created to carry forward its work.[1] This "insider" status gave Forman access to the leading figures who assembled in Worcester. As a result, his account is highly detailed. It is not, however, complete and, while it is usually accurate, his personal support for woman's rights sometimes led him to pull his journalistic punches in both minor matters (his description of speaker after speaker as "eloquent," for example) and major. He did not report, to cite an important case in point, the substance of Abby Kelley Foster's speech during the afternoon session of the first day, a speech which her close friend Lucy Stone later characterized as "odious," although he did include some information about Lucretia Mott's efforts to tone down Kelley Foster's rhetoric in the evening session.[2] Greeley's willingness to print Forman's lengthy, and very positive, "letters" from the convention unquestionably did much to provoke interest in it and in the whole question of woman's rights.

James Gordon Bennett, editor of the New York *Herald*, was Greeley's chief rival. We do not know the name of the Herald's reporter. He too filed a very detailed story but only of the convention's first day. The

---

[1] In this instance one should take the word correspondent literally. Forman wrote letters describing the convention which Greeley published with little or no editing.

[2] Stone's comment came in a eulogy at Kelley Foster's funeral.

Herald apparently lifted much of its coverage of the second day from the *Tribune,* a common journalistic practice. But, since Bennett was intensely hostile to the movement for woman's rights, and intensely scornful of Greeley's support for it, he wove a vituperative commentary throughout his version of the *Tribune*'s basically friendly account. Its editor's bias does not mean that the *Herald*'s account of the first day is untrustworthy. Its anonymous reporter made frequent sport of the speakers, but he also recorded practically verbatim much of what they said, as with their sometimes humorous discussion about the vow of obedience in the marriage ceremony during the evening session of the first day. And, where the *Tribune* refused to go into detail about Abby Kelley Foster's incendiary speech and several other controversial matters, the Herald was only too happy to do so.

The Boston press also gave the convention extensive coverage. The *Chronotype*'s editor-publisher, Elizur Wright, was an even more enthusiastic advocate of woman's rights than Greeley and sent a letter of support which was read aloud at the convention. Unfortunately, his paper's account of the first day—I have been unable to locate a copy of the next day's issue—added little to the detail supplied in the *Daily Tribune.* Also strongly supportive of woman's rights was *The Liberator,* the radical abolitionist weekly edited and published by William Lloyd Garrison. Garrison and his wife signed the "Call" to the convention and both attended. In the weeks before, *The Liberator* printed excerpts of the "Call" along with the list of signers. Garrison also played an active role at the convention itself and gave a major speech on the afternoon of the second day. *The Liberator* for November 15 devoted its entire front page to the "Proceedings" of the convention including the full texts of all resolutions, a list of speakers, and the names of all of the officers. Garrison published the text of Paulina Wright Davis's presidential address on the back page, though without attribution. The following week's issue, that of November 22, contained more convention material in the form of letters read aloud during the sessions. All of this duplicated material available in the Convention *Proceedings.*

The Boston *Daily Mail* was, like the New York *Herald,* highly critical of the woman's rights campaign. In fact, John Milton Earle, editor of Worcester's *Massachusetts Spy,* disparaged the *Daily Mail*'s "exceedingly scurrilous article" on the convention as "a very poor imitation of Bennett's *Herald,* exhibiting all the low vulgarity of that print without any of its wit or humor. It is an article which no man with the feelings of a gentleman could have written, and which no paper with any regard to its character with respectable people, would have published." The *Mail*'s coverage was nonetheless among the most thorough. In fact, it was much more detailed than that in the *Massachusetts Spy,* despite the fact that editor Earle's wife Sarah was one of the principal organizers of the convention. However, as the Mail's anonymous reporter candidly admitted, he decided to skip the concluding session of the convention since he wanted to be sure he could get a train back to Boston that evening and could gain no assurance that the meeting would wrap up by 10:00.

In organizing these materials I have put the various accounts of each session together starting with the convention *Proceedings* followed by relevant news accounts. I have highlighted the central controversies and issues raised at the convention in notes introducing each session. These notes also provide relevant background and contextual information.

I have corrected obvious typographical errors, inserted relevant information (such as first names where known) in brackets, and annotated biblical and other quotations (where possible). I have also attempted to identify contemporary references. I have not corrected the spellings of proper names, such as the New York *Herald*'s spelling of Abby Kelley Foster's name as "Kelly" or of Frederick Douglass's as "Douglas," since some of these were deliberate (as when some papers referred to abolitionist Charles C. Burleigh as "Burley").[3]

• • •

**OCTOBER 23, 1850—MORNING SESSION
FROM: THE *PROCEEDINGS** OF THE WOMAN'S
CONVENTION, HELD AT WORCESTER, 1850**

Although one would not know it from reading the official Proceedings, *the convention's opening session provoked an argument about strategy which continued through the entire two days and which, in somewhat different form,*

---

[3] Kelly is the Irish spelling, Kelley the Scotch-Irish. Hundreds of thousands of Irish poured into the northern states in the 1840s in the wake of the Potato Famine. Their appearance provoked a good deal of hostility. Within a few years, the Know Nothing movement would emerge, committed to limiting the power of immigrants and, especially, limiting the power of the Catholic church. The *Herald*'s misspelling of Kelley, therefore, may have been a deliberate insult.

* Boston: Published by Prentiss Sawyer, No. 11 Devonshire Street. 1851.

rages still among woman's rights advocates. Paulina Wright Davis, the convention's principle organizer and its president, sought in her opening address to preempt certain issues. The task before them, she maintained, was practical. They did not need ringing declarations of rights or wrongs. They needed to launch a broad-based movement which would open new opportunities for women by securing them their rights. To do this, they needed to appeal to men as well as women, she went on, and that meant they must forego the language of blame. They must also foreswear violence "or any [other] form of antagonism." They must instead "be gentle with the ignorance [of "old ideas and habits of mind"] and patient under the injustice which old evils induce."

Lucretia Mott, a long-time antislavery activist and woman's rights advocate, who would play a leading role throughout the convention, immediately demurred.[1] Women should follow the lead of the abolitionists, she argued, and that meant mincing no words about the responsibilities of men for the injustices suffered by women. There was no "abstract" evil, she would point out in a later session. It did not just happen by itself. And the proper response was to confront and condemn the evil-doer. The Daily Tribune *treated this argument with kid gloves, but the* Herald *reveled in the controversy as did the Boston* Daily Mail.

If Davis failed to head off a public argument over the wisdom and propriety of blaming men for women's plight, she had mixed success in forestalling the public airing of other controversies. She largely succeeded in keeping the question of dress reform out of the convention. She had less success in getting participants to avoid taking up "any unmeaning questions of sex and sphere." What she had in mind were such matters as whether women and men were equal in mental and physical abilities or whether women were capable of filling all the occupations then monopolized by men. What she meant by "unmeaning" was not that such questions were unimportant, but that there was no need to raise them and no way, in the light of what was then known, to answer them. Women, she insisted, needed opportunities. Open to them all the occupations and professions. If there were some they were

---

[1] Lucretia Coffin Mott, born in 1793, was recognized by the Quakers in her meeting as an "acknowledged minister" in 1821. In fact, all Quakers "ministered" to the meeting. In 1827 she and husband James Mott became Hicksite Quakers when a major schism among American friends occurred. Hicksite Quakers continued to insist that all members of the Society of Friends might minister to the meeting when inspired by the Holy Spirit. She was active in the abolitionist movement and attended the Seneca Falls Convention in 1848 where she initially opposed the demand for suffrage, not out of any doubt about women's fitness to vote but out of a deep suspicion concerning the morality of politics. By 1850 she had changed her mind and was a stout advocate of women sharing all the rights men enjoyed, including the right to vote.

incapable of doing, experience would soon teach them which they were. So too with education. Offer women the same opportunities as men. If they proved unable to conquer certain branches of study, so be it. But, she argued, it was pointless to affirm or deny that women could do something until they had had a chance to try.

Implicit in Davis's argument was the strategic notion that these arguments might needlessly divide the fledgling movement. Some of those attending the convention, as the debates would make plain, believed that women's "nature" made them different in key ways from men. Others held that the two sexes—we would now say genders—were, obvious physiological differences aside, basically the same. They held, that is, that human "nature" was the same for both men and women. Davis thought that there was no need for convention participants to take up this question and no possibility for them to resolve it. Instead they should focus upon those specific steps, such as opening educational opportunities to women, upon which all could agree.

Pursuant to a call previously issued, a Convention to consider the Rights, Duties, and Relations of Women met at Brinley Hall, Worcester, Mass., on Wednesday, October 23, at 10 o'clock.

The Convention was called to order by Sarah H. Earle, of Worcester.

On motion of Mary A. W. Johnson, of Ohio, Joseph C. Hathaway, of Western New York, was chosen President, pro tem.

On motion of Phoebe Goodwin, of Pennsylvania, Eliza J. Kenney, of Massachusetts, was chosen Secretary, pro tem.

On motion of Eliza Barney, of Massachusetts, a Nominating Committee was appointed by the Chair, namely: Eliza Barney, of Massachusetts; C. I. H. Nichols, of Vermont; Asa Foster, of New Hampshire; Charles C. Burleigh, of Connecticut; Lydia Dennett, of Maine; Pliny Sexton, of New York; M. A. W. Johnson, of Ohio; Rebecca Plumley, of Pennsylvania; Susan R. Harris, of Rhode Island.

The Call of the Convention was then read by the President, pro tem. . . .

The Committee on nominating Officers reported the following list, which was adopted by the Convention:

President
Paulina W. Davis, of Rhode Island.

Vice Presidents
William H. Channing, of Massachusetts.
Sarah Tyndale, of Pennsylvania.

Secretaries
Hannah M. Darlington, of Pennsylvania.
Joseph C. Hathaway, of New York.

The President elect, Paulina W. Davis, took the Chair and offered the following ADDRESS.

Usage assigns to the Chair of such Conventions as this, the duty of stating the objects of the meeting. But the published call under which we are convened presents such a summary of our objects as may suffice for mere statement; and the subject matters to be submitted, the points to be discussed, and the action contemplated by this Convention, are equally familiar to us all.

This leaves me at liberty to occupy your attention for a few moments with some general reflections upon the attitude and relations of our movement to our times and circumstances, and upon the proper spirit and method of promoting it. I do not even intend to treat these topics formally, and I do not hope to do it successfully; for nothing less than a complete philosophy of reform could answer such inquiries, and that philosophy, it is very certain, the world has not yet discovered.

Human rights, and the reasons on which they rest, are not difficult of comprehension. The world has never been ignorant of them, nor insensible to them; and human wrongs and their evils are just as familiar to experience and as well understood; but all this is not enough to secure to mankind the possession of the one, or to relieve them from the felt burden and suffering of the other. A creed of abstract truths, or a catechism of general principles, and a completely digested list of grievances, combined, are not enough to adjust a practical reform to its proper work, else Prophets and Apostles and earnest world-menders in general would have been more successful, and left us less to wish and to do.

It is one thing to issue a declaration of rights[1] or a declaration of wrong to the world, but quite another thing wisely and happily to commend the subject to the world's acceptance, and so to secure the

---

[1] This was most probably a reference to the 1848 Seneca Falls *Declaration of Sentiments*.

desired reformation. Every element of success is, in its own place and degree, equally important; but the very starting point is the adjustment of the reformer to his work, and next after that is the adjustment of his work to those conditions of the times which he seeks to influence.

. . . . Right principles and conformable means are the first necessities of a great enterprise, but without right apprehensions and tempers and expedient methods, the most beneficent purposes must utterly fail. Who is sufficient for these things?

Divine Providence has been baffled through all the ages of disorder suffering for want of fitting agents and adapted means. Reformations of religion have proved but little better than the substitution of a new error for an old one, and civil revolutions have resolved themselves into mere civil insurrections, until history has become but a monument of buried hopes.

The European movement of 1848[2] was wanting neither in theory nor example for its safe direction, but it has nevertheless almost fallen into contempt.

We may not, therefore, rely upon a good cause and good intentions alone, without danger of deplorable disappointment.

The reformation which we purpose, in its utmost scope, is radical and universal. It is not the mere perfecting of a progress already in motion, a detail of some established plan, but it is an epochal movement—the emancipation of a class, the redemption of half the world, and a conforming re-organization of all social, political, and industrial interests and institutions. Moreover, it is a movement without example among the enterprises of associated reformations, for it has no purpose of arming the oppressed against the oppressor, or of separating the parties, or of setting up independence, or of severing the relations of either.

Its intended changes are to be wrought in the intimate texture of all societary [social] organizations, without violence, or any form of antagonism. It seeks to replace the worn out with the living and the beautiful, so as to reconstruct without overturning, and to regenerate without destroying; and nothing of the spirit, tone, temper, or method of insurrection is proper or allowable to us and our work.

Human societies have been long working and fighting their way up from what we scornfully call barbarism, into what we boastfully call

---

[2] Davis had in mind the revolutions in France, Prussia, and other European states. Many German refugees migrated to the United States and became known as '48ers.

modern civilization; but, as yet, the advancement has been chiefly in ordering and methodizing the lower instincts of our nature, and organizing society under their impulses. The intellect of the masses has received development, and the gentler affections have been somewhat relieved from the dominion of force; but the institutions among men are not yet modelled after the highest laws of our nature. The masterdom of the strong hand and bold spirit is not yet over. . . . But the age of war is drawing towards a close, and that of peace (whose methods and end alike are harmony) is dawning, and the uprising of womanhood is its prophecy and foreshadow.

The first principles of human rights have now for a long time been abstractly held and believed, and both in Europe and America whole communities have put them into practical operation in some of their bearings. Equality before the law, and the right of the governed to choose their governors, are established maxims of reformed political science; but in the countries most advanced,[3] these doctrines and their actual benefits are as yet enjoyed exclusively by the sex that in the battle-field and the public forum has wrenched them from the old time tyrannies. They are yet denied to Woman, because she has not yet so asserted or won them for herself; for political justice pivots itself upon the barbarous principle that "Who would be free, themselves must strike the blow."[4] Its furthest progress toward magnanimity is to give arms to helplessness. It has not yet learned to give justice. For this rule of barbarism there is this much justification, that although every human being is naturally entitled to every right of the race, the enjoyment and administration of all rights require such culture and conditions in their subject as usually lead him to claim and struggle for them; and the contented slave is left in slavery, and the ignorant man in darkness, on the inference that he cannot use what he does not desire. This is indeed true of the animal instincts, but it is false of the nobler soul; and men must learn that the higher faculties must be first awakened, and then gratified, before they have done their duty to their race. The ministry of angels to dependent humanity is the

---

[3] By Davis's standard, the "advanced" countries would be Great Britain, the United States, and France. No other country had yet adopted the principles and declarations of rights she used as the criterion of "advanced."

[4] Lord Byron, *Childe Harold's Pilgrimage*, Canto ii, Stanza 76:

Hereditary bondsmen! know ye not,

Who would be free, themselves must strike the blow?

method of Divine Providence, and among men the law of heaven is, that the "elder shall serve the younger." But let us not complain that the hardier sex overvalue the force which heretofore has figured most in the world's affairs. "They know not what they do"[5] is the apology that crucified womanhood must concede in justice and pity to the wrong doers. In the order of things, the material world was to be first subdued. For this coarse conflict, the larger bones and stronger sinews of manhood are especially adapted, and it is a law of muscles and of all matter that might shall overcome right. This is the law of the vegetable world, and it is the law of the animal world, as well as the law of the animal instincts and of the physical organization of men; but it is not the law of spirit and affection.

. . . . Besides the feebler frame, which under the dynasty of muscles is degraded, there remains, even after justice has got the upper hand of force in the world's judgments, a mysterious and undefined difference of sex that seriously embarrasses the question of equality; or, if that is granted, in terms of equal fitness for avocations and positions which heretofore have been the monopoly of men. Old ideas and habits of mind survive the facts which produced them, as the shadows of night stretch far into the morning, sheltered in nooks and valleys from the rising light; and it is the work of a whole creation-day to separate the light from the darkness.

The rule of difference between the sexes must be founded on the traits which each estimates most highly in the other; and it is not at all wonderful that some of woman's artificial incapacities and slaveries may seem to be necessary to some of her excellencies; just as the chivalry that makes man a butcher of his kind still glares like a glory in the eyes of admiring womanhood, and all the more because it seems so much above and unlike her own powers and achievements. Nature does not teach that men and women are unequal, but only that they are unlike; an unlikeness so naturally related and dependent that their respective differences by their balance establish, instead of destroying, their equality.

Men are not in fact, and to all intents, equal among themselves, but their theoretical equality for all the purposes of justice is more easily seen and allowed than what we are here to claim for women. Higher views, nicer distinctions, and a deeper philosophy are required

---

[5] A reference to Luke 23:34 [King James Version]: Then said Jesus, Father, forgive them; for they know not what they do. And they parted his raiment, and cast lots.

to see and feel the truths of woman's rights; and besides, the maxims upon which men distribute justice to each other have been battle-cries for ages, while the doctrine of woman's true relations in life is a new science, the revelation of an advanced age, —perhaps, indeed, the very last grand movement of humanity towards its highest destiny, —too new to be yet fully understood, too grand to grow out of the broad and coarse generalities which the infancy and barbarism of society could comprehend.

The rule of force and fraud must be well nigh overturned, and learning and religion and the fine arts must have cultivated mankind into a state of wisdom and justice tempered by the most beneficent affections, before woman can be fully installed in her highest offices. We must be gentle with the ignorance and patient under the injustice which old evils induce. Long suffering is a quality of the highest wisdom, and charity beareth all things for it hopeth all things.

. . . . The tyrant sex, if such we choose to term it, holds such natural and necessary relations to the victims of injustice, that neither rebellion nor revolution, neither defiance nor resistance, nor any mode of assault or defence incident to party antagonism, is either possible, expedient, or proper. Our claim must rest on its justice, and conquer by its power of truth. We take the ground, that whatever has been achieved for the race belongs to it, and must not be usurped by any class or caste. The rights and liberties of one human being cannot be made the property of another, though they were redeemed for him or her by the life of that other; for rights cannot be forfeited by way of salvage, and they are in their nature unpurchasable and inalienable.

We claim for woman a full and generous investiture of all the blessings which the other sex has solely or by her aid achieved for itself. We appeal from men's injustice and selfishness to their principles and affections.

For some centuries now, the best of them have been asserting, with their lives, the liberties and rights of the race; and it is not for the few endowed with the highest intellect, the largest frame, or even the soundest morals, that the claim has been maintained, but broadly and bravely and nobly it has been held that wherever a faculty is given, its highest activities are chartered by the Creator, and that all objects alike—whether they minister to the necessities of our animal life or to the superior powers of the human soul and so are more imperatively needed, because nobler than the bread that perishes in the use—are, of common right, equally open to ALL; and that all artificial restraints, for whatever reason imposed, are alike culpable for their presumption, their folly, and their cruelty.

It is pitiable ignorance and arrogance for either man or woman now to prescribe and limit the sphere of woman. It remains for the greatest women whom appropriate culture, and happiest influences shall yet develop, to declare and to prove what are woman's capacities and relations in the world.

I will not accept the concession of any equality which means identity or resemblance of faculty and function. I do not base her claims upon any such parallelism of constitution or attainment. I ask only freedom for the natural unfolding of her powers, the conditions most favorable for her possibilities of growth, and the full play of all those incentives which have made man her master, and then, with all her natural impulses and the whole heaven of hope to invite, I ask that she shall fill the place that she can attain to, without settling any unmeaning questions of sex and sphere, which people gossip about for want of principles of truth, or the faculty to reason upon them.

But it is not with the topics of our reform and the discussion of these that I am now concerned. It is of its position in the world's opinion, and the causes of this, that I am thinking; and I seek to derive hints and suggestions as to the method and manner of successful advocacy, from the inquiry. Especially am I solicitous that the good cause may suffer no detriment from the theoretical principles its friends may assume, or the spirit with which they shall maintain them. It is fair to presume that such causes as have obscured these questions in the general judgment of the governing sex, must also more or less darken the counsels of those most anxious for truth and right. If our demand were simply for chartered rights, civil and political, such as get acknowledgement in paper constitutions, there would be no ground of doubt. We could plead our common humanity, and claim an equal justice. We might say that the natural right of self-government is so clearly due to every human being alike, that it needs no argument to prove it; and if some or a majority of women would not exercise this right, this is no ground for taking it from those who would. And the right to the control and enjoyment of her own property and partnership in all that she helps her husband to earn and save, needs only to be stated to command instant assent. Her appropriate avocations might not be so easily settled that a programme could be completed on theoretical principles merely; but we need discuss no such difficulties while we ask only for liberty of choice, and opportunities of adaptation; and the question of her education is solved by the simple principle, that whatever she can receive is her absolute due.

Yet all these points being so easily disposed of, so far as they are mere matters of controversy, the advocates of the right need none the less the wisest and kindest consideration for all the resistance we must encounter, and the most forbearing patience under the injustice and insolence to which we must expose ourselves. And we can help ourselves to much of the prudence and some of the knowledge we shall need, by treating the prejudices of the public as considerately as if they were principles, and the customs of society as if they once had some temporary necessity, and so meet them with the greater force for the claim to respect which we concede to them. For a prejudice is just like any other error of judgment, and a custom has sometimes had some fitness to things more or less necessary, and is not an utter absurdity, even though the reason on which it was based is lost or removed. Who shall say that there is nothing serious, or respectable, or just, in the repugnance with which our propositions are received? The politician who knows his own corruption may be excused for an earnest wish to save his wife and daughter from the taint, and he must be excused, too, for not knowing that the corruption would be cured by the saving virtue which he dreads to expose to risk.

There may be real though very foolish tenderness in the motive which refuses to open to woman the trades and professions that she could cultivate and practice with equal profit and credit to herself. The chivalry that worships womanhood is not mean, though it at the same time enslaves the objects of its overfond care.

And it is even possible that men may deprive women of their property and liberties, personal and political, with the kindly purpose of accommodating their supposed incapacities for the offices and duties of human life. Harsh judgments and harsh words will neither weaken the opposition, nor strengthen our hands. Our address is to the highest sentiment of the times; and the tone and spirit due to it and becoming in ourselves, are courtesy and respectfulness. Strength and truth of complaint, and eloquence of denunciation, are easy of attainment; but the wisdom of affirmative principles and positive science, and the adjustment of reformatory measures to the exigencies of the times and circumstances, are so much the more useful as they are difficult of attainment. A profound expediency, as true to principle as it is careful of success, is, above all things, rare and necessary. We have to claim liberty without its usually associated independence. We must insist on separate property where the interests are identical, and a division of profits where the very being of the partners is blended. We must demand provisions for differences of policy, where there should be no shadow of controversy; and the free choice of industrial avocations and general education, without respect to the distinctions of sex and natural differences of faculty.

In principle these truths are not doubtful, and it is therefore not impossible to put them in practice, but they need great clearness in system and steadiness of direction to get them allowance and adoption in the actual life of the world. The opposition should be consulted where it can be done without injurious consequences. Truth must not be suppressed, nor principles crippled, yet strong meat should not be given to babes. Nor should the strong use their liberties so as to become a stumbling block to the weak. Above all things, we owe it to the earnest expectation of the age, that stands trembling in mingled hope and fear of the great experiment, to lay its foundations broadly and securely in philosophic truth, and to form and fashion it in practical righteousness. To accomplish this, we cannot be too careful or too brave, too gentle or too firm; and yet with right dispositions and honest efforts, we cannot fail of doing our share of the great work, and thereby advancing the highest interests of humanity.

On motion of M. A. W. Johnson, the Nominating Committee were appointed to nominate a Business Committee, who reported the following names, which were approved by the Convention:

M. A. W. Johnson, of Ohio; Wm. Lloyd Garrison, of Massachusetts; Ernestine L. Rose, of New York; Harriet K. Hunt, of Massachusetts; Lucretia Mott, of Pennsylvania; Lucy Stone, of Massachusetts; W. H. Channing, of Massachusetts; E. W. Capron, of Rhode Island; Abby H. Price, of Massachusetts; Wm. Fish, of Massachusetts, Samuel May, Jr., of Massachusetts; Susan Sisson, of Rhode Island; Anna Q. T. Parsons, of Massachusetts; Frederick Douglass, of New York.

On motion of S.S. Foster, all persons present were invited to take part in the discussions, but those only who enrolled their names as members were allowed to vote

Massachusetts Spy, October 30, 1850

CONVENTION.

On taking the chair, the President read an address, in which the objects which ought to claim the attention of the Convention were set forth, and the means of their accomplishment discussed. The address was elaborate, evincing much and deep reflection, and was written with great clearness and even elegance of style. As a mere literary composition, it was very creditable to the author.

Lucretia Mott, of Philadelphia, took the stand, and alluding to some remarks in the address of the President, expressed a fear that they might be considered as not taking a stand sufficiently high and decided, and urged that the whole truth in relation to the disabilities and wrongs under which women suffer, should be plainly, freely, and yet kindly spoken.

New York *Tribune,* October 24, 1850

WOMEN'S RIGHTS CONVENTION AT WORCESTER, MASS.

Correspondence of The Tribune

Mrs. Paulina W. Davis, on taking the chair, delivered an address to the Convention, on the relations of Woman; her title to the rights and privileges with man, and on the true method of conducting the reform of the evils and disabilities under which she is placed. She took the ground that man has no right to circumscribe the sphere of woman; that she should have freedom for the full development of her nature and capabilities; the right to her own property and earnings, acquired previous to marriage, and an equitable division of their joint accumulations, during that state. She claimed for woman the right of self government, which belongs to every human being, and based her argument not on any supposed similarity in the constitution of the sexes, but on the ground that the Creator has endowed woman with a moral, intellectual nature, and the same inherent and inalienable rights as man. She said that nature does not teach that men and women are unequal, but only unlike, and that the balance of the differences would establish her equality. She described the law of force as the law of the physical world, and of the muscular energies of man, which often tramples on the right. It was the law of the spirit on which woman must rely. She urged that they must not take an antagonistic or hostile position to man; they must appeal to his sense of justice and his affections for a recognition of those rights; they must be patient and rely on the force of moral sentiment, which would in time pervade the life of the world.

Miss [sic] Lucretia Mott suggested whether it would not be well to make some arrangement for the publication of the address of the President. She did not propose to review the sentiments advanced; they would be responded to generally by the friends of reform. There were two or three expressions in the address and in the call for the Convention which she did not fully approve. She thought it might be construed as a profession of too great gentleness in discussing this subject. She thought they should find it necessary to take an antagonistic position, and to meet the prejudices and opposition of the world with directness and an earnest expression of the truth. They must attach blame to those who had persisted so long in depriving woman of her rights, in passing laws which deny her the control of her property and place her beyond the pale and protection of equal laws. She said they must mourn over the admitted inferiority of woman; over her slavish subjection to the evil customs and prejudices of society. It was not strange, after so long a period of degradation, she should be enervated and contented with her inferior position. She desired that we might speak with the earnestness and severity of the truth—with an earnestness and severity that should make the ears of man tingle for the degraded position in which he has kept woman during so many ages, and especially under the influences of the religion and teachings of the Son of God.

New York Herald, October 25, 1850

WOMAN'S RIGHTS CONVENTION.

Awful Combination of Socialism, Abolitionism, and Infidelity.

The Pantalettes Striking for the Pantaloons.
Bible and Constitution Repudiated.

Miss [sic] Davis, on taking the chair, read a very elaborate, philosophical, socialistic address, on the wrongs and rights of woman. She presented the restraints under which woman is bound down to slavery in a very touching manner. It was heart-rending to think of it. From popular prejudices, she knew that reformation was difficult, but the convention proposed to enter upon the great work. She asserted the equality of woman by nature and protested that she was entitled to equality in politics, legislation, and everything else. Woman wanted an equal chance to the unfolding of her great capacities, and she was bound to have it. Society was in a state of barbarism, while it denied equality of privileges, political, religious, and all other privileges, and it must be reformed.

(While she was delivering this highly philosophical exposition of the wrongs and rights of woman, the attention of the audience was somewhat disturbed by the music of a hand organ in another room of the building, in which the American fat girl, sixteen years old and weighing 400 pounds, was being exhibited as a specimen of what woman would be if she had her rights. She ought, by all means, have been made president of the Convention.)

On the motion of Lucretia Mott, who considered the address a little too tame, the question of its adoption was left open for debate. It disclaimed the intention of open hostility against the existing laws of society, and for this disclaimer she [Mott] was not prepared. The sentiment ought to be conditional. Direct hostility might yet become necessary to woman in enforcing her rights. We don't want any milk and water policy of action. If the despotism of man has displaced woman from her proper sphere, we must tell him so—if the thing was wrong, we must declare it—the plain, naked truth, without disguise. From the manner in which woman had always been treated, it was argued that she was an inferior animal; but she contended that woman was the equal of man in everything pertaining to human rights. She justified the plain truth, however severe it might be. It was by bold and severe language of denunciation that William Lloyd Garrison had done so much to shake the foundations of slavery. We must use the armor of love and truth; but we must tell the truth without fear, and call things by their right names.

Boston *Daily Mail,*
October 24, 1850

GRAND DEMONSTRATION OF PETTICOATDOM AT WORCESTER—THE "WOMAN'S RIGHTS" CONVENTION IN FULL BLAST—IMPORTANT AND INTERESTING REPORT.

Miss Davis took the Chair, and being a pretty woman, of course made a very pretty speech. She dilated with much eloquence on the disadvantages her sex lay under. She acknowledged the difficulties the reforms sought by the convention were surrounded with, from popular prejudice; and entered into an elaborate explanation of the objects of the conference. It was so transcendentally philosophical[1] that common minds could make nothing of it; but by reading the 119th Psalm backwards some idea of its purport might be arrived at. Once, here and there, there was a lucid expression; but these were not numerous enough to leaven the lump, and render the whole in any measure palatable to the understanding. Equality in political matters was one of the claims which peeped, naked, from the mass. The whole entertainment was accompanied by a hand organ, which squealed out its liquid notes to the praise of "old Dan Tucker," "Jeannette and Jeannot," and all of these famed characters—mixed up with the original Polka. In the middle of the music the particular fitness of the female sex to legislate and rule was asserted, and her artificial state denuded of all its artificial clothing. The principal plea for woman's equality was drawn from the inequality of mind and other qualifications which exists, confessedly, among men. Society, in denying privileges political to woman, was called an old barbarian of the most barbarous caste for its trouble. Freedom for the natural unfolding of the powers of womankind was wanted, and would have to come, aye, even were the sky to fall. What the details of that development were we could not

---

[1] A reference to Transcendentalism, a philosophy associated with Ralph Waldo Emerson, Margaret Fuller, and others. Emerson did not attend the convention but did sign the "Call." Fuller, author of *Woman in the Nineteenth Century,* died a few months before the convention met. Paulina Wright Davis had intended to nominate Fuller to preside.

guess; but from what crude opinion we could gather, we should say one was the liberty to take the purse and go a marketing without restraint. Custom, in connection with this unfolding, caught it over the pate [i.e., head]; and the Dry Goods business was not spared, as women, it was argued, were as competent as men to do the amiable over a counter. The *Spirit of the Times* was appealed to, to assist in the progress of social revolution, which should place woman on the throne of her rights. There! friend Porter [editor of the *New York Times*]—there's a job for you! No other paper was mentioned, which convinced us that the whole affair was purely a sporting matter. Very likely; nay, most assuredly.

• • •

Lucretia Mott, of Phila., took up the address, and very eloquently reviewed some of its statements. A kind of disclaiming of any hostility of action was one of them; but that sentiment was one that should be qualified. Direct antagonism might yet have to be operated upon; but, in the meantime, it was best to be mum. The severity of truth and justice was recommended at present, and no milk and water proceeding; for if man, in displacing woman from her sphere, was wrong in so doing, he would have to be told so without disguise. The common treatment of womankind was spoken of [by men] as furnishing its own argument that woman was an inferior animal; and a very eloquent appeal made to the authority of Christ that it was not so. Harsh language was justified, too, and William Lloyd Garrison and George Thompson [a British antislavery advocate] quoted as bright examples of the wielders of such power in their treatment of the slave question. Love and truth were to be the panoply of the meeting; but the truth was to be of the very plainest kind, and no mistake. Seriously, the fair speaker was a noble example of female intelligence; but, perhaps the speech was a pocket one?[2] Very likely; Abby [Kelley Foster] has lots of these, and we could furnish notes of them too.

**Boston *Chronotype*,
October 25, 1850**

WOMEN'S RIGHTS CONVENTION AT WORCESTER.

[Following a summary of Davis's speech] .... The address of the President was warmly received by a large audience, but we have not room to give even a barren abstract of a truly philosophical address.

Mrs. Lucretia Mott, of Philadelphia, followed the President in a few remarks upon the manner in which the Reform should be conducted. Mrs. M. thought a portion of the address of the President too mild. She said we must use as strong words as Jesus used when he rebuked Satan, Sin, and the money changers. True we should come armed with the panoply of truth, but should we speak that truth with plainness and force it may be considered pungent and impertinent—truth is to some people. We must be indignant at the monstrous perversion of Scripture and the privileges of woman by the tyrant sex; and we must speak in the language of censure to the woman herself who is hugging her chains.

---

[2] The charge here is that Mott's remarks were not genuinely extemporaneous but prepared in advance.

OCTOBER 23, 1850—AFTERNOON SESSION

Abby Price gave the major address of the afternoon session, one whose controversial nature is difficult to appreciate today. But in 1850 "proper ladies" did not admit even to knowing that there was such a thing as prostitution, much less make public speeches on the subject. Further, Price's view of the causes of the "social evil" was equally daring. Most prostitutes, she held, had been driven into their lives of degradation by poverty and the lack of opportunity to earn honest livings. She quoted extensively from French and English sources to document her argument. Price was a resident of Hopedale, a utopian community located about twenty miles from Worcester. Hopedale's founder, the Rev. Adin Ballou, was, with the Rev. William Ellery Channing, one of the guiding lights of the Universalist movement in American Protestantism. Hopedale was organized on a basis of gender equality.

Historians have not always appreciated how central the concern over prostitution was for the first generation of woman's rights activists, but for many of them it was the strongest possible reason why women needed to demand their rights. Until women could enter any profession for which their abilities qualified them, until they could earn comparable wages to men in those fields, until they could control their own earnings and other property, until they had an equal voice in establishing and enforcing the laws, countless of their "sisters"—and Price and others used that term—would remain the sexual prey of men. It was an argument that even the reporter for the Daily Mail, *whose overall hostility to the woman's rights movement remained unshaken throughout, had to admit was convincing.*

Next the convention turned to considering a resolution sponsored by Mrs. Ernestine Rose which asserted that the "contracted sphere" in which women were forced to live was the ultimate source of her grievances and that no remedy could be effective until women were granted the right to move in their "proper sphere." This notion of a "sphere," contracted or proper or other, was central to the whole discussion of woman's rights in the nineteenth century. And Rose is a good example of those early feminists who accepted the notion that women's natures were sufficiently different from men's that the sexes should occupy distinctive spheres. The trouble, such feminists argued, was that the "spheres" needed radical redefining.

In the midst of the debate over the Rose resolution, Abby Kelley Foster made an incendiary address. According to her long-time friend and admirer Lucy Stone, the other convention organizers found her remarks so "odious" that they almost prohibited her from attending the 1851 convention.[1] *The* Proceedings *notes only that she spoke. The* Massachusetts Spy, *published in her home town of Worcester by a strong supporter of women's rights, did not even mention her speech. Other pro-woman's rights papers are similarly silent. So one has to turn to the openly hostile New York* Herald *and Boston* Daily Mail *to attempt to decide what she did say. However, since Lucretia Mott would attempt to tone down her friend's rhetoric during the evening session, one can use the pro-woman's rights accounts of Mott's remarks to test the reliability of the anti-suffrage accounts of Kelley Foster's speech.*

FROM THE *PROCEEDINGS*

The Convention met at 2 o'clock. The President, P. W. Davis, in the Chair.

The minutes of the morning session were read by H.M. Darlington, and adopted.

Abby H. Price then offered an Address:

In our account of the work of Creation [i.e., the Book of Genesis], when it was so gloriously finished in the garden of Eden, by placing there, in equal companionship, man and woman, made in the image of God, alike gifted with intellect, alike endowed with immortality, it is said the Creator looked upon his work, and pronounced it good—that "the morning stars sang together, and all the sons of God shouted for joy." Since that time, through the slow rolling of darkened ages, man has ruled by physical power, and wherever he could gain the ascendancy, there he has felt the right to dictate—even though it degraded his equal companion—the mother who bore him—the playmate of his childhood—the daughter of his love. Thus, in many countries we see woman reduced to the condition of a slave, and compelled to do all the drudgery necessary to her lord's subsistence. In others she is dressed up as a mere plaything, for his amusement; but everywhere he has assumed to be her head and lawgiver, and only where Christianity has dawned, and right not might

---

[1] At the 1851 convention Kelley Foster made perhaps her most famous speech in which she proclaimed that "my life has been my speech" and that "bloody feet, sisters, have worn smooth the path" you have traveled. In eulogizing her friend, Stone remarked that she had almost not had the opportunity to deliver that speech, so strong was the revulsion against her speech in 1850.

been the rule, has woman had anything like her true position. In this country even, republican, so called, and Christian, her rights are but imperfectly recognised, and she suffers under the disability of caste. These are facts that, in the light of the nineteenth century, demand our attention. "Are we always to remain in this position" is a question we have come here to discuss.

The natural rights of woman are co-equal with those of man. So God created man in his own image; in the image of God created he him; male and female, created he them. There is not one particle of difference intimated as existing between them. They were both made in the image of God. Dominion was given to both over every other creature, but not over each other. They were expected to exercise the viceregency given to them by their Maker in harmony and love.

In contending for this co-equality of woman's with man's rights, it is not necessary to argue, either that the sexes are by nature equally and indiscriminately adapted to the same positions and duties, or that they are absolutely equal in physical and intellectual ability; but only that they are absolutely equal in their rights to life, liberty, and the pursuit of happiness—in their rights to do, and to be, individually and socially, all they are capable of, and to attain the highest usefulness and happiness, obediently to the divine moral law

These are every man's rights, of whatever race or nation, ability or situation, in life. These are equally every woman's rights, whatever her comparative capabilities may be—whatever her relations may be. These are human rights, equally inherent in male and female. To repress them in any degree is in the same degree usurpation, tyranny, and oppression. We hold these to be self-evident truths, and shall not now discuss them. We shall assume that happiness is the chief end of all human beings; that existence is valuable in proportion as happiness is promoted and secured; and that, on the whole, each of the sexes is equally necessary to the common happiness, and in one way or another is equally capable, with fair opportunity, of contributing to it. Therefore each has an equal right to pursue and enjoy it. This settled, we contend:

1. That women ought to have equal opportunities with men for suitable and well-compensated employment.
2. That women ought to have equal opportunities, privileges, and securities with men for rendering themselves pecuniarily independent.

3. That women ought to have equal legal and political rights, franchises, and advantages with men.

Let us consider each of these points briefly. Women ought to have equal opportunities with men for suitable and well compensated employment in all departments of human exertion.

Human beings cannot attain true dignity or happiness except by true usefulness. This is true of women as of men. It is their duty, privilege, honor, and bliss to be useful. Therefore give them the opportunity and encouragement. If there are positions, duties, occupations, really unsuitable to females, as such, let these be left to males. If there are others unsuitable to men, let these be left to women. Let all the rest be equally open to both sexes. And let the compensation be graduated justly, to the real worth of the services rendered, irrespective of sex.

However just and fair this may seem, it is far from actual experience. Tradition so palsies public sentiment with regard to the comparative privileges and rights of the sexes, that but little even is thought of the oppressions that exist, and woman seems to have made up her mind to an eternal inferiority. I say eternal, because development constitutes our greatness and our happiness

. . . [W]oman should have her inalienable rights. She cannot act freely, be true to her moral nature, or to her intellect; she cannot gratify her charity or her taste, without pecuniary independence, that which is produced by suitable and well-compensated employment. Woman, in order to be equally independent with man, must have a fair and equal chance. He is in no wise restricted from doing, in every department of human exertion, all he is able to do. If he is bold and ambitious, and desires fame, every avenue is open to him. He may blend science and art, producing a competence for his support, until he chains them to the car of his genius, and, with Fulton and Morse,[1] wins a crown of imperishable gratitude. . . . Not so with woman. Her rights are not recognised as equal. Her sphere is circumscribed not by her ability, but by her sex. The wings of her genius are clipped, because she is a woman. If perchance her taste leads her to excellence in the way they give her leave to tread, she is worshipped as almost divine; but if she reaches for laurels which they have in view, they scream after her, "You are a woman." She is sneered at for her weakness, while she is allowed little

---

[1] Robert Fulton, inventor of the steamboat; Samuel F. B. Morse, inventor of the telegraph.

or no chance for development. The number of her industrial avocations are unnecessarily restricted, far more than reason demands. And when she is engaged in the same occupations with men, her remuneration is greatly below what is awarded to her stronger associates.

• • •

And why not allow to those who have not become "happy wives and mothers," those who are anxious of leading active and useful lives, of maintaining an honorable independence, a fair chance with men, to do all they can do with propriety?

At present it is well nigh a misfortune to a poor man to have a large family of daughters. Compared with sons their chances for an honest livelihood are few. Though they may have intellect of a high order, yet they must be educated to be married as the chief end of their being. They must not forget that they are females in their aspirations for independence, for greatness, for education. Their alternatives are few. The confined factory, the sedentary, blighting life of half-paid seamstresses, perhaps a chance at folding books, or type setting may keep them along until the happy moment arrives, when they have an offer of marriage, and their fears for sustenance end by a union with the more favored sex. This should not be so. Give girls a fair chance to acquaint themselves with any business they can well do. Our daughters should fit themselves equally with our sons, for any post of usefulness and profit that they may choose. What good reason is there why the lighter trades should not open with equal facilities for their support, and why their labor should not be well paid in any useful and profitable department? Is it fair that strong and able men capable of tilling the soil, should be paid high wages for light mechanical labor that is denied woman because she is a woman, and which she could with equal facility execute? The newspaper press, clerkships, and bookkeeping, not now to mention different offices in Government, (whose duties are principally writing,) would, if they were equally open to our daughters, afford them an opportunity of well-paid and congenial employment; would relieve them from the necessity of marriage or want, and thereby add dignity and energy to their character. What good reason is there why women should not be educated to mercantile pursuits, to engage in commerce, to invent, to construct, in fine to do anything she can do? Why so separate the avocations of the sexes? . . . Man inflicts injury upon woman, unspeakable injury in placing her intellectual and moral nature in the background, and woman injures herself by submitting to be regarded only as a female. She is called upon loudly, by the progressive spirit of the age, to rise from the station where man, not God, has placed her, and to claim her rights as a moral and responsible being, equal with man.

As such, both have the same sphere of action, and the same duties devolve on both, though these may vary according to circumstances. Fathers and mothers have sacred duties and obligations devolving upon them which cannot belong to others. These do not attach to them as man and woman, but as parents, husbands, and wives. In all the majesty of moral power, in all the dignity of immortality let woman plant herself side by side with man on the broad platform of equal human rights. By thus claiming privileges, encouragements, and rights with man, she would gain the following results:

1. A fair development of her natural abilities and capabilities, physical, intellectual, economical, and moral.
2. A great increase of self-respect, conscious responsibility, womanly dignity, and influence.
3. Pecuniary competence, or the ready resource for acquiring it in some department of human exertion.
4. A far higher moral character, etc.

Now take a survey of things as they are. The general opinion that woman is inferior to man, bears with terrible and paralyzing effect on those who are dependent upon their labor, mental or physical, for a subsistence. I allude to the disproportionate value set upon the time and labor of men and women. A man engaged in teaching can always, I believe, command a higher price for his services, than a woman, though he teach the same branch, and though he be in no respect superior to the woman. It is so in every occupation in which both engage indiscriminately. For example, in tailoring, a man has twice as much for making a coat, or pantaloons, as a woman, although the work done by each may be equally good. In the employments which are peculiar to women, their time is estimated at only half the value of that of men. The washer-woman works as hard in proportion as the wood-sawyer, yet she makes not more than half as much by a day's work. Thus by narrowing the sphere of woman, and reducing her remuneration of labor so unjustly, her resources are few and she finds it hard to acquire an honorable independence. Necessity, we are compelled to believe, cruel necessity, often drives her to vice, especially in our large cities; as the only alternative from starvation! Deplorable and heart sickening as the statement is, I have good authority for saying that more than half of the prostitutes of our towns are driven to that course of life from necessity! M. Duchatelet, in his investigation in Paris, established this fact in the clearest manner. In his work, Vol. I., p. 96, we read the following statement: "Of all causes of prostitution in Paris, and probably in all large towns, there are none more influential than the want of work and indigence resulting from insufficient earnings. What are the earnings of our laundresses, our seamstresses, our milliners? Compare the wages of the most skillful with the more ordinary and moderately able, and we shall see if it be possible for these latter to provide even the strict necessaries of life. And if we further compare the prices of their labor with that of others less skillful, we shall cease to wonder that so large a number fall into irregularities, thus made inevitable! This state of things has a natural tendency to increase in the actual state of our affairs, in consequence of the usurpation by men, of a large class of occupations, which it would be more honorable in our sex to resign to the other. Is it not shameful, for example, to see in Paris thousands of men in the prime of their age in shops and warehouses, leading a sedentary and effeminate life, which is only suitable for women?"

M. Duchatelet has other facts, which show that even filial and maternal affection drive many to occasional prostitution as a means, and the only means left them, of earning bread for those depending on them for support. He says, "It is difficult to believe that the trade of prostitution should be embraced by certain women as a means of fulfilling their filial or maternal duties. Nothing, however, is more true. It is by no means rare to see married women, widowed, or deserted by their husbands, becoming abandoned, with the sole object of saving their families from dying with hunger. It is still more common to find young females, unable to procure, from honest occupations, adequate provision for their aged and infirm parents, reduced to prostitute themselves in order to eke out their livelihood. I have found," says he, "too many particulars regarding these two classes, not to be convinced that they are far more numerous than is generally imagined." . . . Poor outcasts! —miserable lepers! Their touch even, in the very extremity of human suffering, shaken off as if it were a pollution! They seem to be considered far more out of the pale of humanity than negroes on a slave plantation, or felons in a Pasha's [a Turkish military official] dungeon! It is thought to be discreditable to a woman even to know of their existence. You may not mention them in public. You may not allude to them in a book without staining its pages. Our sisters, whose poverty is caused by the oppressions of society, who are driven to sin by want of bread, —then regarded with scorn and turned away from with contempt! I appeal to you in their behalf, my friends. Is it not time to throw open to women, equal resources with men, for obtaining honest employment? If the extremity of human wretchedness—a condition which combines within itself every element of suffering, mental and physical, circumstantial and intrinsic—is a passport to our compassion, every heart should bleed for the position of these poor sufferers.

● ● ●

Of the 5,183 Parisian prostitutes, his [Duchatelet's] investigations show that: 2,690 were driven to the profession by parental abandonment, excessive want, and actual destitution; 86 thus earned food for the support of parents or children; 280 were driven by shame [i.e., becoming pregnant out of wedlock] from their homes; 2,181 were abandoned by their seducers, and had nothing to turn to for a living! You may say, this may be the case in the old countries, but not in our own cities. Very little difference exists in the state of actual society here. Women are the same proscribed class here as elsewhere. The same difference is made between male and female labor. Public opinion surrounds them with ten thousand restrictions. The law disfranchises them. Christianity, to whose influence alone woman is indebted for all social dignity that she now enjoys, is appealed to, as sustaining the present degree of dominion over her, and tortured to prove her inferiority. Thus the cause exists, and why may not the evil also? It does exist to a fearful degree. And, painful though the contemplation of the sad picture may be, it is nevertheless our duty to investigate and seek its cause—then to apply the remedy—and to do now what we may to educate a different public sentiment.

I come now to my second proposition. Women ought to have equal opportunities, privileges, and securities with men for rendering themselves pecuniarily independent. And why not? . . . Without a certain degree of pecuniary independence, it is impossible for man or woman to rise in usefulness, excellence, and enjoyment to the height of their natural capabilities. Women at present are cramped, dwarfed, and cowed down. Mothers, with large families of girls, though they may see in them intellect and genius, which, were they boys, might open to them in the future the pathway to independence and perhaps to fame, find that to girls nearly all avenues are closed. There are some branches of the fine arts, if they are very remarkably gifted, where they may find brilliant and dazzling success, as in the case of Jenny Lind.[2] They may perhaps excel as poets and as painters. But these are the exceptions. The bright pinions of their [daughters'] intellect remain unfolded, and they are perhaps permitted to learn the trade of a milliner, already crowded to excess, and miserably paid. For men, too, have monopolized the profits in that business, and hire their milliners at the lowest possible wages. Very few girls can acquire money enough to compete with the aspirants of the other sex, and so they must submit to their destiny. . . . All the education she is allowed, all the resources opened before her, have for their object marriage, that is to say, a husband. "She was made only for man," is the idea, and of what use will this or that be to her, when she is married? To develop all her faculties, as an individual, is not thought of. Does not a woman live for herself, then? Is she not a member of the race, an immortal being, — unless she is married? O yes, for above these titles of wife and mother, which depend upon circumstances, accidental and transitory, are suspended by absence and perhaps broken by death, there is for woman a title, eternal, inalienable, preceding and rising above all, —that of human being, co-existent with man; and with him she can demand the most complete development of heart and mind. In the name of eternity, then, in behalf of the race, we ask her elevation. Do you acknowledge this? Do my sisters here feel that they have relations to the Universe, —capabilities to be developed for immortality? In the name of eternity, we ask our brothers no longer to proscribe our sphere. I say, then, that we are cramped, dwarfed, and cowed down, for the want of pecuniary independence. Is not this a miserable doctrine, that woman is subject to the man, that she must, if married, ask her husband to dole out her charities for her, to say when she may sign a petition, when she may speak out for the dumb, when she may plead for the poor, when she may visit the widow and fatherless in their affliction? Does it not compel her to take off the crown of her womanhood, and lay it at man's feet? No; give her her right to the disposal of her own property, to the disposal of her own earnings. As a wife, do not compel her to explain all her needs to one who can scarcely apprehend them

---

[2] Lind, "the Swedish Nightingale," was in the midst of a triumphal tour of the United States in the fall of 1850.

from his want of attention to her situation and comforts, but let her have an equal right to the disposal of her earnings, equal privileges with man to acquire, hold, and manage property. The rightfulness of this is beginning to be felt and acknowledged. Laws have been recently passed by many of the States, giving to wives the right to control property owned before marriage; and would it not be equally just to give to them also some well-protected rights regarding what they may save and acquire by a faithful discharge of their duties as wives and heads of families.

. . . Look again, and see how things are, and the consequences. Woman degenerates, physically and intellectually. By thus narrowing their sphere, and curtailing their rights and resources, women are doomed to an endless routine of domestic drudgery, to an indoor sedentary life, with little or no stimulus to great or noble endeavors. They feel, indeed, with their narrow views and narrow interests, and their weakened bodies, that they are overcrowded and overdone with cares and labors. Dooming women to satisfy their love for excellence in household arrangements only—their love for beauty in dress, etc., is a great injury to both soul and body. We are so constituted, that exercise and great exertion, with high and soul-arousing objects, are potent to give us strength and powers of endurance. Witness wives in the times of our Revolution, think of the privations, hardships, and toil our grandmothers endured; compare them with the sickly race of wives and mothers whom modern improvements and labor-saving machinery in cloth-making are relieving from so much exertion, yet reducing their physical strength in proportion!

My remedy for this increasing degeneracy in health and consequent weakness of mind, is: give woman her rights; acknowledge her equality with man in privileges for the improvement of all her gifts; lift off the incubus [nightmarish] weight, that crushes half her rights; allow her to feel that she has other obligations resting upon her than the eternal routine of domestic affairs. . . . If married women have too little stimulus and objects, how much less have young girls, whose very dreams of the future are restricted to getting married! Having no encouragement for great endeavors, excluded from the liberal professions by the law, how many poor victims, who are not obliged "to labor" but only "to wait," are yielded up to be the prey of that frightful disease called ennui. To suffer with pain, and to be exhausted with toil, are evils, doubtless very great afflictions, but from these we do not shrink, for they are the necessary consequences of life; but ennui, —that scourge of existence, that living death, that conscious annihilation, that painful, aching nothingness, —that it is which corrodes and destroys the soul. Painful, though true, our country abounds in young ladies whom forced idleness condemns to this torture. . . . Ah, it is work, approved, creditable, well-paid work, that would reanimate these wretched existences. There are hard trials on this earth, but God has appointed labor, and all are cured. Work is a pleasure unequalled in itself; it is the preserver of all other pleasures. All may abandon us, — wit, gaiety, love, —but industry may still be ours; and the deep enjoyment which it produces, brings with it life's greatest pleasure, the approval of a good conscience. It is of this good that woman is deprived. She is accused of being too imaginative, and yet she is left a prey to reverie. She is complained of for being easily impressed, and yet society does its utmost to increase that susceptibility. This is cruel, oppressive. Dispute our rights, envy us our claim as mothers, but leave us our privilege to labor. Give us our just remuneration. Allow us a fair and equal chance, if you would see the genius of woman rising in its peculiar beauty, its free and natural manifestation.

• • •

I come now to my third proposition. Women ought to have equal legal and political rights, franchises, and advantages with men. Why not? Our laws ought to respect and protect all their rights. They ought to have an equal voice in constituting government, in administering it, in making and executing laws. Why not? This follows as the climax of what we have contended for. There may be some offices more suitable to males than females, and let matters be arranged accordingly. These are details of convenience; but for the rest let them be equal. Why not? If a woman may earn property freely, hold and dispose of it freely, etc., should she not have a free and equal voice in the government which regulates and protects her rights? She must, or be a mere ward under guardianship, a serf, a plaything, an appendage. And why should she not? Has she less at stake? Has she less moral sense? Has she less regard to the common good? Would she degrade and brutalize the exhibition at the polls? In the legislature, at the bar, etc., would the State be worse governed than it is by man alone? It is absurd to suppose it.

• • •

Blackstone,[3] in his chapter entitled Husband and Wife, says: "By marriage, the husband and wife are one person in law; that is, the very being or legal existence of the woman is suspended during the marriage, —or at least is consolidated into that of her husband, under whose wing, protection, and cover, she performs anything." So, the very being of a woman, like that of a slave, is absorbed in her master! All contracts made with her, like those made with slaves by their owners, are a mere nullity. Her legal disabilities are too well known to render it necessary to quote many of the laws respecting them. That she sustains the same relation that slaves do to our government is well known. That the laws are unjust towards her is believed by all who candidly give their attention to the subject.

• • •

People echo the cry of "danger to home" without stopping to inquire whether any such danger exists. Our grandfathers saw great danger to home and to the female character in the decline of household spinning. No, no, you do not endanger home by giving woman her true position as equal companion in the affairs of the nation as in the administration of home. So far from these new functions interfering in the least with the sacred and holy duties of wife and mother they would be rather their reward and crown. . . . our imagination looks forward to the time, with pleasure and hope, when experienced and virtuous matrons, who have passed through years of domestic duties with fidelity and care, shall sit in the Councils of the Nation wisely to control and direct their deliberations, to speak from their deep maternal love for the suffering and oppressed, to blend with the sterner element of Government that true affection for the suffering and the erring, which only woman knows, to suppress by their presence that undignified and unworthy ruffianism, which so often disgraces the councils of the nation, and finally to encourage decision, haste, and despatch of business, as only women can do, who are attracted home by an ever abiding love, that with them would be an influence far stronger than eight dollars a day.

I think you must all feel that women's rights as human beings are greatly encroached upon, that they suffer a degree of tyranny the world over, unworthy of the nineteenth century, that in view of their

---

[3] Sir William Blackstone (1723–1780), the English jurist whose *Commentaries on the Laws of England* was a basic text for attorneys in both the British Empire and the United States.

degraded position, women are called upon loudly to remonstrate, that patience has ceased to be a virtue, that it is time we demand our rights. Are we willing to be denied every post of honor and every lucrative employment—to be reckoned as the inferior sex, and but half paid for what we do—to feel that we are a proscribed caste, in all our aspirations for excellence and great and noble exertion, and to receive in return the fulsome, and sickening flattery of perverted taste—to be complimented about our shrinking delicacy, our feminine weakness, our beautiful dependence! And shall we with complacency receive and smile on such praise, bought by the sacrifice of our rights, our noblest endowments, while we know that he who thus compliments us for shrinking and dependence, is but a frail mortal like ourselves, and that to cower before man is to be recreant to God, false to our higher angel natures, and basely slaves! Is there a woman here, who is willing to be disfranchised, to be taxed without representation, to feel that she has no part or lot in the Government under which she lives—that she is a mere thing!

If there is a woman who is willing to be in this position, I do not envy that woman her spirit, and no wonder that such mothers have dough-faced children. . . .

In view of all these oppressions, —this undervaluing our labor, —taking from us our right to choice in our industrial avocations, —infliction of pecuniary dependence, —shutting us from the trades, and the learned professions, —wresting from us our legal rights, —denying us political equality, —denying us the right of free speech, —chaining us to a prescribed sphere, —we say that these, and other usurpations, demand our speedy remonstrance. "Who would be free, themselves must strike the blow." No matter if the yoke we wear is soft and cushioned, it is nevertheless a yoke. No matter if the chain is fastened by those we love, it is nevertheless a chain. Let us arise then in all the majesty of renewed womanhood and say, we must be free. We will attend to our previous home duties faithfully, cheerfully, but we must do it voluntarily, in obedience to our Maker, who placed these responsibilities more especially upon us. If the affairs of the nation demand the attention of our fathers, our husbands, and our brothers, allow us to act with them for the right, according to the dictates of our own consciences. . . . Parents, I appeal to you: are you willing to train your daughters with reference only to marriage? Are you willing they should be the prey of that sickly sentimentality, that effeminate weakness, which is produced by making that one idea the focus of life?

Husbands, are you willing to urge the cowering obedience of that being whom you admit is your "better half," especially when you consider your own frailties, and oftentimes misguided judgment? Will you assume to be her lawgiver and ruler? Are you proud to see her bend her soul to man? Brothers, are you willing to see your sisters, whose sympathy and communion in childhood was the sweetest solace of your life, prevented from future companionship, by the threatening scowl of a narrow, and heathenish public sentiment that must blast their highest aspirations—palsy the wings of their genius—dim the crown of their womanhood, and make them slaves? Again, I say—give us an equal chance. Allow us one free choice. Talk not to us of weakness when you have so long broken our spirits by the iron hand of oppression. Lift off that hand—give us our rights inalienable, and then a new era, glorious as the millenial morning, will dawn on earth, an advent only less radiant than that heralded by angels on the plains of Bethlehem.

"What highest prize hath woman won
In science, or in art?
What mightiest work by woman done,
Boasts city, field, or mart?
She hath no Raphael! Painting saith—
No Newton! Learning cries;
Show us her steamship! her Macbeth!
Her thought-won victories.

"Wait, boastful man! Though worthy are
Thy deeds, when thou art true, —
Things worthier still, and holier far,
Our sisters yet will do.
For this, the worth of woman shows
On every peopled shore,
That still as man in wisdom grows
He honors her the more.

"O, not for wealth, or fame, or power,
Hath man's meek angel striven;
But, silent as the growing flower,
To make of earth a heaven!
Soon in her garden of the sun
Heaven's brightest rose shall bloom;
For woman's best is unbegun!
Her advent yet to come!"

The Business Committee reported the following Preamble and Resolutions, offered by E. L. Rose:[4]

Whereas, The very contracted sphere of action prescribed for woman, arising from an unjust view of her nature, capacities, and powers, and from the infringement of her just rights as an equal with man, —is highly injurious to her physical, mental, and moral development; therefore, Resolved, That we will not cease our earnest endeavors to secure for her political, legal, and social equality with man, until her proper sphere is determined, by what alone should determine it, her Powers and Capacities, strengthened and refined by an education in accordance with her nature.

The resolutions were discussed by W. H. Channing, E. L. Rose, A. K. Foster, and C. C. Burleigh. On motion adjourned to meet at 7 o'clock.

New York *Tribune*, October 24, 1850

Mrs. [Abby] Price of Hopedale, was introduced to the Convention. She described the unequal condition of men and women, and the usurpation of power and right on the part of man. Man has ruled the world by physical force. She claimed equal rights on the ground of creation. God made man in His own image, "male and female created he them." He gave them dominion over all the lower orders of the creation, but not over each other.

She maintained,

Firstly: That woman should have equal rights and opportunities [to] develop her whole nature.

Secondly: That she should have equal opportunities to secure pecuniary independence; a just reward for her labor; an equal chance in the professions and business of life. She described the injustice and evil she suffers from inadequate compensation—the extent of shame and prostitution to which she is driven by the denial of her rights and privileges and of adequate compensation for her labor.

Thirdly: Women should have equal legal rights, franchises and privileges.

These propositions were maintained in an argument of great length, evincing much knowledge of the legal conditions of Woman; dwelling with biting sarcasm on the false ideas that prevail in regard to Woman's sphere and duties. She closed with an appeal to men, to husbands, brothers and fathers to stand up and help forward this righteous reform.

Rev. Wm. H. Channing, from the Committee on Business, read the . . . resolution,

---

[4] Ernestine L. Rose was born in 1810 in Russian Poland. She emigrated to the United States after her marriage in 1836. By the time of the convention she was well known as an advocate of women's rights. Her eloquence had already earned her the title, "queen of the platform."

prepared by Mrs. Ernestine Rose of N.Y. [as printed in the *Proceedings*]:

• • •

Mr. Channing made some very earnest remarks on the subject. He spoke with warm approbation of the address of the last speaker [Abby Price]. He thanked God that one woman had shown the moral courage to stand out and claim the rights that belonged to her nature. He spoke of the evil that had been named, prostitution. He described its corrupting influence upon society, from the child, through all the grades of human life, up to manhood and womanhood. It poisons and vitiates the institution of marriage; it destroys the confidence that should exist between the husband and wife; it spreads its contamination over the whole of human life. He pointed out a remedy. Let men exclude from their society every man he knows to have sacrificed his virtue to sinful lusts. Men pretend to value chastity and virginity in woman. Let him prove it by valuing chastity and virginal purity in man.

Mrs. Ernestine Rose of New York, spoke with great eloquence on the subject of the resolution. Her French [sic] accent and extemporaneous manner added quite a charm to her animated and forcible style. Woman, she asked, who is she? She is the mother, the wife and the sister of man. Is she not coequal with man? Has she not like powers of mind, like sentiments, faculties and affections given her for culture and improvement? Why, in the name of common sense, she would ask, is she not equal in the enjoyment of life, liberty and the pursuit of happiness? But she is not equal before the law. During her minority she is the property of her parent, and when she attains her majority, and enters the relation of marriage, she is transferred from the parent to the husband. If she had her rights and was properly educated, marriage would be the union of two hearts from real affection, instead of being as it now too frequently is, an artificial bond producing often more misery than happiness. She said a just indignation was felt by the community on account of the law which delivers up the fugitive slave to oppression. But it was no more unjust than some of the laws

are toward women. If a woman is compelled, by the tyranny and ill treatment of her husband, to leave him and seek a refuge among her friends, the law will deliver her up into his hands. He may compel her return. She did not propose to examine the laws that bears [sic] so unequally upon woman. What she claimed was that the laws should be made equally for both.

She said, when a father and mother have a son born to them, what do they ask themselves? They sit down and consult together about his education; how he shall be trained and fitted for usefulness in life. If they have a daughter, what do they ask? nothing. Girls are educated with one single aim, she felt ashamed to say it. And what is that aim? It is to catch a husband. She is educated in accordance with man's desires, wishes, and aims, and [it] is no wonder she has not risen to the true level of her womanhood. Woman has never yet received an education for the higher purposes of life. Why should she not be made acquainted with the arts, the sciences and the philosophies of life? With all the obstacles that exist to her elevation, there are brilliant instances of her success in all that has adorned and rendered great the character and fame of man. She had even acquired distinction in the field of battle. She trusted that if ever woman touched the sword, it would be to sheathe it in its scabbard forever.

She mentioned that woman could study successfully any of the professions. Is perseverance necessary? She possesses it. Look at her by the bed of sickness, where toil and sacrifice are needed. Who is it that holds out to the last? It is feeble woman! Look at man when he is ready to give up with despair. Who is [it] that upholds and strengthens him? It is feeble woman. It is the being whom Society assigns an inferior in rank and position in life. She mentioned that woman was as heroic as man, and often exhibited a higher heroism, [compared] with which that displayed in the battle field is cowardice. She contended for woman's rights, not so much for her benefit as for the benefit of the world. She pointed out the evils of Society under its present organization and made a strong appeal to the reason and moral sense of her audience, to give their influence to the cause.

Her speech was received with applause by a large and intelligent audience, as were also the speeches of Mrs. Mott, Mrs. Price, and Mr. Channing. The hall was very crowded, and the audience seemed to have caught the spirit of the speakers.

Abby Kelly Foster also addressed the Convention in a strong speech, and was followed by C. C. Burleigh. I see Wendell Phillips and W. L. Garrison in the audience, having arrived this afternoon.

New York *Herald,* October 25, 1850

Mrs. Price read a manuscript address, on the wrongs and rights of women. Rather tedious.

Audience swelling to five or six hundred persons.

Mr. W. H. Channing submitted the [Rose] resolution . . . which he discussed at length, travelling over the whole ground of woman's inconveniences, with a sprinkling of abolition thrown in here and there by way of seasoning.

Lucretia Mott next followed in some pointed remarks, exhibiting the present degraded condition of woman in civilized society. She has nothing but her outward semblance in her favor; when that ceases all respect for her vanishes; for an old woman is simply an object of ridicule, and anything that is ridiculous or foolish is said to be only fit for an old woman. In no respect had the rights of woman been as yet recognized in society.

The girls in the audience beginning to get tired of this nonsense, began to whisper and titter among themselves, at the ridiculous figure which that row of seven or eight old women on the platform presented, when one of them, a very fat lady, weighing about three hundred (a clear evidence that her rights had been respected) rose to speak.

Abby Kelly, in the crowd—We can't hear you in this corner. Speak louder.

Lucretia Mott—We must have silence. I have addressed audiences of two thousand persons, and there was no difficulty in hearing.

Here we have, perhaps, not over five hundred, and yet we have complaints that we cannot be heard.

The audience became quiet.

Mrs. Abby Kelly Foster here came forward upon the platform. —I am sick, too sick to debate this subject this evening [sic]. (She looked sickly, and had the echo of a bad cold in her voice.) I prefer not to argue about a woman's rights, but to take them. I know what they are instinctively, and shall contend for them, without getting into a theoretical argument about them, and that is what I suppose to be the business of this Convention. Abby disappeared, and

Mrs. Rose rose upon the platform. [the reporter sought to mock her accent by rendering parts of her speech phonetically.]—Madame President and ma dear sisters and bredren, I do regret no one rises better dan myself to speak; but I shall offer you but a few remarks on de subject before us. Mrs. Rose spoke at some length, saying, among other things, dat woman is in de quality of de slave, and man is de tyrant; and dat when de distinction of rights between de sexes ceases, then, and not till then, will woman get her just desserts. [sic] When men and women are trained as human beings, without regard to sex, in schools, in academies, in Church and in State, when their education and thoughts become more spiritual and less animal, then we shall not suffer this inequality any longer. The sphere of woman, oh, how limited! Woman suffers and man suffers—they must both suffer from this inequality. What we most want is this—a determination never to give up the rights of humanity. We have eyes, and we have the right to see; tongues, and the right to speak. We have the same phrenological[1] organization as man, and the same intellectual desires, and the same right to have them gratified.

Abby Kelly Foster—I do not talk of woman's rights, but of human rights, the rights of human beings. I do not come to ask [for] them, but to demand them; not to get down on my knees and beg for them, but to claim them. "Sauce for the goose is sauce for the gander." We have our rights, and the right to revolt, as did our fathers against King George the Third—the right to rise up and cut the tyrants' throats. On this subject I scorn to talk like a woman. We must give them the truth, and not twaddle. We must not be mealy mouthed with our tyrants in broadcloth and tight clothes. In short, in the harangue of Abby, she simply demanded that men and women should be treated as human beings all alike—that the sexes should be for-gotten in society—that property and votes and offices, civil, religious and military, even to the right of cutting throats, should belong to woman as well as to man. She urged that the work should be commenced by educating both sexes together, and that all distinction in society between man and woman should be abolished, and that a woman was just as well qualified to be President as a man. [Applause.]

Charles C. Burleigh (an improved specimen of George H. Munday, the prophet having more beard and a greater amount of hair about his ears) next took the rostrum. He did not exactly agree with Mrs. Abby Kelly Foster, that the sexes should be dispensed with in the reorganization of society. He thought the two sexes were different, and that man and woman were sexes in soul as well as in body. He, however, agreed that the restraints upon woman ought to be removed, and that her freedom to choose her own vocation in life ought to be allowed upon an enlarged scale, as well as the privilege of the ballot box, the right of property, and so forth.

Boston *Chronotype,*
October 24, 1850:

The Convention met at the appointed hour, when Mrs. Abby Price of Hopedale, Mass., read an eloquent and piquant address which was received with applause by an almost [sic] enthusiastic audience.

Rev. W.H. Channing, on behalf of Mrs. Rose of New York reported the . . . Resolution. . . . Mr. Channing supported the resolution with a good speech.

Mrs. Rose of N.Y. gave the resolution a radical support.

She attacked and demolished Dana's theory of *mannish* woman. Mrs. R. is a Polish lady, but she speaks pure English undefiled, with a slight foreign accent. Hers was the speech of the afternoon.

Mrs. Sarah Tynsdale, of Philadelphia, made a few remarks introductory of Lucretia Mott's pamphlet on Woman.

Mrs. Lucretia Mott said that in the Society of Friends to which she belongs, women

---

[1] Phrenology was very popular in the mid-nineteenth century, especially among the reform-minded. It held that character traits and abilities were located in specific regions of the brain and corresponded mathematically to the size of the "bumps" of an individual's cranium. Woman's rights advocates found phrenology especially intriguing because the measurements disclosed no differences between men and women.

are constructed with lungs for use rather than show; but a part of their education is to keep silence. Our voices would, she continued, be heard in all parts of this crowded room if there were no whisperings.

Mrs. Abby Kelley Foster, then addressed the convention in support of Mrs. Rose's resolution. Her Subject, The rights of Humanity; shall women have them? She made a brilliant speech.

Chas. C. Burleigh, of Ct., was introduced and spoke upon the right and duty of woman to judge for herself her own sphere of action. His speech was pointed and often eloquent.

Boston *Daily Mail,* October 24, 1850:

The Conference met at the hour of adjournment, to the tune of "Oh Susanna!" from the organ below, whose mellifluous tones won stray passengers from the sidewalk to view "One of the Wonders," in the shape of a remarkably fat and fubsy [i.e., chubby and squat] fair one, who was showing off in the hall below as being "only 16 years old and 400 pounds weight!" Her physical disease operated, of course, as a contrast to the mental disorganization above:

The minutes of the morning session were read by Miss [Hannah M.] Darlington, the secretary, who took off her bonnet, that the assimilation to the masculine comportment under the same order of circumstances should be perfect.

Thereafter Mrs. [Abby] Price of Hopedale, Mass., read a paper, which commenced at the creation of the world down to physical force, and the degradation which that ugly weapon, in the hands of intolerant man, had conferred upon womankind. Coming down to the middle of the nineteenth century, it was proved that the creation produced the equality of the sexes—absolutely—in the articles liberty of action, and expression of political and social power. The nineteenth century, at the middle, had also proof in connection with it—in some manner unexplained—that women had a right to the same privileges as men, in all things, even down to all and every variety of rowdy craft. These and other things were to be asserted and attained that the souls of females should be saved. The particular dependencies on the purse of the "old feller," when a "love of a bonnet," was wanted or "perfect beauty of a shawl," were commented on in a style which the late Mrs. Caudle[2] would have gloried in. The narrow circle in which social observances confined the dear creatures of womankind, was considerably rated [condemned]; and if it has not extended its circumference, it has no shame in it. The propriety of a girl being constituted a regular *blue* [stocking? A scholarly or educated woman] received an elegant and strong propulse [push forward]; and the reason why she should not be a cabman, a mason, carpenter, sailor, or anything of that sort, was arraigned and abused to its [sic] heart's content. This reason was simply that girls would believe that they were only women—*only,* observe; and that they would not generally allow that they were anything else. A very sensible appeal was made to the cheap tailors to pay the girls better wages for their labor; and their conduct characterised as the prevailing cause of prostitution. This

---

[2] A reference to Douglas William Jerrold (1803–1857), *Mrs. Caudle's Curtain Lectures.* By "Punch." (Hartford: S. Andrus & Son, n.d. [1845?]). [Mrs. Caudle is the stereotypical nagging wife; Mr. Caudle, the original henpecked husband.]

prostitution was a natural result of low prices, and scarcity of work. It was also certain that the adoption, by men, of trades peculiarly feminine, was a great cause of occasional immorality of young women. The fair speaker quoted several instances and authorities in proof of these very plain truths— for it must be confessed that they are such. To throw open to women equal resources to those of the men, the lady speaker considered the best cure for the evils she had described. The whole of the various incentives to prostitution were enumerated; and the general conclusion drawn that the cause of all was man's inhumanity towards the gentler sex, in denying them the full privileges, and profits, and enjoyments—cigars and champagne included we suppose—that they arrogated to themselves. Women, at present, were "flat—prostrate—worn down by this tyranny of man." One might rise now and then as a Jenny Lind, or as a poetess—but none were allowed to become lawyers, physicians, mechanics or anybody else; but favored individuals were sometimes allowed to be milliners. Her resources were nothing, it would be seen: still she was a human being and ought to be privileged, so that her natural developments should be seen. Ahem! Special privileges were specified, viz: the power of women to spend money she [sic] earned, the abolition of domestic drudgery, and household duties hitherto saddled upon them. A strong appeal was made to allow woman her rights, that she should renew the physical strength our blessed old grandmothers were reported to have enjoyed: those excellent ladies who milked their own cows, and were not too gentle to make and sell their own butter, and who could drive a team to and from the field on a pinch. Work! healthy well paid work! *that* was the panacea. The whole race of copying, recording and other clerks were busying themselves with this healthy kind of work; and all the secretaryships in this vast continent were just in the same category—not excepting that one [Secretary of State] held by the

godlike Daniel [Webster]. The country could not possibly be worse governed by women than it is now; and Blackstone was quoted to prove that his opinion regarding women was just no opinion at all, for he said they ought not to be enfranchised, as they were incapable of the necessary degree of intelligence to qualify them. But would the meeting suffer this opinion to pass unnoticed? No Madam! no such thing! Woman had, in this republic, being themselves free and intelligent, and not criminal, or wanting in physical ability, a right to vote at elections, and they would. No doubt of that! If such objections regarding woman legislators did exist as those quoted by the enemies of emancipation of women, how did it come that the so-called thoroughly qualified men contrived to send so many old women to Congress and elsewhere? This was a truth that the audience assented to with a semi-cheer—the other half of which was a grunt. The very stupid thing called gallantry was used up like an old pair of boots, and no mistake. In the community at Hopedale every body did what they blessed pleased in voting, and doing up politics, women as well as men. This very rambling affair ended with Dan O'Connell's[3] pet couplet—

Hereditary bondsmen! know ye not
Who would be free himself must
strike the blow!

Mrs. [Ernestine] Rose, of New York, moved a resolution declaring that the most earnest endeavors would be used to secure to womankind her rights in all their details.

Mr. Channing, of New York, [sic] spoke in a complimentary strain of the preceding speaker. He thanked God that he had lived to see the day when a woman could be found who could utter such sentiments. Mr. C. had but one word to say; but that word would fill two columns in the *Mail*. That one word, being interpreted, signified that it was a blasting shame on the face of manhood that the men of this country had not risen and

---

[3] Daniel O'Connell (1775–1847), an Irish patriot who led the battle in the British Parliament for the Catholic Emancipation Act which granted religious toleration to British Catholics in 1829.

prevented the evils which assail woman-kind—and carry, even into the hearts of youth low, foul, bestial, infernal associations and practices—constituting things so that a man could not bring virgin purity to his breast, but a mass of pollution, arising from the corruption of the social condition of the female sex. This sweeping inference, insinuation—calumny—that's it! singularly to say, was not received by the groanings of the audience. This led the speaker to arraign every soul in the universal community as a reprobate who cultivated this pollution, and the lie was applauded by not more than ten or fewer than three. He proposed a Senate of women to correct the universal evil; and the remainder of his speech was so grossly indecent as to be unfitted for the lowest brothel. He knew all about what he said—he confessed—and we well believe him. He may have the hats of half the brothel supporters in the United States.

Mrs. [Ernestine] Rose, next spoke of the misery which arose from the false state of society, and the degradation of woman, its consequence—and wished its nature could be fathomed that it might be known and corrected. Mrs. Rose spoke with eloquent pleadings in behalf of the mother, sister, wife of man, and in favor of her equality with her brother man, in all the privileges, enjoyments and liberties that life produces. She was recognised not as being her own property, but the property of another, from her cradle to her grave. Marriage was a transfer, only, from the custody of the parent or guardian to the husband: a woman went ever to him as a common piece of goods. Talk of Fugitive Laws! The same were in operation against the oppressed wife. If she broke the bonds of slavery the law would bring her back—she was a fugitive slave. The law of marriage was a mistake—a great fundamental error, and operated all on one side, furnishing the penalty, but none of the privileges to women—who were nonetheless the moulders of society—and had her influences, especially in the ordering of social details. If the error of the inferiority of woman was once trampled under foot, and other necessary reforms instituted, woman would not only have a higher knowledge and estimate of herself, but she

would impart her improvement to society at large. Elevate her to the position she should occupy, and charity, morality, and every other humanising sympathy and principle would flow from her in its essence and purity. This was, in utterance, manner, and treatment, the most eloquent speech of the day. Mrs. Rose was loudly applauded at the close. Her sonorous, German style of expression, and the use of certain idiomatic phrases, more than her accent, shewed this lady to be a native of the land [Germany] of Goethe and Gessner. Mrs. Rose's intelligence conferred a respectability on the conference that it would not, without her aid, have deserved in name. Of course we do not mean that the meeting was characterless in a moral sense—but that the means specified to advance the object it professed to serve had no status in the list of rational speculations.

Mrs. Tisdale [Tyndale], of Philadelphia, next spoke, but simply to puff Mrs. Mott's and Mr. Dana's lectures, copies of which were on hand for sale.

Mrs. Lucretia Mott asked all the good folks to keep as quiet as possible, as there was no hearing at all.

Mrs. Abby Kelly Foster could not endure to have the resolution pass unless she had a finger in the pie. She said her life was her best argument in connection with the movement; and as the bottom of it had not been found she would make a dive at it. Every woman was not able to go to the bottom of the well, for they were so enslaved, that they could not attempt the search. She said she appeared not as a woman, but as humanity itself. (Well, humanity has been called a lovely thing but—that's all on this subject for present.) She continued to deny that girls were trained in schools, academies, churches or senates as human beings, but everything went to foment the sensual and debasing. Brother Channing's filthy speech received a very undeserving compliment. Woman's sphere, was then described to be anything else than the fallen star it is now recognized generally to be—and no nebulous matter at all, but a fixed planet, where equality of rights, privileges and their exercise in social and political respects shone most conspicuously. This planetary system was claimed as the proper sphere of existence for woman kind. Its relation to the *moon* was not mentioned.[4] A very excellent physiological lecture followed this definition, mixed up with phrenology, biology, and all the ologies, showing that women were, physically and mentally, the equals of men. In the love of power, rule and general influence she was also his equal, and he was superior to her in nothing but a tyranny which would be a justification for women to rise and cut men's throats. She came not into the meeting to mince words, but to speak plain; and what she had just said was plain enough in all conscience—as plain as—Ahem! Humanity in tights [men] and humanity in flowing clothing [women] were at issue, and force of arms was justifiable, and not unlikely to be arrived at soon. Women had a right to cut the throats of the men of Massachusetts who taxed them without their consent. She said she had the locomotive power in her organization, (and no one could doubt the share the tongue had in the distribution.) She also had the intelligence— (no one could question that, but the *quality* was open to dispute.) She had the physical strength too, and that would be used to pull down the barrier between woman and her rights; (no one could doubt of the Amazonian temper and disposition of Abby). She was perfectly right in saying she did not appear as a woman. There was little of a woman about her and very much of the tigress. Her poor hubby, she described, as a savage in unwhisperables—which was a consequence of his going to educational institutions, et cetera, and women had as good [a] right to go to such institutions as men—therefore women had a right to cultivate the savage passions.

Honor was paid to women so gifted with a sanguine propensity. Mademoiselle Jagelli was one instance. That women had a right to the Presidency, the fact of Queen Victoria reigning over the British, was alluded to as a noble example of the heaven-born right to wear the breeches, and rule with such rod—iron or cork, as might best please themselves. This about closed Abby's remarks, who was allowed to proceed and sit down without one word of applause.

Mr. C. C. Burley [Burleigh] spoke from behind an abominably arranged mass of whiskers and beard, consequently we could not allow ourselves to listen to him. The trouble the gentleman had in commencing his speech particularly struck us as being funny; but that the misty introduction should constitute soul and substance, Alpha and Omega, of said speech, was a curiosity in oratory that we never heard of only in the cure of a stuck oration—some of which we have heard—but never one with such pretence as Grizzly Burley's had. He closed with a lecture on Hydraulics, and a string of common-places regarding the philosophy of something or other that our spectacles could not see through. Very dirty, very diffuse, and very hairy was Grizzly Burley.

By the time Burley had sputtered his foolishness forth it was dark— very dark—as dark as was his arrangement of ideas and a movement at adjournment was made in the shape of a stampede for the door. As the last flicker of sunlight came in at the window and went out at the door, we closed our labors, as we had hoped, for a day; but a meeting was called for the evening, to be held at 7 o'clock. Adjourned.

---

[4] Popular wisdom associated insanity with the moon as the word lunatic exemplifies.

OCTOBER 23, 1850—EVENING SESSION

The evening session began with Abby Kelley Foster's speech still ringing in everyone's ears. The opening speaker, the Rev. William H. Channing, who had introduced the Rose resolution of that afternoon, however, made no reference to it. Instead, he advanced a notion of his own, that there ought to be an Annual Congress of Women who would exercise moral influence on the issues of the day. However farfetched this scheme might seem today, it reflected an important trend within the early woman's rights movement, that is, to argue that women possessed by "nature" a higher moral sense than did men and that they therefore should occupy a separate, albeit equal, sphere from men.

Lucretia Mott, who spoke next, set the tone for the rest of the session. She expressed dismay at those "friends" of the movement who spoke of women being "given" their rights. They should demand their rights. She also expressed misgivings about those who worried overmuch at biblical injunctions about wives being subject to their husbands, a topic which would loom even larger the next day. Clergy were always condemning something for being unbiblical, she argued, only to backtrack after that something, such as the new science of phrenology, proved its worth. Mott then turned to Abby Kelley Foster's defense of women's right to rise up against their oppressors as their forefathers had risen up against King George III during the American Revolution.

Mott doubtless appreciated the irony of her situation. It had been she, only that morning, who had rejected Paulina Wright Davis's argument that convention participants had to avoid inflammatory rhetoric. Kelley Foster had only carried her own argument a step further. But, for Mott who, like Kelley Foster, grew up in the Quaker tradition of nonviolence, it was a fatal step. Interestingly, it was the anti-woman's rights Boston Daily Mail *which gave the fullest treatment of Mott's remarks. More interesting still, its reporter had nothing but praise for her entire speech.*

It might seem at this point that Davis's efforts to control the course of the convention's deliberations had failed utterly. A reading of the official Proceedings, *which she edited, shows that the situation was more complicated. Most of those who learned of the convention would do so from the* Proceedings, *and it contained not a word of Mott's or Kelley Foster's views. Further, the resolutions reported by Wendell Phillips for the Business Committee reflected Davis's views to the letter. There was no language in them about woman's "sphere," in the manner of the Rose resolution which they replaced. Nor did they take up the vexed issue of gender equality. Instead, they proclaimed certain universal human rights and then called for specific actions.*

If Davis's influence continued, despite her inability as president of the convention to participate in the debate, it remained partial at best. Phillips, seconded by Ernestine Rose, asserted that women bore much of the responsibility for their situation. Mott, seconded by Abby Kelley Foster, avowed that it was the "despot" man who was to blame. Phillips tried to find a middle position by putting the responsibility where Davis had suggested it lay, on custom and tradition. The Mott contingent, joined by Abby Kelley Foster's husband Stephen S. Foster, agreed that antiquity in general and the views of St. Paul in particular should have no authority in determining the rights of women, but rejected the notion that the hold custom and tradition had over men's minds was any sort of excuse.

FROM THE *PROCEEDINGS:*

P.W. Davis in the Chair.

Business of the Convention—the discussion of the preamble and resolution offered at the morning [sic, actually afternoon] session. Speakers—W. H. Channing and Lucretia Mott. Wendell Phillips, on behalf of the Business Committee, reported several resolutions, which were discussed by W. Phillips, E. L. Rose, L. Mott, A. K. Foster, J. N. Buffum, and S. S. Foster. The resolutions were as follows:

Resolved, That every human being of full age, and resident for a proper length of time on the soil of the nation, who is required to obey law, is entitled to a voice in its enactments; that every such person, whose property or labor is taxed for the support of government, is entitled to a direct share in such government. Therefore,

Resolved, That women are clearly entitled to the right of suffrage, and to be considered eligible to office; the omission to demand which, on her part, is a palpable recreancy to duty; and the denial of which is a gross usurpation, on the part of man, no longer to be endured; and that every party which claims to represent the humanity, civilization, and progress of the age, is bound to inscribe on its banners, Equality before the law, without distinction of sex or color.

Resolved, That political rights acknowledge no sex, and therefore the word "male" should be stricken from every State Constitution.

Resolved, That the laws of property, as affecting married parties, demand a thorough revisal, so that all rights may be equal between them; that the wife may have, during life, an equal control over the property gained by their mutual toil and sacrifices, be heir to her husband precisely to the extent that he is heir to her, and entitled, at her death, to dispose by will of the same share of the joint property as he is.

On motion, adjourned, to meet to-morrow morning, at half past nine.

New York *Tribune,* October 25, 1850:

The Convention reassembled this evening at 7 o'clock, in Brinley Hall. The room was crowded to excess, every seat, and aisle, and the space around the platform being filled, men and women standing on their feet during the whole evening. A heartfelt interest evidently pervaded the audience.

The first speaker was Rev. Wm. H. Channing—He advocated the wisdom, the propriety and duty of opening our institutions of learning, our medical schools, our colleges and high schools to both sexes indiscriminately. Women should be admitted to all these privileges as her right. He alluded to the remark quoted from a gentleman [Richard Henry Dana?] who had objected to women having equal rights, because it would make them *manish.* He said it was a foolish expression. There was no possibility that such a thing could ever happen. God's law of spiritual order could never be set aside. He spoke of Woman in the industrial pursuits. She should have the opportunity to use all her powers, in every form of industry she may choose. There should be no obstacle in the way of her raising herself to personal independence. She should be trained for the coequal of man in every respect. She should be represented in the legislation of the country and the administration of the laws. She should have the right to sit on a jury; to be tried by her peers.

He did not know whether this would ever be obtained by suffrage or not; but woman's judgment and woman's heart shall yet be felt in the very center of legislation. The purity of wisdom and of heart which belongs to woman is not expressed in the church nor in the state. It is shut out from the pulpit and the halls of legislation. But there is a method he would suggest, by which it could be made to bear on the public heart and mind. Let there be an *Annual* Congress of Women, to whom there shall be a standard of moral appeal, and their influence shall be felt far and wide. He alluded to the appeal of Miss Catharine Beecher[1] in behalf of her friend. He honored her for the skill and noble manner in which she executed her work, and especially that it evinced her true womanhood. Suppose such an annual meeting of a Congress of Women could be held, in which women of years and full of honor should be found, and young women; and then let an association of orthodox clergymen uphold a young man in a course of conduct

---

[1] Catharine Beecher (1800–1878) was the eldest daughter of Lyman Beecher, one of the most celebrated clergymen of the day. Two of her brothers, Edward and Henry Ward, followed their father into the pulpit and both achieved national renown. Her sister, Harriet Beecher Stowe, became a best-selling novelist. Catharine was also a best-selling author, of advice books on homemaking and childrearing; she led the crusade to open the teaching profession to women. She also campaigned for dress and nutrition reforms.

so dishonorable and unmanly [breach of promise], and the moral sentiment of such a body of women, in their congregated might, would fall upon them like an avalanche. In such a Congress they might make their higher sentiments bear on the evils of war, of slavery, and on the interests of power and freedom. He advocated the wisdom and propriety of establishing orders of women. Our Catholic friends established orders of this kind, and he did not know why Protestants might not do the same thing. Why should there not be an order of women, composed of those who do not choose to encumber themselves with the ties of marriage? and why might they not plant themselves on a domain, invest their property, and engage in such industrial operations as might suit their capacities and tastes; and here would be a place, where woman, driven from the family circle, by the tyranny of a husband, a brother, son, might find a home, and a place for the employment of her powers. Said he "Sisters, you know I am speaking the solemn fact when I say that there are thousands of women, who wet their pillow with their tears every night, in consequence of the tyranny to which they are subjected by their position, and who do not know where to stand." Such an order of women would give them hope and reliance in attempting their own emancipation.

Mrs. Lucretia Mott said: The language of those who favor our cause implies a degree of kindness when they speak of *giving* us our rights, *permitting* us to receive them; but she was not disposed to receive them in this way; she was in favor of *demanding* them, in the name of our common humanity. She wanted a resolution framed that should express this demand. She wanted Woman's freedom and independence acknowledged as a right; that they should be secured to her, yielded, not given; that those restrictions which have prevented her from rising to her true position should be removed, leaving her a fair opportunity to rise in the scale of being, and make herself what God designed she should be. That she sometimes does this despite the obstacles that surround her, is evidence of her capacity. There are some signs of progress and encouragement to cheer us onward. A Medical School is instituted in Philadelphia

for the education of female physicians, and a large number have already entered their names as students. An Academy of Design is also established, where Women may learn a knowledge of drawing and design, which shall enable them to find useful employments. Journeymen tailors and tailoresses are forming associations so as to do business for themselves, and the value and dignity of labor is rising and will command its proper reward to the Woman as well as to the Man. Woman's labor has not been appreciated. And many Women, by suffrance, to some extent, are raising their voices in the name of religion and humanity. In the Society to which she belonged [of Hicksite Quakers], and among one or two other Societies she named, Women stand on an equality with Men, and have the same rights of speech. But this was not generally the case.

She regretted that so much time had been wasted in applying the Bible argument to these reforms. All we have to do is to step forward in the right, and the theologians will have to do this work, of reconciling the Bible with these principles of everlasting truth and right. She alluded to the writings of George and Andrew Combe as have at first encountered this objection, that the truths they taught of Phrenology and Philosophy were opposed to the Bible. A work was written to refute them on this ground. But while the works of these men had reached many editions, it had fallen into oblivion, and now an appendix is written by an American Divine to show the *harmony* between them. Mr. Combe, probably, had no objection to this, but it was not his work. He left that to the ecclesiastics. And so it had been with the other sciences and in the Anti-Slavery reform. She was not [to be] understood to want [i.e., lack] reverence or respect for the Bible, but the work of reconciling any apparent or imaginary conflicts was not their appropriate work. They should stand forth on the great principles of justice and humanity; and she alluded to the fact that there were "honorable women, not a few," who had dared to prophesy in the name of Christ.

She made reference to the language of Mrs. [Abby Kelley] Foster, who she feared would be construed to favor the use of violence and bloodshed as one of the means of obtaining these rights. She thought she [Kelley Foster] might not be understood. What she said on the subject was based upon the supposition that certain other things were right. She wished her friend had given her own views of the subject. Mrs. Mott then went on in a few eloquent and powerful remarks, to urge that the weapons of their warfare were not carnal, but spiritual, and might through God, lead to the pulling down of strongholds. That they must fight with the sword of the spirit, even the works of God; they must appeal to the pure sentiments of the mind, and the justice of their cause. She was opposed to any twaddle on that subject, as was her friend. We want to speak earnestly and truly the words of honest and sober conviction. We want to speak in tones of reproof to those on whom the guilt of these wrongs rests. We want to say as Jesus did "Ye fools and blind," "Ye hypocrites," and to our Sisters, who are still indifferent and contented with their position "O, thou slothful and slow of heart, rise up in the strength of thy Womanhood, and Christ shall give thee light." There is no greater mistake than to suppose that what is called non-resistance is a timid and inefficient method of meeting those evils. It is the strongest kind of resistance—the resistance of moral sentiment, of justice and truth. It will not permit us to injure our fellow beings, to take their lives, but it leaves to us that higher resistance which comes from God.

Wendell Phillips, on behalf of the Business Committee, read the . . . series of resolutions [as printed in the *Proceedings*]:

• • •

Mr. Phillips remarked that he felt interested in this movement, because it promises to bring to the cause of humanity, in its struggle with wrong, the intellect and heart of one half the world, who, by their position, have been kept from exerting their full share of influence and power. The rights to which Woman is entitled are of two kinds, natural and political rights. Whichever of these is first secured the other will soon follow. He was inclined to think the former would be realized first—the right to determine for herself what shall be her profession; what kind of industry shall engage her attention; what studies she shall pursue, and how she shall dispose of her property. But he regarded the question of political rights [as being] of great importance. He thought Women ought to be equally eligible to offices of responsibility and trust in the Government; to vote, and to a voice in the enactment of laws. She should be represented in the Courts and in the Jury box. He differed from Mr. Channing so far as Mr. C. would compose a Jury exclusively of one sex or the other. He would not have a woman tried by a jury entirely of her own sex, nor a colored person by those of his own color. But he thought sex and color should be mingled up before the law. The Jury is one of the means of making us feel our rights and responsibilities. DeTocqueville[2] had said of the French nation, that they never could have a Republic till the trial by jury was consummated. The influence of the Jury box is very great. But Woman is denied all this by her exclusion from it.

The feudal ages and customs, he said, had given us our laws, and they abolished Woman. Our social customs have come from the Hebrews, with a touch of the classic, and these abolished Woman. We need, therefore, to run the ploughshare of reform deep through the soil which has given growth to our present institutions and customs. This is, therefore, a most thorough and radical reform.

He did not think all the guilt of these wrongs to which women are subjected rested on Man. He thought Woman must share equally the guilt with him. We are in part the creatures of circumstances; we are what the past has made us, and these wrongs have grown up, or continued to exist, not

---

[2] Alexis de Tocqueville was the most celebrated of all the foreign travelers to visit the United States in the first half of the nineteenth century. His *Democracy in America* (1835, 1840) was an international best-seller. He also wrote a history of the French Revolution.

from an intention of wrong on the part of man, but from ignorance. We have inherited these customs; very few men ever get beyond the smoke of their father's cabins.

He thought the annual sessions of this Convention of great importance. He would place the papers that have been read here to-day on record and have them printed, and they would be looked at hereafter as a Declaration of Rights. A series of these Conventions will gather around them the sympathy and moral sentiment of society. He would leave it to a Standing Committee to call them annually at a convenient time and place. No other organization is needed. What we want is to change public opinion. Women had as much influence as men in the formation of public opinion, and here again was there responsibility rested upon them. It is public opinion that deprives Woman of most of her rights. When this public opinion is reformed, the barriers and restrictions thrown around Woman will fall almost imperceptibly. What we want is martyrs in this cause—martyrs to public opinion. The dear friend who preceded him [Lucretia Mott] had done more by her example, in discussing and speaking on great moral questions, for the cause than a thousand tracts. The Legislature will open its doors when the pressure of public opinion outside becomes too great to bear, and no sooner. Politics will change as public opinion changes. This public opinion is slow in its growth and formation. The public mind is like stone on which the water drops continually till it is worn away. The public mind is silly and foolish. It is affected more by epigrams, and jokes, and ridicule, than by the power of reason and truth. It was by such means that Louis Philippe [so-called "Citizen King" of France overthrown in revolution of 1848] in one night lost his crown. If he had possessed the courage of his wife his throne might have been standing to this day. The influence of truth and right upon the public conscience and heart is gradual and slow. The massive architecture of the Romans looks as if it were built to stand through eternity; but the weeds grow out from its crevices and send their roots among its huge masses, and the frosts of an Italian sky gradually separate them, undermining the monuments of the

Cæsars, until they crumble down in piles of broken ruins.

Mrs. Rose of New York, made another of her effective and eloquent speeches, in which she alluded to our Pilgrim *Fathers,* and the pride and reverence with which they were often referred to. But, said she, "Who has heard of the Pilgrim *Mothers?* Did they not endure as many perils, and encounter as many hardships, and do as much to form and fashion the institutions of New England, as the Pilgrim Fathers? Yet they are hardly remembered."

Mrs. Lucretia Mott, made another impressive speech, in which she fixed the blame of these wrongs of Woman on the wrong doer. She did not believe in *abstract* wrong. Where there is oppression there is an oppressor. She thought the wrong in this case rested on man, and he should be held responsible for it. She marvelled that her friend Wendell Phillips should take the view he did. He did not reason thus when he spoke of the wrongs of the Slave.

Mr. Phillips said he cheerfully submitted to the criticism of his friend, while he maintained his position that the guilt of these wrongs should be divided between the sexes. There were none who would ridicule these conventions more than those for whose benefit they were designed. It will be more difficult to meet the sarcasm of the women than to reach the conviction of men on this subject.

He maintained Woman's rights to property, from the fact that she was capable of *earning* property, and therefore she had the right of ownership. She could be punished by the laws, and therefore she was entitled to a voice in their enactment.

Mrs. Foster made a speech in which she argued that the responsibility of these wrongs rests upon men. She replied to the argument that Women are contented with their sphere, and [that women] ridiculed this movement to secure their rights. They were dependent for bread upon their husbands; they were afraid of their displeasure. Many of them lament over their inferior and degraded and helpless position. But they are like the slave on the southern plantation. Ask him in the presence of his master if he is contented, and will he answer no, or murmur at his condition? No! he is afraid. And so it is with Woman. She may not be afraid of the cowhide; but she feels her dependence, and is afraid of the displeasure of her lord and master.

Mr. James M. Buffum of Lynn made a few remarks, urging the movement onward.

Mrs. Mott made some further remarks, touching on the promise of the Woman, in the marriage ceremony, to love, honor, and obey. She said these words were put in the Woman's mouth by the priest, or rather, repeated by the priest and not the Woman, though she reluctantly answers "Yes." In the religious society of which she is a member it

was not so; there was a perfect reciprocity of obligation as they stood in the presence of heaven, without priest or magistrate, and invoked the Father's blessing. And she believed there were as happy and harmonious unions formed in that society as in any other religious association.

Mr. S.S. Foster made a speech of some length, which we have not time nor space to give.

The Convention adjourned at 10 o'clock to meet again in the same place at 9½ o'-clock to-morrow morning.

New York *Herald*, October 25, 1850:

Hall crowded to excess.

Mr. [Wm. H.] Channing resumed the thread of the argument upon the rights of woman, in the consideration of some practical measures. As one of these measures, he recommended that the sexes should be mingled together in schools and academies. They would stimulate and improve each other. He next proposed an annual congress of women to regulate society, and complimented Miss Catharine Beecher for her exposure of that celebrated breach of promise case. He proposed the establishment of orders of women to aid and assist each other.

Lucretia Mott was determined not to ask as a boon what she could demand as a right. She complained that woman's labor was not appreciated—that she was a slave, and the slave of superstition, and paid too much devotion to the Bible. Let theology take care of itself. Theology had always given way when compelled to do it by the light of truth, as in the case of George Combe and phrenology. He was first attacked, and then the theologians found out, when science was too strong for them, that it [phrenology] was according to revelation. (Laughter) She

thought the right of woman to cut throats, in resisting despotism, was a debatable question because many contend for the doctrine of moral suasion. But in demanding woman's rights, she wanted no twaddle, no milk-and-water, but the plain and naked truth.

Mr. Wendell Phillips offered a series of resolutions. . . . Mr. Phillips argued these several points at length, maintaining that the cobwebs and the superstitions of the Bible ought to be swept away. Woman, without culture, without capital, and shut off from commerce, the mechanic arts, the professions, and politics, dwindles down, like the poor colored man in slavery, into an inferior caste. He wished her to be mingled up in society, in the trial by jury, in representation, and in suffrage for her self defense. We should not give too much reverence to the law; laws were but pieces of paper, signed by [President] Millard Fillmore (applause) and public opinion is the silliest thing in the world. (Laughter) He spoke with energy, urging that to secure woman's rights, it was necessary to break down the barriers of the law and the Bible, of feudal and Hebrew despotism, and begin at the very foundation of society.

Mrs. Rose—We are not contending here for the rights of the women of New

England, or of old England, but of the world. And our greatest opposition is from the prejudice of our own sex. Man is as much the victim of his despotism as woman. We had heard a great deal of our Pilgrim Fathers; but who ever tells us anything of our pilgrim mothers? And were not their trials, and is not their glory equally great. Two positions we have assigned to woman. Either to play the puppet in the parlor, or the drudge in the kitchen. And till all these old prejudices, and restrictions, and this whole system of woman's slavery from beginning to end, were done away with, and not till then, would man and woman be brought to a happy state of existence. (Applause.)

Mrs. Lucretia Mott—It strikes me, Madame President, that Mrs. Rose has made a better apology for man than he could make for himself. (Laughter) Woman is crushed, but nobody is to blame; it is circumstances that have crushed her. So of the poor slave. He is crushed, but nobody crushed him. It just happened so. (Laughter) It is an abstract evil, that's all. When we begin to denounce the slaveholder as a man-stealer, all scripture had to be searched before people would believe it, or venture to use the term. And with us, it is monopolizing, despotic man that we have to deal with, in our exclusion from offices, from the schools and colleges. The learned philosopher [Mott] then proceeded to show that the men would prefer to be called knaves, rather than such fools as the idea that his ignorance of her rights was the cause of woman's wrongs. Men are cunning and crafty. They are not such innocent Abigails as you would suppose. (Laughter) She recommended agitation of woman's rights. It was the agitation of the slavery question that had shaken the capitol to its foundations, and that was the cause of the good fruit it will bring forth, in the liberation of the Southern slave. (Applause)

Wendell Phillips contended that woman was largely responsible for her grievances. In the marriage ceremony it is woman that declares she will love, honor, and obey. It was the assent and the prejudice of woman that were the greatest obstacles to her rights.

Mrs. Abby Kelly Foster took up the glove. Woman is a slave, and is obedient in the presence of her master. Ask the slave of Henry Clay,[3] in his master's presence, if he is satisfied and happy; he will say yes. So with woman, though she might not get a cowhiding like the slave if she answered no! Still, she would be fearful to displease her husband, her lord and master, as he is. And her whole life, and her whole education was adapted to please him and serve him like a slave. And do you suppose that woman so situated can dare to assert her rights. If disobedient, she is fearful she will never get a husband. But don't believe her when she ridicules this movement or opposes it. She is a slave, and has to do it. Our only safety is to rebuke the oppressor, and to demand our rights.

Mr. J. M. Buffum, of Lynn, came to the rescue of Wendell Phillips and Mrs. Rose. It appeared [to Buffum] the debate was coming to a contest between the two sexes. Frederick Douglass says all that the slave wants is, that the tyrant shall take his foot off his neck, and let him get up. So of woman. It is not for us to elevate, but to release her, and she will elevate herself. As for the marriage relation, laws cannot control it altogether. It must regulate itself, as between man and woman. Now, I married a white woman myself, but although the law might oppose the marriage of whites and blacks, I do not suppose it would be regarded [i.e., the law obeyed] in some cases. The great outrage upon woman is that she has no right of property to herself; and this and all the other restrictions against her political equality, it is our duty to endeavor to remove.

---

[3] Henry Clay (1777–1852), long-time Whig senator from Kentucky, author of the Missouri Compromise (1820), founder of the American Colonization Society which sought to "return" freed American slaves to Africa, and slaveholder, was a principal author of the Compromise of 1850 which included the Fugitive Slave Law.

Lucretia Mott—My friend, Wendell Phillips, says that it is the woman in marriage who says that she will "love, honor, and obey." As I understand it, the priest says the words, and she only answers "yes." (Laughter) The priest says "love, honor, and obey." Woman has been taught to pin her faith to the sleeve of the priest. Now, in our society [i.e., the Hicksite branch of the Society of Friends to which she belonged], there is nothing of this; but perfect equality and reciprocity. It is all the result of education. Sometime ago, if a woman could make a shirt, turn a pancake, and write her name at her marriage, she was educated. But she is beginning to understand that she is entitled to something more.

Mr. Foster (husband of Abby Kelly, a tall, ungainly figure, in big whiskers and spectacles) next took the platform. He was proceeding to remark that the question of woman's right to take the sword was irrelevant to the objects of the meeting, when

Mr. Burleigh raised a question of order against the Speaker himself. His object, however, was to move when the meeting adjourned that it adjourn to meet again at half-past nine in the morning. Agreed to.

Wm. Lloyd Garrison gave notice that the friends of the abolition of the gallows would meet at half-past eight.

Mr. Foster (husband of Abby Kelly), returned to the question of woman's right to use the sword. He thought it ought to be left an open question, for there were a million and a half of women in the South, in a condition which makes us shudder to think of, and God only knows how soon the sword may be drawn for their deliverance, and I would not like to see her hands tied in the struggle. For this reason he considered it inexpedient to discuss the question of woman's right to use the sword. After a long rigmarole on woman hugging her chains, he concluded by charging that the pulpit and St. Paul were responsible for the enslavement of the sex. When the priest says to the woman, "Love, honor, and obey," what can she do?

Abby Kelly Foster—Do! Do as the wife of the Rev. Joseph Bancroft, of Worcester, did. Say "I won't." (Laughter) She was a good woman, and a much better man than her son George.[4] She said I won't," and she compelled them to leave that part out.

Mr. Foster (husband to Abby Kelly)—yes; and there was a lady of seventy years old at dinner to-day, who said when she came to the word "obey," she dropped her husband's hand. (Laughter) The orator then went on to show that many women who did not appear so, were friends of this movement. He was once lecturing on the necessity of dissolving the Union, to get rid of the curse of slavery, when a man who dared not openly avow it, slipped a three dollar bill into his hand very quietly. So there are women who dare not speak, who will slip a three dollar bill to the advocate of woman's rights, if they had a chance.

Very stout lady, in a grey dress—My friend says that many a woman will slip a three dollar bill to the advocate of her rights. She cannot do it for she cannot get the three dollars, if she has a husband. (Laughter)

Mr. Foster—Ah, yes, I should have said if she can get it. He next argued that the slavery of woman degraded both sexes, and man the most, for that woman was naturally better than man.

And at a quarter past ten p.m. the Convention adjourned, to meet again at half past nine in the morning, to finish up the resolutions.

---

[4]George Bancroft (1800–1891) wrote a best-selling ten-volume *History of the United States* (1834–1874) and served as Secretary of the Navy (1845–1846).

Boston *Daily Mail*, October 25, 1850:

The Conference was again called to order at half past 7 o'clock, and the business of talking was substituted for the more useful business of stocking darning.

Mr. Channing defended the Utopianisms of the scheme contemplated (but not explained) by the conference; but he proceeded at last to state them. They were to declare that woman was thus far independent of man that she should judge of her own sphere—a right she had as a human being, and in accordance with God's design. A full benefit of educational facilities to woman was a preliminary step; and we [i.e., the reporter] were in ignorance till now that such was not the provision in New England. The *modus operandi* received explanation in such shape as to convince us after all, that our notions had been correct. Passing the initiatory steps the first practical one afterwards was a college education; secondly, a sphere to dispense her collegiate knowledge; and, thirdly, if she was thus trained and favored, woman would prove that she was not dependent on man, but herself *per se*. This position would not tolerate a denial of legislative honors to woman. Connected with this concession of right to woman was the abolition of war, which was an inconsistency their pure hearts would never tolerate. An annual Congress and legislation of women were recommended to be held in every State. Miss [Catharine] Beecher's case was alluded to, and an appeal made to the sympathies of the audience in her behalf. Such congresses and legislatures would operate as a court of appeal against such judgments as followed Miss Beecher's case. As no one seemed to have heard of the lady, or her case, the appeal went down very coldly, and the very specially modest Mr. Channing went on to pick up the social sphere, and show how women could roll round in it and be thoroughly independent of any wheel in the masculine clock work. An order of women was recommended, which could organize by clubbing their means and furnishing a retreat for women who were compelled to marry when they did not want to. Dear brother Channing! where are there

any such? Speak out, experienced brother, do!

Lucretia Mott desired speakers not to say that they would *permit* women to do so and so; women would *do* so and so just as they thought proper themselves, and in accordance with their rights—all considerations social, civil and ecclesiastical to the contrary notwithstanding—and this she would do on the foundation of her own just desserts [sic] and nothing else. Much more she said, and did not fail to give the priesthood a well merited rebuke because of the obstructions they always had thrown in the way of science, and did at present respecting the science of reforming the condition of woman. Her address was one of much power of argument, and was a fair match for that of Mrs. Rose, spoken in the afternoon. She gave Abby Kelly Foster fits on account of her "cut throat theory," which she said was not a justifiable one. Mrs. Foster was handsomely asked to retract; and people pricked up their ears in anticipation of a scene—the rebuke was so pointed, and yet so gentle. Mrs. Mott would recommend moral suasion—an appeal to the moral mind—as a much more powerful weapon. A carnal weapon could never affect a spiritual deliverance from slavery, such as the emancipation of womankind was in truth. The boldness of Christianity was sufficient to attain the ends sought.

Mr. Wendell Phillips of Boston, reported three resolutions, viz: That every human being had a right to vote, if of full age and good character; that all people, of whatever sex or color, taxed from property or labor, had a right to suffrage. That no sex being acknowledged politically, therefore the word "male" should be stricken from the constitution. He then went on to say that the political machinery was entirely out of joint, and the enterprise of the age had lost one half its momentum, because the elective suffrage, and social facilities, and advantages, were denied to women. This he proceeded to prove at great length, and exhibited the superiority of a contrary action, as it would affect the general welfare of society, and the emancipation of woman from the thraldom of a slavery of custom and prejudice. The "Mister Chairman's" of the orator were

received with much mirth. Religious prejudices, which narrowed the field of operation
of female labor were calculated to be a main
cause of the depreciation of her condition.
By removing these the number of trades
would be extended at which woman could
find employment, and their status and condition put in a way of improvement. In the
same way did the prejudice named keep
women out of the professions and mechanic
arts, and this artificial condition of hers was
fatal to self reliance, and the assumption of
independent rights. Promiscuous juries—a
mixture of men and women—would be the
sure result of such independence as the just
rights of woman being granted—would
follow in the train of the concession; as also
legislative privileges, and many other improb-
abilities too tedious to mention.

Mrs. [Ernestine] Rose of New York concurred in what had been said by Mr. Phillips
with one exception, which was that this
Convention was not for the women of New
England, or Old England, but for the world.
She went on to show that the reform was
one depending alone on the concurrence of
the female sex—united and one. The only
discouragements the fair speaker had ever
met with were from her own sex, who had
the false idea that they were naturally inferior to man. That great error would have to
be attacked boldly, and [the truth of woman's
equality] would be ultimately prevalent [i.e.,
prevail] over common prejudice. Due cultivation of the physical, mental and moral condition of woman would prove the falsehood of
her being an inferior being to man. It was not
a whim, but a necessity of her nature that
woman should have her rights, and she would
have them. She would demand, and have, a
principle of right, instead of one of oppression and wrong. Much had been said of the
Pilgrim fathers, but what had been said of the
Pilgrim mothers? Had they not suffered as
their husbands had done? Had not the sons
of these very pilgrim fathers burnt
the daughters of the pilgrim mothers—thus
showing the prejudice against the sex was
present even in those boasted [of] times.
The right of claim which woman had to
equality with man was elaborately and eloquently argued, and a very touching appeal

made to the sense of justice extant to assist
truth to conquer falsehood and prejudice,
which combined to deny woman her rightful
share of social and political justice. The natural predilection of woman was to rise above
her present degraded condition, and she had
the power if she would only command the
will. Instances of recent occurrence were
quoted in proof of woman's claim to equality
in scientific discoveries, et cetera, —the
speaker concluding that society never would
strike its natural tone until woman's equality
with man, in action, in every public shape,
was recognized. (Loud applause followed
Mrs. R's speech.)

Mrs. Mott again spoke, recapitulating
some of her former statements; and hitting
Wendell Phillips over the knuckles for some
of his remarks purporting that man was not
to blame for crushing woman. Men *were* the
despots, and the time was come when they
were to be dethroned. It was not circumstances, or accident, that had made woman
what she was; it was man. There was no provision made in the public high schools for
girls, but all for boys. Men would certainly
prefer to be called knaves rather than such
fools as to father this great omission. It was
not ignorance in man that caused this neglect—it was their cunning and their crafti-
ness that did it, as a matter of protective
policy securing the ascendancy of their sex.
Otherwise it would not have held its head so
high at the present day. (Applause, repeated
several times.)

Mr. Phillips was glad that the mistake
had been made, as it produced a good
speech—a sentiment in which the meeting
concurred. He then spoke briefly in explanation of some misapprehension of his lady
friends regarding what he had said. Woman
had, he said, her full share in the creation of
the prejudices which militated against her in
society. Her power to do so was acknowledged; but whatever might be the cause the
prejudice subsisted largely among the female
sex, whose ridicule of the present reform
would be worse to bear than that of the men.

Mr. [sic] Abby Foster rose not to make
a speech; but she could not rest easy till she
spoke in vindication of women. She was in
fault—so said Mr. Phillips—and he said the

bitterest taunts came from them [women]. So said every slave holder; but what was the reason? Why, women dared not, as the slave dared not say, for fear of the cowhide, in presence of his master, that he was abused. Abby said that Phillips knew nothing about the matter, for her extensive experience had shewn her the contrary; and she actually perpetrated a very long, and a very *manly* speech, and she gave the priests Harry [slang term for Hell] for the share they had in woman's degradation. If Abby could be believed, the country was in an awful situation because of the horrible persecutions that women had to submit to. Caudledom had *riz* in internal shape, but weak policy had advised no public demonstration. Woman was wronged even by her advocates—she said—and the fact she demonstrated there and then on the spot, in terms of not overly gentle, or specially reasonable, or correctly logically; but everybody knows Abby. She said that there were women present who would sneer at what then was passing before them; but these were children of the present pulpit, not the petticoat one that was on the tapis [ready for immediate use], and would soon be set up. But woman was not to be believed when she sneered thus, for she gave expression to an altogether contrary sentiment to that her heart entertained. Abby sat down.

A muss was brewing evidentially; and some fun was anticipated, when James M. Buffum started up and caught at Abby's sentiments, as a cur grabs a bone. He did not see any harm in a woman reconciling herself to a man in marriage, or a man to a woman, as Abby did. Her ungodly distinctions were like the laws of Massachusetts, which, sometime ago laid down law as to who should, and who should not marry. Marriage was a copartnership, and ought to be mutually broken if the parties choosed [sic]—a very unblushing recommendation of the Socialist principle relative to the bond of marriage. His oration was a lame one, but sufficiently vicious in tone to prove that James M. Buffum was very silly, and remarkably prone to disorganize the recognized marriage system, if his feebleness only could encompass so much.

Mrs. Lucretia Mott again got up to arraign Wendell Phillips' notions, and the priesthood at large. She backed up Abby like a brick, and prostrated Buffum like a trodden squash. Marriage, its various forms, its results, and all connected with it, and unconnected with the business before the convention, was discussed ad nauseam. Lucretia had to be corrected in some of her statistics, and went adrift again on the well ploughed sea of her former prelections [sic]. We can't afford to follow her throughout this heat.

Mr. Foster of Boston [sic] opened his mouth and spake following the fashion of Balaam's ass[5]—and he commenced his little campaign of talking by deprecating all differences of opinion, at the same time throwing a brand into the fire of excitement and opposition which was smouldering, and ready to burst out in the meeting.

Mr. Grizzly Burley [C. C. Burleigh] interrupted Foster, and told him that he was not doing what he ought. There was a question before the Convention, and that question he was keeping at a very respectful distance.

A motion to meet at half past nine next morning was put and carried.

Mr. Foster defended his line of argument, and was going ahead in glorious style, when William Lloyd Garrison said he was spoiling valuable time; when Foster said he was not, and then he went on again on the wartrack—the stereotyped anti-war eloquence that saves original speech making. The man had got up to give a speech, and he gave the head of an old and very stale one, which having no more connection with the business of the meeting than the "Lay of the Last Minstrel,"[6] nobody paid any attention to. Having "roared him a roaring which outroared all roarings," he sat down, but not before he had said enough to disgust all the

---

[5] A reference to the Hebrew prophet Balaam whose ass was enabled by the Lord to speak. See Numbers 22.

[6] A popular poem by Sir Walter Scott.

world present, "and the rest of mankind"—if that section of it had been on hand—with a socialist harangue, mixed with anti-slavery. There was a very industrious hum and bustle during all the time Foster spoke.

Abby chimed in, and told an anecdote about something that we could not catch the skirt of. It was something concerning the impolicy of women obeying their husbands. Hasn't Foster caught a Tartar?[7] Heaven preserve all mankind from these dreadfully wise women, who know all about politics and nothing about sewing and darning! The two emptied the Hall well, between them.[8] The meeting then adjourned.

OCTOBER 24, 1850—MORNING SESSION

The opening session of the second day began with the reading of a letter from Elizabeth Cady Stanton, the organizer of the 1848 Seneca Falls convention whose family responsibilities prevented her from attending. The letter shows the hand of Paulina Wright Davis at work in continuing to attempt to shape the convention's deliberations. Stanton noted that Davis had assigned her the task of addressing the concerns of women over the propriety of their voting. Propriety was a word to conjure with, and Stanton rang all the changes on that theme.

William H. Channing then introduced another set of resolutions which, with the exception of his own scheme for establishing an annual Congress of Women, again reflected Davis's views quite closely. This is particularly the case in their insistence that any limits on women's activities were to be first "tested by experiment." The resolutions are notable too for establishing the first permanent woman's rights organization, the Central Committee which would establish other committees and have the authority to call future conventions.

Next came an address by Harriet K. Hunt, a Boston physician, calling for the opening of the medical profession to women. Hunt's argument is another

---

[7] An idiom meaning, according to *The American Heritage Dictionary*, "to grapple with an unexpectedly formidable opponent." The Tartars were the Mongol tribes who invaded central Asia in the twelfth and thirteenth centuries.

[8] A joke. The reference is to the Mother Goose rhyme about Jack Sprat, who could eat no fat, and his wife, who could eat no lean, but who, between them, "licked the platter clean."

early instance of what is today called "difference" feminism, that is, it rested upon the notion that women possessed by "nature" certain qualities of patience and sympathy which particularly fitted them for medicine. She also argued for the propriety of women physicians attending women patients, especially during childbirth.

The resolutions introduced next by Wendell Phillips, reflecting as they did the views of Paulina Wright Davis, made no reference to women's "nature" but instead called for the opening up of all avenues of work for women as the necessary precondition for them successfully utilizing the educational opportunities the convention would also call for. These resolutions are also important because they explicitly linked the call for woman's rights to one for the rights of slaves and free persons of color. As the debate between Jane Gray Swisshelm and Parker Pillsbury, excerpted below, shows, this proved highly contentious. It also foreshadowed the controversy of the post–Civil War years when the woman's movement split over the question of granting the vote to black males.

Once again, however, much of the session's interest derives from questions arising from the floor. Mrs. C. A. K. Ball of Worcester challenged the views of those such as Lucretia Mott who downplayed the importance of biblical arguments about woman's proper role. And she challenged too the practicality of "equal pay for comparable work," as we would phrase it today, an argument advanced by Abby Price and several other speakers during the first day's sessions.

FROM THE *PROCEEDINGS:*

The Convention met at half past nine, A.M.

The minutes of yesterday's afternoon and evening sessions were read by J. C. Hathaway, and adopted.

Letters addressed to the Convention were read from Elizabeth C. Stanton[1] and O. S. Fowler, by M. A. W. Johnson, and one from Samuel J. May, by Mr. Hathaway.

[Here follows the Stanton letter.]

---

[1] Elizabeth Cady Stanton (1815–1902), daughter of a wealthy lawyer in upstate New York, attended the Troy Female Seminary which offered girls the same curriculum as found in schools for boys. In 1840 she married Henry B. Stanton, an activist in the abolition movement, and attended the World Anti-Slavery Convention in London while on her honeymoon. There she met

From Mrs. Elizabeth C. Stanton.
Seneca Falls, Sunday, Oct. 20.

My Dear Friend: As you have handed over to me the case of those women who have fears in regard to the propriety of woman's exercising her political rights, I would gladly embrace this opportunity to address them through your Convention.

No one denies our right to the elective franchise, unless we except those who go against all human governments, and the non-resistant, who condemns a government of force, though I think the latter might consistently contend for the right, even if she might not herself choose to exercise it.[2] But to those who believe in having a government—to those who believe that no just government can be formed without the consent of the governed—to them would I appeal, and of them do I demand some good reason why one half of the citizens of this Republic have no voice in the laws which govern them.

The right is one question, and the propriety of exercising it quite another. The former is undeniable, and against the latter I have never heard one solid objection that would not apply equally to man and woman.

Some tell us that if woman should interest herself in political affairs, it would destroy all domestic harmony. What, say they, would be the consequence, if husband and wife should not agree in their views of political economy? Because, forsooth, husband and wife may chance to differ in their theological sentiments, shall woman have no religion? Because she may not choose to worship at the same altar with her liege lord, must she of necessity do up all her worshipping in private, in her own closet? Because she might choose to deposit her vote for righteous rulers—such as love, justice, mercy, truth, and oppose a husband, father, or brother, who would, by their votes, place political power in the hands of unprincipled men, swearing, fighting, leaders of armies, rumsellers and drunkards, slaveholders and prating northern hypocrites, who would surrender the poor panting fugitive from bondage into the hands of his blood-thirsty pursuers—shall she not

---

Lucretia Mott and first became interested in the question of women's rights. Stanton was the leading spirit at the 1848 Seneca Falls Convention and author of its "Declaration of Sentiments." Family responsibilities—she had three small children by then and would have four more—prevented her from attending either the 1850 or the 1851 conventions in Worcester.

[2] Stanton may have had Lucretia Mott in mind here. Mott had opposed the suffrage resolution at the Seneca Falls Convention in 1848 on these grounds. Mott had changed her mind by 1850.

vote at all? It is high time that men learned to tolerate independence of thought and opinion in the women of their household.

It would not make much difference in man's every day life, in his social enjoyments, whether his wife differed with him as to the locality of hell, the personality of the devil, or the comparative altitude of the saintships of Peter and Paul; as to one's right to as much air, water, light, and land as he might need for his necessities; as to the justice of free trade, free schools, the inviolable homestead, and personal freedom—provided the husband had a great head and heart, and did not insist upon doing up all the thinking and talking in the establishment himself, or the wife was not a miserable formalist, like Mrs. Swisshelm's Deborah Elmsley.[3] Much of this talk about domestic harmony is the sheerest humbug. Look around among your whole circle of friends, and tell me, you who know what transpires behind the curtain, how many truly harmonious households have we now. Quiet households we may have, but submission and harmony produce very different states of quietness. There is no true happiness where there is subordination—no harmony without freedom.

But, say some, would you have women vote? What, refined, delicate women at the polls, mingling in such scenes of violence and vulgarity! By all means, where there is so much to be feared for the pure, the innocent, the noble, the mother surely should be there to watch and guard her sons who are to encounter such stormy, dangerous scenes at the tender age of twenty-one. Much is said of woman's influence: might not her presence do much toward softening down this violence, refining this vulgarity? Depend upon it, that places which, by their impure atmosphere, are rendered unfit for woman cannot but be dangerous to her sires and sons. But if woman claims all the rights of a citizen, will she buckle on her armor and fight in defence of her country? Has not woman already often shown herself as courageous in the field, as wise and patriotic in counsel, as man? Have you not had the brave Jagello in your midst, and vied with each other to touch but the hem of her garment? But for myself, I believe all war sinful; I believe in Christ; I believe that the command, "Resist not evil," is divine; I would not have man go to war; I can see no glory in fighting with such weapons as guns and swords, while man has in his possession the infinitely superior and more effective ones of righteousness and truth.

---

[3] A reference to Jane Gray Swisshelm, editor-publisher of the *Saturday Visiter* [sic].

But if woman votes, would you have her hold office? Most certainly would we have woman hold office. We would have man and woman what God intended they should be, companions for each other, always together, in counsel, government, and every department of industry. If they have homes and children, we would have them stay there, educate their children, provide well for their physical wants, and share in each other's daily trials and cares. Children need the watchful care and wise teachings of fathers as well as of mothers. No man should give up a profitable business, leave his wife and children month after month, and year after year, and make his home desolate for any false ideas of patriotism, for any vain love of display or ambition for fame and distinction. The highest, holiest duty of both father and mother is to their children and each other, and when they can show to the world a well-developed, wisely-governed family, then let the State profit by their experience. Having done their duty at home, let them together sit in our national councils. The violence, rowdyism, and vulgarity which now characterize our Congressional Halls, show us clearly that "it is not good for man to be alone."[4] The purifying, elevating, softening influence of woman is a most healthful restraint on him at all times and in all places. We have many noble women in our land, free from all domestic incumbrances, who might grace a Senate chamber, and for whose services the country might gladly forego all the noise, bluster, and folly of one-half the male dolts who now flourish there and pocket their eight dollars a day.

The most casual observer can see that there is some essential element wanting in the political organization of our Republic. The voice of woman has been silenced, but man cannot fulfil his destiny alone— he cannot redeem his race unaided. There must be a great national heart, as well as head; and there are deep and tender chords of sympathy and love that woman can touch more skillfully than man. The earth has never yet seen a truly great and virtuous nation, for woman has never yet stood the equal with man. As with nations, so with families. It is the wise mother who has the wise son, and it requires but little thought to decide, that as long as the women of this nation remain but half developed in mind and body, so long shall we have a succession of men dwarfed in body and soul. So long as your women

---

[4]A reference to the near violence that characterized the congressional debate over the Compromise of 1850. The quotation is from Genesis 2:18 [King James Version]: And the lord God said, It is not good that the man should be alone; I will make him an help meet for him.

are mere slaves, you may throw your colleges to the wind—there is no material to work upon. It is in vain to look for silver and gold from mines of copper and brass. How seldom now is the father's pride gratified in the budding genius of his son? The wife is degraded, made the mere creature of his tyranny and caprice, and now the foolish son is heaviness to his heart. Truly are the sins of the father visited upon the children.[5] God, in his wisdom, has so linked together the whole human family, that any violence done at one end of the chain is felt throughout its length.

.... Adieu.

Yours truly,
E. C. STANTON

W. H. Channing, from the Business Committee, reported a series of resolutions.

Resolved, That as women alone can learn by experience, and prove by works, what is their rightful sphere of duty, we recommend, as next steps, that they should demand and secure

1. Education in primary and high schools, universities, medical, legal, and theological institutions, as comprehensive and exact as their abilities prompt them to seek, and their capabilities fit them to receive;
2. Partnership in the labors, gains, risks, and remunerations of productive industry, with such limits only as are assigned by taste, intuitive judgment, or their measure of spiritual and physical vigor, as tested by experiment;
3. A co-equal share in the formation and administration of law, Municipal, State, and National, through legislative assemblies, courts, and executive offices;
4. Such unions as may become the guardians of pure morals and honorable manners—a high court of appeal in cases of outrage which cannot be and are not touched by civil or ecclesiastical organizations, as

---

[5] A reference to Exodus 34:7 [King James Version]: Keeping mercy for thousands, forgiving iniquity and transgression and sin, and that will by no means clear the guilty; visiting the iniquity of the fathers upon the children, and upon the children's children, unto the third and to the fourth generation.

at present existing, and a medium for expressing the highest views of justice dictated by human conscience and sanctioned by Holy Inspiration.

Resolved, That a Central Committee be appointed by this Convention, empowered to enlarge their numbers: on (1) Education; (2) Industrial Avocations; (3) Civil and Political Rights and Regulations; (4) Social Relations; who shall correspond with each other and with the Central Committee, hold meetings in their respective neighborhoods, gather statistics, facts, and illustrations, raise funds for purposes of publication; and through the press, tracts, books, and the living agent, guide public opinion upward and onward in the grand social reform of establishing woman's co-sovereignty with man.

Resolved, That the Central Committee be authorized to call other Conventions, at such times and places as they shall see fit; and that they hold office until the next annual Convention.

Harriet K. Hunt[6] read an able essay upon the medical education of women.

We are living in a struggling age, in a transition age, in an age when, through the leadings of Divine Providence, the minds of the community are asking the why and the wherefore of all things. Old established customs are examined as to their worth, and habits and tendencies are brought to the light, that their soundness may be proved, or that they may vanish like dew before the sun. Noble men and women have been working upon the outer skin, and thus preventing a palsy in the community; but still the heart, the central point of circulation has not been reached. Surface remedies have been applied, and irritants and stimulants have performed their uses; but now we need something internal, and therefore we demand equal freedom of development, equal advantages of education, for both sexes.

To discern the signs of the times, and to seek for remedies to meet existing wants, is the part of wisdom. In asking your attention to the professional sphere of woman, as a PHYSICIAN, I speak from the experience

---

[6] Harriet K. Hunt (1805–1875) began practicing medicine after an apprenticeship in 1835. In 1847 she applied to Harvard Medical School but was turned down. In 1850, the year of this address, she received permission to attend lectures at the school but was unable to enroll as a regular student. The all-white and all-male Harvard class of 1851 protested to the faculty against the mixing of sexes and races in their classes (three African Americans were attending the lectures as well). Her address was excerpted in the *Proceedings*.

of many years, and bear testimony to duties of vital importance. I have lived in this work, loved it, felt its power, enjoyed its privileges, been sustained in it by kind and intelligent spirits, —and I would here gratefully acknowledge that "the lines have fallen to me in pleasant places and I have had a goodly heritage."[7] For fourteen years in the City of Boston, the place of my birth and education, my path has been public, as a physician for my own sex and for children; and although at the first, ridicule busied herself about me, and ill nature furnished her weapons, yet the consciousness of right, and the deep enjoyment growing out of that consciousness, opened to the mind a state of religious trust and a dependence upon the Lord as the source of all life, which have amply sustained me. My own experience is my standpoint, in offering the following remarks, which I cannot but think will meet with a response in many minds.

Although society is yet in a confused state, the sphere of the sexes is as confidently defined by some persons, as the boundaries on a map; while, to others, the subject presents a serious and perplexing riddle. This question will be met in as many varied ways, as there are mental or moral qualities engaged in the investigation, until we base our thoughts upon mind, and not upon sex alone, —and realize that the qualities of mind will ever bear upon them the distinctive character of their innate organization, either masculine or feminine. It is mind that must direct, it is mind that must be developed. No one, who realizes how strong is the religious element in woman, will for a moment fear for the use she will make of the highest educational advantages, for in drawing largely from the great book of human life, she will reverently look above to its Author. This element in her nature, this dependence upon the Lord, gives to the true woman a consciousness of responsibility which will safely direct her through professional life, business trials, or any other emergencies.

It is to the right and duty of opening for woman a legitimate sphere, around which too many obstacles have been placed, that I ask your particular attention. The medical education of woman is a positive necessity, indicated by the signs of the times. It will fit her—if she become a mother—(for no change can alter the highest law of her nature) not only to understand the delicate organizations committed to her care, but so to guard her own system that she may not become

---

[7] A paraphrase of Psalms 16:6 [King James Version]: The lines are fallen unto me in pleasant places; yea, I have a goodly heritage.

a victim to the thousand wearing, weakening, prostrating, protracted diseases, which so often unfit woman for life and duty. Her affections need truths to guide them; but wan and anxious countenances around us denote ignorance. Woman needs her own sex to guard and guide her, particularly at those times when she is moulding her children for a life of joy or sorrow, and to impress upon her the importance of guarding herself. When the time comes that physiological knowledge is diffused among our people, and there is a oneness in our medical departments, then and then only will the influence of states of mind and qualities of thought be thoroughly searched out in reference to ourselves and our children. Trace out in your minds the thousand situations in which a mother needs medical knowledge, or the assistance of one of her own sex on whose superior knowledge she can rely!

Then look at the nurse, acting either privately among her family and friends, or in a public capacity. Who requires medical knowledge more than she to whose fidelity life is thus committed? How often physicians have to deplore the ignorance of nurses! How many a death has occurred through neglect during the period of convalescence! Now—since this department is universally admitted to belong to our sex—we demand light to guide woman's quick perceptions, and a thorough and systematic education, instead of a confused and miscellaneous crowd of notions. The community are now awake to the subject of midwifery, and all must acknowledge that woman should be carefully trained for this profession. Those whose perceptions are intuitive, to whom sympathy and propriety are text books, and to whom a consciousness of duty brings attending energy, are especially fitted for this path. But others may be called to a different task; to lead a physician's life may be their great desire, as the means of developing their powers, and meeting the wants of their natures, and I demand for them every medical advantage.

I must utter myself strongly here, for there are dreamers on this subject as well as thinkers. We ask for no separate medical colleges, we ask for no appropriation of public money; but we do ask, —in the fear of the Lord, in the trust that our claim is right and proper, in the hope that this question may be thoroughly looked into, involving as it does, such important interests, —we do ask for women EQUAL medical advantages with those enjoyed by men. Read the daily papers carefully, and then you will feel that woman must come into this path with every advantage of co-operation that man can offer, to meet not only physical diseases, but the spasms of fanaticism, the fever of infidelity, the St. Vitus' dance of levity, and the delirium tremens of fashion, —incipient states which are precursors of melancholy and derangement of mind. We ask the philanthropist, the political economist, yes, and even the conservative, to join with the physiologist in investigating this momentous question. Can there be complete integrity in discharging a function like this, when it is open only to man? We ask that the medical colleges may be opened to MIND, not to sex, that the whole of human nature may aid in promoting the well being of humanity. "Male and female created he them and blessed them," are the words of Holy Writ. We ask for the recognition of this great truth in the medical department; we ask for our own sex, and we ask it earnestly, that they should be the healers of their own diseases; we ask for physicians who by nature understand woman's nature, who being organised like us, know directly through sympathy how to treat us, and who have experimental knowledge which can be applied to meet our wants. We ask for perfect harmony with our brethren in this great work. We ask to investigate social institutions in relation to their influence on health. Cannot woman, by her very nature, best look into the thousand petty physical ills so common among women, and direct others to suitable clothing, proper food, the importance of a cheerful mind, and a quiet spirit? When woman stands side by side with man in the healing art, —then and then only will society, its claims, its pleasures, be examined in their physiological bearings. Will not there be more completeness in our hospitals when physicians of both sexes meet there to perform their duties, and the nurses are their intelligent and educated aids?

• • •

The great increase of quackery has produced a distrust of physicians, and, vice versa, this distrust has but increased quackery, while the confidence formerly felt in the medical faculty has been gradually decreasing for many years. Physicians are conscious of this fact, as their journals testify. I am sorry to say, too, that kind but ignorant women are travelling through the country, advertising to cure all diseases. Woman, longing to consult one of her own sex, encourages them. There is a gap in society here which must be filled. The want and the need cry aloud. Must separate institutions arise? Must woman go forth unprepared for this work? Or is the truth to be felt, and a response given to the demand for EQUAL privileges?

What duty can be more delicately feminine, more truly womanly, than to take the hand of a sister, afflicted in body and mind, and to show her the cause of her diseases, in the transgression of those eternal laws which know no escape nor evasion, —to lead her by kind sympathy and wise advice not only to health again, but to a desire for perfect obedience? Here is a worthy and elevating vocation for woman; it is a living life. No intellectuality will ever impair her true consciousness of the feminine; no profession or business can smother her innate feeling. Many are the hindrances which lie in her path, but we trust in the influence of truth, and in the prayers of earnest spirits that light may be shed on this question. There is already a consciousness in the community that something must be done. We have had physiological lectures, societies have been formed, books have been published, and a sort of spasmodic action has seized the public; but this is a convulsion only which will do no good, unless we have medical knowledge for our sex, which may be appropriated day by day. Action must be founded on the firm basis of thorough, scientific education.

• • •

We need female physicians to guard the young girl against those influences which, scarcely perceptible in their first approach, will prove her ruin. We need them to impress on young minds the religious nature of their physical duties. Your moral reform societies need such women as lecturers. Your maternal associations need them to awaken mothers to the serious nature of the habits formed in childhood, and to guide their powerful but blind affections. We need them to visit our schools for girls, and to trace those insidious forms of disease, destructive of normal harmony, those nervous tendencies so rapidly accelerated by unwise study and exciting emulation. The moral character of society depends more upon this reform, than at first appears. It is demanded by the heart of true delicacy and refinement. It is through the presence of woman, as a physician, that many evils now disregarded will be looked upon as sins, and shunned as such, and that the masculine and feminine elements of communities will be brought nearer to a religious co-operation. . . .

Wendell Phillips reported another series of resolutions, which were discussed by Mrs. Ball, of Worcester, Antoinette Brown, of Ohio, and C. C. Burleigh.

Resolved, That since the prospect of honorable and useful employment, in after life, for the faculties we are laboring to discipline, is the keenest stimulus to fidelity in the use of educational advantages, and since the best education is what we give ourselves in the struggles, employments, and discipline of life; therefore, it is impossible that woman should make full use of the instruction already accorded to her, or that her career should do justice to her faculties, until the avenues to the various civil and professional employments are thrown open to arouse her ambition and call forth all her nature.

Resolved, That every effort to educate woman, until you accord to her her rights, and arouse her conscience by the weight of her responsibilities, is futile, and a waste of labor.

Resolved, That the cause we are met to advocate, —the claim for woman of all her natural and civil rights, —bids us remember the million and a half of slave women at the South, the most grossly wronged and foully outraged of all women; and in every effort for an improvement in our civilization, we will bear in our heart of hearts the memory of the trampled womanhood of the plantation, and omit no effort to raise it to a share in the rights we claim for ourselves.

On motion, adjourned till 2 o'clock, P.M.

New York *Tribune,* October 24, 1850:

The Convention assembled this morning at 9½ o'clock. The day is fine and the Hall filled with many persons standing in the aisles.

The President [Paulina Wright Davis] read a Poem from a Woman of the Nineteenth Century, whose heart had been stirred by this Convention.

A Woman's Rights Convention!
There's music in the word;
Through every vein of living frame
My warm life's-blood is stirred.

A Woman's Rights Convention!
Deny it every Man!
Then right the evil done her,
That instant if you can.

A Woman's Rights Convention!
Is not laid low in dust,

A better time is coming,
Because it will and must.

A Woman's Rights Convention!
Ring out the word on high;
If my brother, Man, will help me
To help myself, I'll try;

And with the power given me
By our all-gracious Lord,
Obtain my Rights, in every light
By plowshare, not by sword.

"A Woman of the 19th Century"

Letters were received and read from Elizur Wright of Boston, Mrs. Elizabeth C. Stanton of Ohio [sic], Samuel J. May of Syracuse, N.Y. and others. . . .

Miss Harriet K. Hunt, of Boston, read a very forcibly written address on the Medical Education of Women. She urged the need of this branch of reform, showing that Woman needs the sympathy and counsel of one of her own sex in certain critical periods of her life, and when suffering from disease. She showed Woman's peculiar fitness for the duties of the medical profession; and urged that she should stand side by side with man in the healing art. She had devoted herself, for the last fourteen years, to the practice of medicine. She took it up from inclination and a sense of duty, and she had met with great encouragement and success.

At the close of her address, which was delivered in an impressive manner, and received with applause, she gave an account of an application she made in 1847 to attend the lectures of the Massachusetts Medical College, and the refusal of that institution to grant her request. She read the letters that passed between herself and Dr. O. W. Holmes,[1] the Dean of the College, on the subject. The Government of the College passed a vote that it was "inexpedient."

The . . . Resolutions [as printed in the Proceedings] were offered by Wendell Phillips:

• • •

The following preamble and resolution was read from the Business Committee:

Whereas, The great fundamental law of truth, that moral and intelligent beings are bound to *obey God rather than man,* is as much binding on woman as man, therefore,

Resolved, That it is the imperious duty of every woman to obey the dictates of her own enlightened conscience, in all matters of religion and benevolence, without asking the consent of her father or husband.

The . . . resolutions were read by Mr. Channing, from the Business Committee [as printed in the Proceedings]:

• • •

In accordance with the foregoing resolutions, the following persons were appointed to constitute said Committees [as printed below in the Proceedings]:

Mrs. [C. A. K.] Ball of Worcester, expressed her interest in the objects of the meeting; but she did not know that she could go so far as the Convention on this subject. There were some difficulties and objections which she should like to hear fully met. The power of religious influence over woman had been referred to as an obstacle to her emancipation. It was true, that she was greatly under the control of religious influence; and here is the difficulty to be met. The Scriptures must be harmonized with the principles and objects of this movement, in order to secure the cooperation of the women of the country. We read in the Bible that God said unto Eve: "Thy desire shall be unto thy husband, and he shall rule over thee."[2]

Another difficulty. The unequal compensation of woman for her labor, compared with man, has been referred to. It has been said, that a washerwoman is entitled to as much compensation for her day's work as a woodsawyer. She supposed the case of a woodsawyer's wife, unable by sickness, or the care of her children, to do her own work. It would cost her husband all his wages to procure a woman to do her work. How would the husband buy bread for his children?

Miss [Antoinette] Brown of Oberlin was introduced to the Convention as a young lady who had studied Theology in the Oberlin Institute, and fitted herself to preach the Gospel, with a view of devoting her life to that work. She was of the orthodox [i.e., Presbyterian] faith, but had been refused ordination. She intended, nevertheless, to devote herself to that calling. She addressed the Convention in a very clear, logical and eloquent

---

[1] Oliver Wendell Holmes (1809–1894), author and physician, whose *Autocrat of the Breakfast Table* (1858) was his most popular book, taught at Harvard from 1847 to 1882.

[2] Genesis 3:16 [King James Version]: Unto the woman he said, I will greatly multiply thy sorrow and thy conception; in sorrow thou shalt bring forth children; and thy desire shall be to thy husband, and he shall rule over thee.

speech, delivered extemporaneously. She took up the objections drawn from the Bible against Woman's rights. And *first*, of the passage, "Thy desire shall be to thy husband and he shall rule over thee." This, she maintained, was not given as a law of God, but a prediction of what should befall her in the state of sin and moral death to which they had fallen. She quoted language of the same tenor addressed to the Serpent: "Thou shalt bruise his heel."[3] Now, she said, it would be absurd to suppose Satan had the divine authority for trying to injure Christ and his cause. And yet the language was the same in both cases. She showed that man had ruled over woman in the exercise of his tyranny and superior physical force. But she denied the right.

She took up the language of Paul, "Wives submit yourselves to your husbands,"[4] and showed that this was an injunction to submit to a necessary evil, in that condition of human society, which she could not remove, and to do this in a Christian spirit. It did not by any means recognize the authority of husbands to rule. They were expressly directed not to rule one over another. She dwelt also on the objection that women have no time for mental improvement, and showed how labor-saving machines were relieving her of toil, and would give her time. Spinning and sewing are now done by machinery. This portion of her argument was full and interesting, much of which we are obliged to omit. The young lady showed herself an ingenious theologian, a good scholar, an easy speaker, and her spirit was truly religious and modest.

Everyone felt her vindication of the Rights of Woman from objections urged on Bible grounds was triumphant.

C. C. Burleigh next addressed the Convention. The objection had been made that Woman had no time for the culture and improvement of her mind and the exercise of those rights which were claimed for her. He regarded this fact, if it were true, as an argument that there is something in woman's position and relation. But there is no reason why a woman should not have time. If she has a family of children, her husband should share the care of them. And if mankind would be more simple in their habits, their diet and clothing, there would be plenty of time.

He would add one thought to what had been said on the Bible argument. The same language that has been quoted in reference to the man ruling the woman, occurs in regard to the elder son ruling the younger.[5] This was a command or a prediction that the elder should rule the younger, and if the same mode of interpretation is applied to this as to the other, it follows that the law of primogeniture is the right one. Yet in this country, where is the man that will stand up and say it is the will of God that the elder son shall rule over his younger brother?

He also answered the objection raised against Woman's receiving an equal compensation for her labor. He would change the supposition somewhat. Suppose the woodsawyer is taken sick, and the wife's earnings are only a half or a third as much as a man's, how is the family to be supported then? And

---

[3] Genesis 3:15 [King James Version]: And I will put enmity between thee and the woman, and between thy seed and her seed; it shall bruise thy head, and thou shalt bruise his heel.

[4] Third Epistle to the Ephesians, 5:22 [King James Version]: 22: Wives, submit yourselves unto your own husbands, as unto the Lord. 23: For the husband is the head of the wife, even as Christ is the head of the church: and he is the saviour of the body; 24: Therefore as the church is subject unto Christ, so let the wives be to their own husbands in every thing; 25: Husbands, love your wives, even as Christ also loved the church, and gave himself for it.

[5] First Epistle of Peter 5:5 [King James Version]: Likewise, ye younger, submit yourselves unto the elder. Yea, all of you be subject one to another, and be clothed with humility: for God resisteth the proud, and giveth grace to the humble.

here Mrs. Rose suggested another supposition: Suppose the woman has no husband, and is a widow left with little children to bring up? Does she not need the full value of her earnings as well as man? He [Burleigh] maintained that every woman should have the right to save her own earnings, and to keep them separate, and then she may provide against such contingencies. He claimed for her the right to procure for herself pecuniary independence.

New York *Herald,*
October 26, 1850:

The Convention met, pursuant to adjournment, at half-past nine this morning. Present—Generalisimo [sic] Lucretia Mott, Abby Kelly, [William Lloyd] Garrison, [Wendell] Phillips and company, looking as solemn and important as a court martial.

The leading orator to-day, was Mrs. [Harriet K.] Hunt, of Boston—a regular brick. She spoke chiefly upon the superior capacity of woman for the study and practice of medicine; probably from the fact that every old woman in the country is a quack doctor, and always ready, with her all healing nostrums of sage tea, yarbs, salves, and lotions. And she was also of the opinion, (from the tenor of her argument) that woman was adapted in a superior degree to wrangle with lawyers—to delve into matters of science—and to conduct the affairs of legislation in the most splendid style. In regard to science, she sustained the argument of sister [Ernestine] Rose, yesterday, in which the scientific capacity of woman was proved from the fact, that a young lady had discovered a comet, with the aid of a telescope.

After which, various letters were read from sympathizers who had wisely resolved to stay at home, and throw the burden of the expenses of this convocation upon those enthusiastic disciples, possessed of more money than brains.

Mrs. Ball, of Worcester, next rose in vindication of a proper compensation for the labors and employments of women, and in the course of her argument, she pounced upon Mr. Charles C. Burleigh, for some distinctions which he made yesterday in reference to the pay and the employment of the two sexes. In discussing this subject Mrs. Ball applied the broomstick with great vigor against the despotism of man, in his extortions upon the labor of woman. Master Burleigh attempted a defence; but, to the infinite satisfaction of Mrs. Mott, he was compelled to surrender, amid the applause and laughter of the assemblage.

Mrs. Johnson [Mary A. W. Johnson], of [Salem] Ohio—Notwithstanding the prevailing odor of infidelity in the Convention, a sentiment of skepticism so strong, that, with several reverend gentlemen present, and a host of venerable ladies ambitious of elevating their sex to the cabinet and the camp, the usual form of opening their proceedings with prayer was dispensed with—notwithstanding this prevailing odor of infidelity, the lady from Ohio argued from Scripture the equality of woman with man, in all the rights and privileges which he socially enjoys.[6]

---

[6] The *Herald* reporter apparently confused M. A. Johnson with Antoinette Brown.

Boston *Daily Mail*, October 25, 1850:

This morning the business of Woman's Rights was preceded by a meeting on the subject of Capital Punishment, at which there was an audience of some 300. Speeches were made by Lewis Ford, W. H. Channing, and J. M. Spear, which were levelled at the gross impolicy and impropriety of Capital Punishment. The following were appointed a committee to act in whatever capacity they might see fit in order to secure its abolition: John M. Spear, Wendell Phillips, Robert Rantoul, jr., Adin Ballou, and John A. Andrews.

At 25 minutes to 10 o'clock, the Woman's Rights Convention was called to order by the Lady President, who read three or four verses of miserable doggerel, which she complimented as being the result of inspiration. The organ grinder having removed from below there was no accompanying music, but the rhyme could be said or sung to any tune from "Sich a getting up stairs" to "Ah! non giunge uman pensiero." The minutes of yesterday afternoon and evening's meetings were read, and the resolutions presented yesterday repeated—the general question of Woman's Rights remaining open.

A letter was presented by Mrs. Johnston [sic, actually Mary A. W. Johnson], of Ohio, from Mrs. [Elizabeth Cady] Stanton, whose views on the political rights of women were very novel and very *outre*. The reconciliation of domestic differences, politically and religiously, was attempted on the principle of what *ought* to be, but what *would* assuredly be, and could not possibly fail to be was studiously, or rather *naturally* avoided. The infusion of the peaceful element of woman into the mass of masculine political excitement, was argued as furnishing a good reason why woman should be admitted to vote in political matters; and the same incentive was upheld as endorsing her claim to fight her own countries [sic] battles, and to take share in the rowdy council of her Senates and Houses of Representatives. Moreover woman was capable of taking the $8 per diem which rewarded the old womanism of our Statesmen. These, and a great many more things came up in consecutive, but very ragged array.

Another letter was read from Sam. A. May, of Syracuse. It started by a plea of poverty on account of expenses paid in aid of the progress of fugitive slaves toward freedom. The letter was an anti-slavery one, and bore the sentiment that nothing could be done for women until slavery was abrogated; also the belief expressed that the agitation supported by the conference was a natural one, and the document wound up by a detailed disquisition on what reforms were necessary to establish Woman's Rights.

O. S. [Orson Squire] Fowler, of New York, travelled over the same ground in *his* letter. He believed that the "imperial absolutism of the importance of the work" was beyond decided. The mutual relation subsisting between husband and wife was defined; and the *impropriety* of women meeting, alone, for the management of their *own* business shewn up in very plain terms, which were not so palatable as truth ought to be.

At this point the organ below struck up, and threw the influence of music upon the close. The tune was "Go to the devil and shake yourself." Verily music hath charms, et cetera—everyone knows the quotation.[7]

Harriet K. Hunt, of Boston, described the age, and what kind of animal it was; by her account it was "a very queer beast"—a kind of cross between the unicorn and the "sea-sarpint." The signs of the times too were ocularly reviewed, without *specks,* and these important significations characterized as peculiarly favorable to female ascendancy. The remainder was pathological, theological, conchological, and horological—the latter particularly the case, as its length and *Tempus fugit* were sworn brother and sister—on an equality in all respects—and it wound up by

---

[7] William Congreve, *The Mourning Bride,* Act I, Sc. 1:

Music hath charms to soothe the savage breast,
To soften rocks, or bend a knotted oak.

St. Vitus' dance, Intermittent Fever, and Human Nature. As the world renowned philanthropist Wackford Squeers has it—"She's a rum 'un, human natur, she is."[8] The arrival of the end of the address was as anxiously looked for as dinner time to a very hungry man. Mrs. H. took care before she ended her inexplicable harangue to give her business of female doctoring a very barefaced puff. All right! the *utile cum dulce* [the practical with the sweet] is justifiable now and then; but Mrs. H. had no business at all to depreciate the medical faculty in the manner she did. What right had she to abuse the great undiploma'd doctors who *infest* every nook and corner of Boston—and dispense surgery and medicine as if they were butchers or West India goods men? None whatever. Let quackery and imposture feel secure in its position; for although Mrs. Hunt gave them a withering rebuke, we will not mention it— oh, not at all! The scoundrels are safe from us; but let them beware of Mrs. Hunt! for she is a Tartar and nothing else. Ye serpent excavating surgeons, beware! Mrs. Hunt is on hand, and will be down on you like a hundred[weight] of brick.

W. H. Channing, from the Business Committee, put forth a series of Resolves claiming the full rights of Education, Partnership, a co-equal share with men in the making of the Laws, and such social and political privileges as mankind claim to hold themselves and to deny to women.

Mrs. Ball of Worcester took up some objections to the proceedings of the meeting, particularly on account of some omissions of the speakers relative to the true relationship between man and wife. She repudiated the idea that no scripture proof should be brought to bear on the relationship. She had a great veneration for the ladies who spoke [presumably a reference to Lucretia Mott and Abby Kelley Foster], but she had still a greater veneration for "thus saith the Lord!"[9] As to the propriety, or right, of paying the washerwoman as much as a wood-sawyer,

which had been enforced by some [Abby Price for one], she could not see what the wood sawyer could do if his wife was unwell and he had to pay all his earnings to her nurse. (Loud applause.) This matter had not been clearly put before the meeting.

Dirty-face Burley [C. C. Burleigh] roared out—"The wood-sawyer will pay the nurse out of his wife's earnings!" But suppose, most filthy of all mankind! that the wood-sawyer's wife had nine children "and one at the breast" to take care off [sic]? Eh? what sayest now to this thing? Where would be the price of her labor? In her children's health and comfort; and can she part with her labor in this shape? Verily no, most sage Burley.

Mrs. [Antoinette] Brown, of Oberlin, Ohio, next spoke, and defended the equality of her sex with man. The Scripture aspect of the argument was taken up by this beautiful and very talented lady, who urged probabilities and expediencies as being in every shape against the literal interpretation of the texts which occur in the Bible regarding the subjection of woman to man's rule; and, even were this subjection scriptural, it was not to be wielded if the conscience of the woman said it should not. A woman was situated in a similar position to a child, which was bound to submit to the instruction of its parents, but who was not filially, or morally bound to give obedience to the parent, if he instructed it to do wrong. The word subjection was not properly interpreted, and only meant instruction, which was a mutual duty on the parts of both man and woman. The woman was said to be subject to the man, who was 'head" over her. The word *head* was used only in scripture, to signify precedence of creation, and not of power—consequently equality of position augured equality in the possession of social and political rights. After an appeal to the public on the propriety of their casting off the prejudices which militated against woman, and prevented her from joining in the common business and

---

[8] A character in Charles Dickens's *Nicholas Nickleby*.

[9] A refrain in Exodus [King James Version] where the phrase appears numerous times.

professions of life, her qualifications to conduct, and prosper in public pursuits, were fully and very eloquently described. The modest deportment of the lady was a special recommendation of the good sense, mixed with some alloy, which characterized Mrs. [sic] Brown's speech. Her domestic economics were very markedly heterodox.

C. C. Burley (with the alias) next got up and spoke to the objection to woman's participation in public forums and occupations, because of a want of time. This argument was moulded out of custom, manufactured by man, and was of no account, therefore, only as it stood to condemn the terrible organization of society. He deprecated the necessity to tend the children, wash the clothes, and mend the stockings, if it interfered with this time to improve. Better go with a dirty shirt, no shoes, or forget to wash the children, than hinder this improvement! Most stupid argument in favor of a maggot, which the practices of our New England repudiate, and ever will! Although Burley's oration in this department was one of much power of eloquence; and we really

liked him for it—particularly after it was finished, we believe he was speaking against the grain of his own better conviction; and the lop-sided character of his statements showed this. Mrs. Ball's query concerning the payment of the nurse was a poser to Burley. He labored like an overladen man to make out a case, but Mrs. Ball nailed him up in a corner, and kept him there until he owned beat. Mrs. [Ernestine] Rose also gave him the benefit of a supposition than [sic] a woman was unmarried, and had no one to depend on for assistance in case of sickness—how was she to pay as much as she earned to have her wood cut? Burley could not say how the sick woman would get out of the difficulty; but some one suggested to him that the gas-light of public sentiment would furnish heat. He would have taken the advantage of this metaphysical caloric [source of heat], but could not recognise its definite capabilities to boil the kettle. The rest was all Buncombe [meaningless claptrap], and very obscure at that.

The Convention here adjourned for two hours. Intimation was made that the room had been secured for an evening hour.

OCTOBER 24, 1850—AFTERNOON SESSION

The high moment of this session was the speech of Sojourner Truth, born Isabella Van Wagenen. She was a former slave emancipated when the "peculiar institution" was abolished in New York. In the 1850s she became almost as well known in anti-slavery and woman's rights circles as Frederick Douglass and, as the most prominent woman of color in these movements, has attracted much interest from historians. Truth's speech in Worcester was her first major address on the subject of woman's rights. Most scholars, including Nell Painter whose recent biography has established itself as the definite work on Truth, base their account of what she said on the one-paragraph summary in the New York Daily Tribune. *The Boston* Daily Mail *account, also reprinted here, is much more detailed and differs from that in the* Tribune *in important ways. Did*

Truth, as the Rev. Fowler wrote in the Tribune, *say that "Woman set the world wrong by eating the forbidden fruit, and now she was going to set it right"? So scholars have assumed. But, according to the* Daily Mail, *she actually said:*

> *It was not fair to let woman suffer because she ate the apple, and to say that she was the weaker vessel, and turned the world upside down accordingly. If she had really done so, what should hinder her to turn it back again? Nothing but the intolerance of man! Knock down that, and all would come right; that was a plain truth, and it was wonderful that truth which could be so easily told was not invariably and plainly told.*

Reformers, particularly woman's rights advocates, were always putting words in Truth's mouth. One of them, for example, ghosted her autobiography as Truth herself was illiterate.[1] So historians would dearly love to have access to one of her speeches more or less exactly as she delivered it. Indeed, if we could choose, we would probably select this one. Not only did it do much to establish Truth as a major figure in reform circles, but it also contains her version of the impact of the abolition of slavery in the North upon the woman's movement. Historians have long emphasized the links between the campaign to abolish slavery in the South and woman's rights but have not explored the connections Truth saw between the ending of slavery in the North and the rise of reform.

The Daily Mail *account of this speech is as close as we are likely to get to a verbatim transcript. But, because the reporter's bias against woman's rights is so glaring, we must read it with much care. An important clue as to how he wrote these dispatches immediately precedes his version of Truth's remarks.*

Frederick Douglass also made an influential address, the central theme of which, that women must take their rights rather than wait for them to be given to them, echoed through subsequent speeches in subsequent conventions. Douglass offered convention participants a means of reconciling Lucretia Mott's call for action with Paulina Wright Davis's strictures against any sort of overt hostility to men.

---

[1] *Narrative of Sojourner Truth* (Boston: 1850) written by Olive Gilbert. Painter's biography contains a thorough account of the production of this and other works attributed to Truth.

FROM THE *PROCEEDINGS:*

The President, P.W. Davis, in the chair.
Business before the Convention—the discussion of the resolutions offered at the morning session. Speakers—W. A. Alcott, E. L. Rose, Sojourner Truth, A. Brown, L. Mott, Frederick Douglass, Wm. Lloyd Garrison, C. C. Burleigh, and A. K. Foster.
Adjourned, to meet at 7 o'clock, P.M.

New York *Tribune,*
October 26, 1850

Dr. Wm. A. Alcott spoke on the physical Education of Females. He corrected an error of George Combe in his book of travels, that the women of America were very beautiful, because of their white, transparent skin. This was not true beauty; it was an indication of diseased skin. It had been thought that a high development of physical power was incompatible with high intellectual and moral power. This is not true. They are perfectly compatible. He argued for simplicity of habits, Nature, and the equal rights of both sexes to a full opportunity for the development of their powers.

Mrs. Rose addressed the Convention in a short but animated speech, showing that women were inventive, and that the reason they have not produced high inventions is that they have been continually employed with trifling duties, as drudge in the kitchen, or a puppet-show in the parlor. She maintained that the wrongs they were laboring to remove were not so much the guilt as the misfortune of mankind. She should not use the language of censure and blame. So far as there was blame, she thought both sexes entitled to their share of it. She dwelt earnestly and eloquently on the objects of the reform.

Sojourner Truth, a colored woman, once a slave, spoke, and gratified the audience highly. She showed that beneath her dark skin, and uncomely exterior there was a true, womanly heart. She uttered some truths that told well. She said Woman set the world wrong by eating the forbidden fruit, and now she was going to set it right. She said Goodness never had any beginning; it was from everlasting and could never die. But Evil had a beginning, and must have an end. She expressed great reverence for God, and faith he will bring about his own purposes and plans.

Miss Brown of Oberlin, again addressed the Convention. She took up this time the injunction of Paul, that women should keep silence in churches.[2] She showed this meant she should not disturb the church with questions, asking for information which she could obtain at home from her husband; for Women were then kept in ignorance, and they would be wanting to know many things, which, if they were allowed to ask at the moment would disturb the good order and demeanor of churches. It was enjoined that all things might be done unto edification. But

---

[2] First letter to the Corinthians 14:34 [King James Version]: Let your women keep silence in the churches: for it is not permitted unto them to speak; but they are commanded to be under obedience, as also saith the law.

Woman was not prohibited from teaching and speaking. She quoted passages of Scripture to prove this.

Lucretia Mott said she was glad their young friend from Oberlin had stated so clearly a part of the scriptural argument on the subject. These expositions had been familiar to her for years, and she had come to the conclusion that it would not be profitable to consume too much time with the Bible argument. Let those who are interested in that branch of the subject take a favorable opportunity to investigate it. She thought the true ground to take is to address themselves to the justice, the humanity and the common sense of those who hear. She would, however, say that it was very plain, from the Bible, that Women did preach the gospel. They had the gift of prophecy. She quoted the passage, "I will pour out my spirit upon all flesh, and your sons and daughters shall prophesy."[3] To be a prophet or prophetess was to be a teacher. She quoted several other passages, showing the equality of woman's privileges from the Bible, and said she had many more at her fingers' ends. But she did [not?] think the argument necessary. Yet she would not have had the young friend, who had spoken on this subject, say one word less than she did.

Frederick Douglass addressed the Convention in a forcible and interesting manner, and with much eloquence. He said, this Convention has now been in session two days, and no one has attempted to offer anything against the sentiments and principles advanced here. It is not because there is no opposition to *this* movement; but because the truths on which it is founded are invulnerable. The arguments advanced cannot be met except by ridicule, and this will be the great weapon that will be used against us. He said he had some experience of the character of public opinion. He had been its victim, and the lesson he had learned was to *take* his rights wherever he could get them—to assume them, at any rate, as properly his. This principle of action had brought him into some difficulties; he had been turned out of railroad cars in Massachusetts, and out of steamboat cabins, and knocked on the head. But he found the continual exercise of his rights was wearing out their prejudices against color. He closed by urging strongly that women should take their rights. Seize hold of those which are most strongly contested. You have already free access to the paths of literature; Women may write books of poetry, travels, *et cetera* and they will be read avidly. Let them strike out in some other path where they are not now allowed to go. If there is some kind of business from which they are excluded, let some heroic Woman enter upon that business, as some of these noble Women have entered upon the practice of medicine. Let Woman *take* her rights, and then she shall be free.

Wm. Lloyd Garrison addressed the Convention at much length, and was listened to with deep interest. He felt that he might rightfully stand on that platform. For years he had borne the stigma, and he considered it an honor, of being a Woman's Rights man. He came here almost doubting whether there would be more than a small gathering of friends on this occasion; but he had been most happily disappointed. This hall had been crowded from the beginning this far with attentive and interested listeners. He felt that the spirit of God had brooded over this assembly, and that the word of God had been spoken. He could not but feel how much we had lost—how much had been lost to the world of the eloquence, the wisdom and the power of Woman by the deprivation of her rights. What eloquence, what burning words we had listened to at this Convention from the lips of Woman.

---

[3] Book of Joel 2:28 [King James Version]: And it shall come to pass afterward, that I will pour out my spirit upon all flesh; and your sons and your daughters shall prophesy, your old men shall dream dreams, your young men shall see visions.

He made a distinction between rights and duties. Woman's rights are coequal with Man. With many there is a confusion of rights and duties. There might be different spheres of duty to different individuals, and to some extent to the sexes; but there was no difference of rights. It did not follow that Woman would quit her appropriate sphere if these rights were secured to her. The law of God will regulate all this. Let there be freedom, and every one will find his or her true level and place in the arrangements of the social world.

Mrs. Mott made some remarks, and was followed by C. C. Burleigh, who spoke with much power and in a manner highly argumentative and convincing.

The Convention adjourned to meet again at 7 o'clock.

Boston *Daily Mail,*
October 25, 1850

After a dinner at Tucker & Booney's "American House"—which by the way is one of the best regulated Hotels we ever put our foot in—and whose well bred and clever attendants are patterns of their order—we found ourselves in an unusually good-natured mood—our heart expanded to its full tension, and full of a holy indignity because of the wrongs social, political and general of that unfortunate, but excellent and very lovable creature—woman. We were not as we "used to was" to a certainty; and those around us were apparently in the same mood; for, whether closer acquaintanceship among the fair conferees loosed their tongues—or whether the natural disposition to tattle came out in its most elastic shape—because it would come, we don't know, but the above was written amid a Babel-like confusion of tongues which was peculiarly interesting, and very much divided in its interest. Order having been called, Dr. W. A. Allcott, of Newton, took the platform. He called attention to a physical error in the education of woman, viz: the incompatibility of a high state of mental culture with physical strength—the physiological reasons for this notion being erroneous.[4] His experience told him that education had no effect on the physical organization of woman, neither did it influence the quality of her beauty. The *mens sana in corpore sano* [a healthy mind in a healthy body] was a balance that education only equalized and did not vitiate. The speaker was not adverse to the exercise, by woman, of the domestic duties, as some had argued she should. It was a natural thing that woman should attend to these matters, but not that she should make herself a slave to the wants of the stomach. He had been among slave States, and had seen slavery in every shape, but he had witnessed more slavery to the pot and kettle at home than he had witnessed abroad. Improve this state of affairs, and woman would be furnished with sufficient time to attend to her mental wants and improvements, and have some to spare in order to devote to social and political duties. The necessity of opening up the several branches of scientific education—particularly

---

[4]The belief that education, particularly in subjects such as mathematics and philosophy, endangered the health of young women was widespread in the medical community throughout the nineteenth century. The notion was that such "brain work" diverted blood from the developing sex organs and could lead to infertility. Dr. Edward H. Clarke's *Sex in Education: or, A Fair Chance for the Girls* (Boston: James R. Osgood and Co., 1873) is an example of this belief. The first printing sold out in a week, and the work went through seventeen editions in thirteen years.

medicine—was eloquently pleaded, and the appropriateness of the transfer pointed out by instances quoted in confirmation. Let woman take hold of the medical profession, and her nature and sympathies would confirm the propriety of the step. In this, as in every department, woman would have to take the initiatory steps herself. Men would not do it—would not come up to the work—and an individual and collective effort would have to be made on the part of woman, that her interests might be heeded, and her elevation sure.

Mrs. [Ernestine] Rose, of New York, urged her sisters to make use of the talents that they had, but which men had practically denied them to have, in emancipating themselves from their present condition. Because there was a difference of organization and occupation between men and women, that was no reason that the latter should be neglected; for if the mother, the trainer, the partner and the counsellor of mankind was to do her duty, no advantage should be denied her in the performance of that duty. If she was to leave behind her living, speaking models of her work, she ought to have every facility in building them up to positions and principles of honor. Popularity, fashion, everything but right should be thrown from the mind of womankind, until she had assumed the proper position which that right, and good human policy, justified and demanded. Woman had no right to be underrated; and if she would only think and act for herself she would soon attain to a recognised superiority to her present state. It had been said that woman was incapable to do great things—she could not invent. Could she not? Put her into an empty house, and their [sic] call upon her powers of invention; then she would show them when a man would despair. Her intellect and genius was equal to anything—and this was certain, although man and herself had narrowed the sphere of her inventive power. All the powers and faculties of the mind were referred to in rotation to favor a similar conclusion to the above, viz: that women were not, by nature, unequal to man in the extent or operation of mind, if assisted and directed in a proper manner. Before Mrs. Rose finished an ill-bred fellow behind us commenced reading the above crude abstract of her address, and commenting on the quality of our observations with another worse-bred fellow at his side. (The close of the last sentence was received with a sneer by both the parties alluded to, who afterwards took the trouble to look after their own business, leaving us to ours.)

Sojourner Truth (a colored woman) next spoke. She advocated woman's rights. She had looked on men and was sorry for them. The slaves all came on them, and now the women came on them. This sorrow was great last night when Wendell Phillips spoke, and had to defend himself against saying what he did not know was wrong [i.e., that women had as much responsibility as men for their lack of rights]—and was not convinced when he saw he was clearly wrong. One curious thing was to be thought about, viz: when man's rule began, and what gave him authority to rule. There was nothing in Adam's fall to tolerate his rule, and certainly nothing in his general conduct that said he was fit to rule himself—let alone others. If people would only think, they would see that man was only one half of himself, and the other half very well used up. It was said that, in the treatment of woman in this country was a proof of its civilization; but the heathen would have to come yet and teach them civilization. It was time for the heathen to commence, for things could not be worse. It was not fair to let woman suffer because she ate the apple, and to say that she was the weaker vessel, and turned the world upside down accordingly. If she had really done so, what should hinder her to turn it back again? Nothing but the intolerance of man! Knock down *that*, and all would come right; that was a plain truth, and it was wonderful that truth which could be so easily told was not invariably and plainly told. Sojourner said she had no education; and she was not ambitious of having it, as she saw that those who boasted of it had all of it in their feet and none of it in their heads. Respecting the present agitation she said it was wonderful how things came round. Slaves used to do all the rubbing [scrubbing?] in New England, and they complained of the hard work; they were emancipated and the hard work fell on the wives and daughters of New England, and they had begun to complain. The men, seeing that they had got into a fix, were, too, beginning to squirm and complain; and improvement in the condition of their wives and daughters would have to come before their complaints would have cause to be at an end; and all this arose out of the abolition of slavery. Sojourner made one of the best speeches that were spoken at the Convention, and was several times loudly applauded.

Mrs. [Antoinette] Brown, of Ohio, again spoke, and argued the right of women to speak in public places. She based her arguments on Scripture which she quoted with great facility and aptitude. The extent of the Scriptural law of tolerance towards women, in respect to public teachings and duties, received a very elaborate and ingenious description of treatment from the fair speaker.

By this time the hour appointed for the [railway] cars to leave had arrived, and we were forced to come away. The time to be spent in the afternoon and evening would be occupied with mere repetitions of what had already been spoken.

We have come to the close of our duties in connection with this particular stage of the Woman's Right Reform; and we cannot conclude without giving expression to the belief that such eloquence as had been spent upon it might have done honor to any feasible object of reform—but only served to make the ridiculous character of the present effort the more lamentably apparent.

Our very excellent and chaste[5] brother Channing not being willing to pledge himself that the talking would be over by ten o'clock in the evening, we felt restrained [sic] to take advantage of the last day train home. As for what may have followed, behold! is it not among the things that are of non-importance!

OCTOBER 24, 1850—EVENING SESSION

As the Daily Mail *correspondent made clear, he decided to catch the late afternoon train back to Boston. This meant that the Rev. Fowler's account in the* New York Daily Tribune *is the only source we have for what was said during the final session. Fortunately, like his* Daily Mail *counterpart, he closed with a brief account of how he wrote his dispatches. I have included the New York* Herald's *treatment of the close of the convention as well, not because it contains any new information but simply to illustrate how opponents of the movement could turn Fowler's sympathetic prose to their own purposes.*

If Sojourner Truth's speech in the afternoon helped establish her reputation, so did Lucy Stone's in the evening. Coming as it did near the end of the two days, her peroration that "We want . . . to be something more than the appendages of Society. . . . we want that when [a woman] dies, it may not be

---

[5] This was another gibe at Channing's alleged familiarity with the conditions inside brothels.

*written on her grave-stone that she was the 'relict' [widow] of somebody" pro-
duced a storm of applause and made her famous overnight.*

FROM THE *PROCEEDINGS:*

Convened at 7 o'clock, P. W. Davis President in the chair.

W. H. Channing read the resolutions presented in the morning meeting, and accompanied the reading with remarks upon the measures proposed for the coming year, and the principles which should govern the movement for establishing woman's co-sovereignty with man.

Sarah Tyndale, of Philadelphia, spoke of the business capacities of women, and the necessity of engaging in active duties to promote their own development.

Martha H. Mowry, physician, of Providence, Lucy Stone, S. S. Foster, L. Mott, and A. Brown, occupied the floor till a late hour. The resolutions were unanimously adopted, and, with the other documents of the Convention, referred to the Central Committee for publication.

Proceeds of the contributions, $119.65.

Adjourned, sine die

• • •

CENTRAL COMMITTEE.
- PAULINA W. DAVIS, Providence, R.I., Chairman.
- SARAH H. EARLE. Worcester, Mass., Secretary.
- WENDELL PHILLIPS, Boston, Mass., Treasurer.
- MARY A.W. JOHNSON, Salem, Ohio.
- WILLIAM H. CHANNING, Boston, Mass.
- GERRIT SMITH, Peterboro, N.Y.
- JOHN G. FORMAN, West Bridgewater, Mass.
- MARTHA H. MOWRY, Providence, R.I.
- LUCY STONE, West Brookfield, Mass.
- JOSEPH C. HATHAWAY, Farmington, N.Y.
- ABBY K. FOSTER, Worcester, Mass.
- PLINY SEXTON, Palmyra, N.Y.

- J. ELIZABETH JONES, Salem, Ohio.
- WILLIAM ELDER, Philadelphia, Penn.
- WILLIAM STEDMAN, Randolph, Stark Co., Ohio.
- EMILY ROBINSON, Marlborough, Mass.
- ABBY H. PRICE, Hopedale, Mass.
- WILLIAM L. GARRISON, Boston, Mass.

COMMITTEE ON EDUCATION.
- ELIZA BARNEY, Nantucket, Mass., Chairman.
- MARIAN BLACKWELL, Cincinnati, Ohio, Secretary.
- ELIZABETH C. STANTON, Seneca Falls, N.Y.
- ELIZA TAFT, Dedham, Mass.
- C.I.H. NICHOLS, Brattleboro, Vt.
- CALVIN FAIRBANKS, Maine.
- HANNAH DARLINGTON, Kennet Square, Penn.
- ANN ELIZA BROWN, Brattleboro, Vt.

COMMITTEE ON INDUSTRIAL AVOCATIONS.
- CHARLES F. HOVEY, Boston, Mass., Chairman.
- PHILINDA JONES, Worcester, Mass., Secretary.
- HARRIET K. HUNT, Boston, Mass.
- ELIZABETH BLACKWELL, London, England.
- BENJAMIN S. TREANOR, Boston, Mass.
- EBENEZER D. DRAPER, Hopedale, Milford, Mass.
- PHEBE GOODWIN, Delaware Co., Penn.
- ALICE JACKSON, Avondale, West Chester Co., Penn.
- MARIA WARING, Dublin, Ireland.

COMMITTEE ON CIVIL AND POLITICAL FUNCTIONS.
- ERNESTINE L. ROSE, New York, Chairman.
- LUCY STONE, West Brookfield, Mass., Secretary.
- WENDELL PHILLIPS, Boston, Mass.
- HANNAH STICKNEY, Philadelphia, Penn.
- SARAH HALLOCK, Milton, N.Y.
- ABBY K. FOSTER, Worcester, Mass.
- CHARLES C. BURLEIGH, Plainfield, Conn.
- ELIZABETH C. STANTON, Seneca Falls, N.Y.
- WILLIAM L. GARRISON, Boston, Mass.

COMMITTEE ON SOCIAL RELATIONS.
- LUCRETIA MOTT, Philadelphia, Penn., Chairman.
- WILLIAM H. CHANNING, Boston, Mass., Secretary.

- ANNA Q.T. PARSONS, Boston, Mass.
- WILLIAM H. FISH, Hopedale, Milford, Mass.
- REBECCA PLUMLEY, Philadelphia, Penn.
- ELIZABETH B. CHASE, Valley Falls, R.I.
- JOHN G. FORMAN, West Bridgewater, Mass.
- HENRY FISH, Hopedale, Milford, Mass.
- MARY GREW, Philadelphia, Penn.

COMMITTEE OF PUBLICATION.
- PAULINA W. DAVIS,
- WILLIAM L. GARRISON,
- WILLIAM H. CHANNING.

• • •

Note. As there was no phonographic reporter present, and the speeches were most of them brought out by the interest of the occasion, we are able to give a very meagre sketch only to our readers. The rich gems of thought and the thrilling eloquence of the extempore speeches are lost to those who were not present to listen.

Many of the speakers are already well and widely known, and it needs no word of ours to prove how eloquently Lucretia Mott, Wm. L. Garrison, Wm. H. Channing, W. Phillips, C. C. Burleigh, S. S. Foster, and A. K. Foster, advocated the right; but there are others less known to the public who were not less eloquent, for they spoke from full hearts, and feeling always burns, and glows, and imparts to others its own rich life.

Sarah Tyndale, of Philadelphia, spoke with great effect. There was an affecting earnestness combined with real womanly dignity in the narration of her own personal experience that could not fail of producing a deep impression.

Antoinette Brown, a graduate of Oberlin College, and a student of the Theological Seminary, occupied a portion of the time and chained the attention of the audience with her logical statement of the Bible arguments in favor of Woman's Equal Rights.

Ernestine L. Rose, of New York, gave utterance to her clear, strong thoughts in her own peculiarly graceful style of eloquence.

Lucy Stone, of Massachusetts, expressed her lucid views in her usual simple and effective manner. All who listen to her feel that the truths she utters have had their influence in shaping out her life and destiny.

Martha Mowry, M. D., of Providence, gave a neat finished address near the close of the Convention, evincing a fearless and truthful spirit.

Dr. W. A. Alcott introduced his views of the necessity of a better physical education for women, and dwelt on its importance very earnestly.

P. W. D. [Paulina Wright Davis]

New York *Tribune*, October 26, 1850:

The Hall was filled long before the hour to which the Convention adjourned. Every spot in the large room was filled with persons standing in solid phalanx, where there are no seats. There must have been over a thousand people present through nearly all the meetings. If a larger place could have been had many thousand more would have attended. Many have gone away, not being able to find admission.

Wm. H. Channing is delivering a thrilling and powerful address on the sin of licentiousness. He does not spare the licentious man. He looked to the pure and elevating influence of Woman as the remedy. He then dwelt upon the objects of the Convention, and read the series of resolutions before the meeting, and explained the objects of the appointments of the Committees.

The resolutions were unanimously adopted, and the appointment of the Committees confirmed.

Mrs. Sarah Tyndale gave her experience in business for the encouragement of her sisters. She was left a widow, and her husband's estate in debt. She had risen from these embarassments, and met with abundant success. Mrs. Mott arose at this point and stated that Mrs. Tyndale was the proprietor of one of the largest and most beautiful China establishments in this country or the world. Mrs. Tyndale continued. She said her children, if they could see her standing up before such an audience, would say, Why, mother, how can you expose yourself so? She said she did it for the encouragement of her sisters, and from a sense of duty. She went on to say

that her child had grown up to succeed her in business, and now she was employing her faculties for the good of others. She finds that her energies had been rendered greater and more active by attention to business, and she could not remain idle and at ease. She desired still to be usefully employed. Her friend, Mrs. Mott, here arose and said, she must state what the modesty of her friend would not allow her to state. She had, with another friend, visited all the houses of bad repute in Philadelphia; they had established a place of retreat for them [prostitutes], and had induced over three hundred young women to return to the path of virtue, and found homes and places of useful employment for them. This fact was received with great applause and many moistened eyes in the audience. Mrs. Tyndale urged her sisters onward in the path of improvement, usefulness, and happiness. Her remarks were delivered with great simplicity, natural eloquence and pathos.

Mr. Channing rose to thank his sister for her noble conduct. If he were her son he should be proud of a mother who could stand up here and give such words of encouragement, and who had done such noble deeds. There were not many dry eyes in the house during this scene.

Mrs. Mercy, a female physician of Providence, R.I. made some very stirring and eloquent remarks, urging Woman to effort and God-like action.

Lucy Stone spoke with great simplicity and eloquence on the character of the meeting, the misgivings with which she came to it, the triumphant success which had attended it, and said she could not go away without unburdening her heart. She said Woman must take her rights as far as she can get them; but those she cannot take she must ask for—demand in the name of a common humanity. She recommended the circulation of petitions to the Legislatures of the several States, asking for the *Right of Suffrage,* and the *Right of Married Women* to hold Property, and as much more as one felt it proper to ask for. She continued, speaking of the inferior and slavish position of Woman, and urged the objects of the movement as worthy of the labors of all true-hearted men and women in every land. We want, she said, to be something more than the appendages of Society; we want that Woman should be the coequal and help-meet of Man in all the interests, and perils and enjoyments of human life. We want that she should attain to the development of her nature and womanhood; we want that when she dies, it may not be written on her grave-stone that she was the "relict" of somebody. [Great applause.] She closed with an earnest appeal for Woman.

S. S. Foster spoke at much length upon the Bible argument. He was not satisfied with it, he was not convinced that the Bible did not give the Woman an inferior position in the scale of being than man. His object seemed to be to make his remarks bear against the plenary inspiration of the Bible, and the equal authority of all its parts. He thought the words of Christ taught the equality of the sexes. He expressed greater reverence for the teachings of the Saviour than for Paul. He was interrupted by other speakers and finally yielded the floor.

Lucretia Mott then made the closing address to the Convention. She alluded to the Bible argument, and said that many of those injunctions of Paul were applicable only to the circumstances of the Christians of that age; and suggested whether Paul and the other Apostles might not have imbibed some of the spirit and ignorance of their age on the subject; whether they were not influenced somewhat by the prevailing view that obtained at the time respecting Woman; and whether Paul, never having lived in the marriage relation, was fully competent as an authority on this subject. There could be no doubt that the general tenor, the spirit and the teachings of Christianity were all on the side of Woman's Rights.

She then delivered a most affectionate valedictory, dwelling for a moment on the simple and truthful words of Sojourner Truth, the poor woman who had grown up under the curse of Slavery, "that goodness was from everlasting and would never die, while evil had a beginning and must come to an end." She portrayed the mountains of difficulty that stood in the way of this reform, and said, "Are ye able to bear all this?" Then she uttered words of encouragement and hope. She pictured Jesus Christ, the Messiah, encountering the same difficulties; but the common people heard him gladly and many there are who shall rise up in behalf of our cause, and call it blessed. Mark, said she, the words of Jesus: "Lift up your eyes and behold the harvest, white for the reaper. Pray ye that laborers may be sent into the harvest."[1] We must be living agents of this work. If ever there was an age, since the Messiah, when the people should do those "greater works"[2] which he said they should do who obey his word, this is that age. She alluded to the success of the Temperance and Anti-Slavery reforms. Look at all these movements, and be not discouraged—persevere unto the end. Quoting from the *sainted* Channing [William Ellery, father of William H. Channing], she said, "Mighty powers are at work, and who shall stay them?" She said the sainted Channing because of the good works he had done. It seemed to her, after his death, as she sat

---

[1] John 4:35 [King James Version]: Say not ye, There are yet four months, and then cometh harvest? behold, I say unto you, Lift up your eyes, and look on the fields; for they are white already to harvest.

[2] Probably a reference to John 14:12 [King James Version]: Verily, verily, I say unto you, He that believeth on me, the works that I do shall he do also; and greater works than these shall he do; because I go unto my Father.

alone in her room, thinking of him, his presence was with her, and the halo of his divinity round about her. In regard to this movement she said—he or she who is least in the kingdom, is greater than these.[3] She alluded to the writings of Jane Eyre [sic], Harriet Martineau, Mary Howitt, in terms of approbation, and as a sign of promise; to Catherine Beecher's appeal twenty years ago on behalf of woman. Then she passed to her closing remarks. Are we not now separating from each other with grateful hearts? The day spring from on high hath visited us. We have met around this altar of humanity, and though no vocal prayers have been offered, she trusted an oblation had arisen from our hearts. "And now, Lord, let thy servants depart in peace; for our eyes have seen thy salvation."[4]

Following this tender and pathetic address, of which the foregoing is but an imperfect sketch, there were many warm congratulations, and the Woman's Rights Convention broke up under circumstances most cheering and happy. To-morrow morning there is to be a meeting of the [Central] Committee, and the people returning to their homes, will certainly feel that it has been good for them to be here.

In concluding this report I must apologise for any errors it may contain. I have been compelled to write in great haste amid much speaking and without assistance or aid. It does not profess to be a verbatim report but only a substantial account of this interesting meeting,

Yours very truly, J.G. Forman

New York *Herald*, October 28, 1850:

That motley gathering of fanatical mongrels, of old grannies, male and female, of fugitive slaves and fugitive lunatics, called the Woman's Rights Convention, after two day's discussion of the most horrible trash, has put forth its platform and adjourned. The sentiments and doctrines avowed, and the social revolution projected, involve all the most monstrous and disgusting principles of socialism, abolition, amalgamation [i.e., intermarriage], and infidelity. The full consummation of their diabolical projects would reduce society to the most beastly and promiscuous confusion—the most disgusting barbarism that could be devised; and the most revolting familiarities of equality and licentiousness between whites and blacks, of both sexes, that lunatics and demons could invent. Doctrines like these contemplating the overthrow of society, law, religion, and decency, might occasion some alarm, but for the notoriously vagabond character of the leaders in the movement; and the fanatical and crazy mongrels, in breeches and petticoats, who make up the rank and file. Aided and abetted, however, as they are, by their special organ, Horace Greeley, whose identity with all the fag ends [i.e., the frayed ends of a length of cloth or rope] of all the insane and infidel factions of the day, constitutes his claim as a moral teacher, supported, as these creatures, are by their leading organ of this city [Greeley's New-York *Daily Tribune*], they

---

[3] Probably a reference to Luke 7:28 [King James Version]: For I say unto you, Among those that are born of women there is not a greater prophet than John the Baptist: but he that is least in the kingdom of God is greater than he.

[4] Luke 2:30 [King James Version]: For mine eyes have seen thy salvation.

are entitled to a passing notice, if it were only to throw off the paltry disguises with which their fiendish designs are concealed.

A few brief extracts from the proceedings of the Woman's Rights Convention will sufficiently disclose their crack-brained and detestable projects: [here followed quotations from earlier stories—the *Tribune*'s as well as its own—from Lucretia Mott, Mrs. (Abby) Price, Mrs. (Ernestine) Rose, Abby Kelly, Mr. (James M.) Buffum, (Wendell) Phillips, Mr. Hubby Kelly Foster (Stephen S. Foster), Mr. Elizur Wright's letter, Samuel J. May's letter, the letter of L. A. Hine (twice), and finally the resolutions Wendell Phillips introduced.]

These resolutions were adopted as the platform of the society, and half a dozen committees were appointed to keep this delectable association in harness.

The tail end of this gathering of abolition infidels, and deluded blue stockings [i.e., pedantic women], it appears, was extremely delicious. Sojourner Truth, a lady of color, being a sojourner in the convention, and being called upon to speak the truth, did so by declaring that woman, in the first place, had put every thing wrong, by eating the forbidden fruit, and that she must now set everything to rights again. Frederick Douglas figured largely. He had learned to take his rights. He had been turned out of railroad cars and steamboats, knocked on the head, and kicked and cuffed like a dog, but he didn't mind it. He urged that the ladies should also take their rights—not wait for them to be doled out occasionally, but to take them! [William] Lloyd Garrison felt that the spirit of God had brooded over the Convention, and that the word of God had been spoken, and was affected to tears with this blasphemous hypocrisy. Sarah Tyndale recommended the women to be encouraged, for it appeared that she herself had been remarkably successful in the crockery business. Mrs. Mott said Mrs. Tyndale had visited all the houses of bad repute in Philadelphia, and had established a retreat for the Mary Magdalenes [prostitutes], three hundred of whom she had reclaimed, and given useful employment. Very good for Mrs. Tyndale. Mrs. Mercy, a female physician, of Providence, came also bravely up to the rescue. Mrs. Lucy Stone was very ambitious. She wanted woman put ahead, so that when she died, it should not be written upon her grave-stone that she was the "relict" of somebody. Mr. Hubby Kelly Foster was not satisfied with the Bible doctrine of the inferiority of woman; of course not, when his spouse, Abby Kelly Foster, was at his elbow. Mrs. Lucretia Mott, the ruling spirit of the establishment, thought that St. Paul, being an old bachelor, was a perfect ninny, and didn't know anything about women, was no sort of a judge, and not entitled to respect, in recommending "Wives, be obedient to your husbands." St. Paul, after all, was only a barbarian, full of the ignorance and prejudice of that time of day. Mrs. Mott, in winding up the conventicle, was affecting and solemn to an extraordinary degree. Quoting from the sainted Channing, she said: "Mighty powers are at work, and who shall stay them?" She said the sainted Channing, because of the good works he had done. It seemed to her, after his death, as she sat alone in her room, thinking of him, his presence was with her, and the halo of his divinity round about her. In regard to this movement, she said, he or she who is least in the kingdom, is greater than these. She alluded to the writings of Jane Eyre [sic], Harriet Martineau, Mary Howitt, in terms of approbation and as a sign of promise; to Catherine Beecher's appeal, twenty years ago, on behalf of women. Then she passed to her closing remarks. Are we not now separating from each other with grateful hearts? The day spring from on high hath visited us. We have met around this altar of humanity, and though no vocal prayers have been offered, she trusted an oblation had arisen from our hearts. "And now, Lord, let thy servants depart in peace; for our eyes have seen thy salvation."

Oh, most stupid presumption. "There is no peace for the wicked,"[5] as you will find

---

[5] Isaiah 57:21 [King James Version]: There is no peace, saith my God, to the wicked.

out, old lady; but "they shall be cast into hell fire, where there is weeping and gnashing of teeth."[6]

Now let us see what all this balderdash, clap-trap, moonshine, rant, cant, fanaticism, and blasphemy, means. One of their poetesses, worthy to have been appropriate for the $200 Jenny Lind song says [contest?], in a poem submitted to the Convention, says:

> "A Woman's Rights Convention.
> Ring out the word on high;
> If my brother man will help me,
> To help myself I'll try."

All right. But what does the Convention mean:—and [?] wise are the materials?

Mrs. Lucretia Mott, Quakeress, skeptic, abolitionist, and general in chief

Abby Kelly Foster or Meg Merrilies,[7] aid de-camp.

Hubby Kelly Foster, a wretched fanatic

Wm. Lloyd Garrison, a rampant, raving Judas

Charles C. Burleigh, or Grizzly Burley, a Judy

Mrs. Sarah Tyndale, merchant and general philanthropist

Frederick Douglas, fugitive slave

Mrs. Rose, Polish Jewess turned infidel philosopher

Sojourner Truth, a deluded lady of color

Wendell Phillips, abolition demagogue

Wm. H. Channing, ditto

Mrs. Mercy, female doctor of medicine

Miss Brown, professor of theology

Such are some of the leading geniuses of this assemblage. Their platform of principles comprises in behalf of women of color: The right to vote—the right to hold office—the right to be doctors, lawyers, professors, et cetera—the right to visit oyster houses and all other places—the right to fight when necessary—the right to do as they please.

And they recommend all womankind to put on the breeches—to refuse obedience, and to do just whatever they like. It will refine, improve, and elevate society.

And they declare their disbelief in the Bible, their contempt of St. Paul and the Apostles, a savage and vindictive agency in the doctrines of abolition, amalgamation and disunion; a desire for civil war, promiscuous intercourse of sexes and colors, and the reign of the goddess of reason. There is not a lunatic asylum in the country, wherein, if the inmates were called together to sit in convention, they would not exhibit more sense, reason, decency and delicacy, and less of lunacy, blasphemy, and horrible sentiments, than this hybrid, mongrel, pie-bald, crack-brained, pitiful, disgusting and ridiculous assemblage. And there we drop them, and may God have mercy on their miserable souls. Amen.

---

[6] Matthew 2:12 [King James Version]: But the children of the kingdom shall be cast out into outer darkness: there shall be weeping and gnashing of teeth.

[7] A reference to a poem by John Keats which begins:

> Old Meg she was a gypsy;
> And liv'd upon the moors:
> Her bed it was the brown heath turf,
> And her house was out of doors.

3

Reactions

Almost as important as what happened at the 1850 convention were the responses to it. A critical mass of opinion shapers—editors, popular writers, influential intellectuals, ministers, reformers, and the like—agreed that an important new movement had begun. And, whether they approved or not, they agreed that it had to be treated seriously.

This may seem an odd characterization of some of the opponents' reactions, such as that of the vituperative James Gordon Bennett, editor of the New York *Herald,* who concluded that the triumph of the convention's principles would realize "the jubilee of the Devil and his angels." Yet his no-holds-barred attack on the 1850 convention contrasted sharply with his dismissive reaction to the Seneca Falls meeting of 1848. It was "not the business . . . of the despot to decide upon the rights of his victims," he editorialized then, and he would therefore not "undertake to define the duties of women."[1] The very ferocity of his attack in 1850 showed that he had started to take the issue of woman's rights far more seriously.

---

[1] Bennett even commented in 1848 that Lucretia Mott would "make a better president than some of those who lately have tenanted the White House."

New York *Herald,*
Tuesday, October 29, 1850
[p. 4 editorial]

THE WORCESTER FANATICS— PROGRESS OF SOCIALISM, ABOLITION, AND INFIDELITY.

಄ಌ಄

It has been known ever since Fourier,[1] Brisbane,[2] and Greeley first promulgated their social theories, that society is all wrong. It is known also that their attempts to reform it have signally failed. Social phalanxes, on the Fourier principle of common stock, common privileges, and dividends to members of the establishment, have been tried in various parts of the country with the worst sort of success. In some cases, the speculators upon the credulity and spare cash of their followers, have pocketed the proceeds of these enterprises, and left the

phalanx the privilege either to starve or disperse. Monsieur Cabet and his Icarians,[3] in their wanderings over the plains of Arkansas in search of their promised land, afford a striking example. Fourierism, therefore, has fallen into contempt, the experiments not justifying the plan of the philosophers to make "labor attractive," because there is nothing in it by which your lazy philosophers can be made to work.

The next experiment by our delectable reformer of the *Tribune* was anti-rentism, which is simply the doctrine of occupying other people's property free of cost. All the good that has resulted, after repeated outbreaks and acts of bloodshed in the practical working of this doctrine, has been the creation of a political faction [of Thurlow Weed and William Seward, the nucleus of the future of Republican party in New York] controlling the politics of the State. The existing laws, however, upholding the right of the landowner to collect rents for the use of his property, still continuing in force, the experiment of anti-rentism as a social reform, has also proved to be inefficient.

But Philosopher Greeley is not the chap to drop the cause of suffering humanity. Not he. Union associations were prosecuted, until he lodged a bevy of unfortunate tailors in jail—the Rochester knockings[4]

---

[1] Fourier, Charles (1772–1837): A well-known proponent of utopian socialist ideas (so-called after Marx's distinction between his own "scientific" socialism and the ideas of his predecessors), he was born in Besançon, France, and worked as a clerk before publishing his first work, *The Social Destiny of Man, or, Theory of the Four Movements* (1808). After inheriting his mother's estate in 1812, he devoted himself to working through the details of his ideas in such works as *The New Industrial World* (1829). He advocated a reorganization of society into self-sufficient units (*phalanstères* or phalanxes) which would offer a maximum of both cooperation and choice to members. A number of so-called utopian communities in the United States adopted Fourier's principles. Perhaps the best known of these was Brook Farm.
[2] Albert Brisbane, author of *Social Destiny of Man* (1840), was the leading American exponent of Fourier's ideas.
[3] Étienne Cabet (1788–1852) founded the utopian socialist community of Nauvoo in Illinois on the principles laid out in his *Colony or Republic of Icaria in the United States: Its History* (Nauvoo, Il, 1852).
[4] A reference to Kate and Margaret Fox, two sisters aged twelve and fifteen, who lived outside Rochester and who, in 1848, began their careers as mediums to the spirit world by deciphering the meaning of mysterious rapping sounds. Forty years later, Kate and Margaret confessed they made the sounds themselves, by cracking the joints of their big toes.

were consulted, as likely to afford to the "laboring millions," some new attractions to labor, or some spiritual expedient by which cold victuals, at least, might be got without labor. Phrenology was tried, and found wanting. There was nothing disclosed in "Combe's Constitution of Man," of practical utility in securing a distribution of "every thing to every body." [??]litttlebat Titmouse, elected to Parliament on that platform, dodged the question, as J. B. [James Buchanan?] dodged the Fugitive Slave bill in Congress. Grubby [Greeley] next delved into the mysteries of Mesmerism,[5] but although clairvoyance can tell where Kidd's gold is to be found, if he had any, it could not tell how society is to live without work being done by somebody. Another kink of our friend "Grubby" is land reform, which means that all the public lands are to be given to actual settlers, in small parcels [later the nucleus of the Homestead Act], the deficiency to be supplied upon Big Thunder's [?] doctrine of the right from occupation of lands belonging to other people.

But all of these expedients have been found to be mere palliatives, while a radical reform of society has been the great object of the philosophers, Fourier, Brisbane, Greeley, Big Thunder, Combe, Fowler,[6] Collyer[7] and the Model Artists, the Rochester knockers, and Davis,[8] with his revelations, all having failed, all having proved unsatisfactory, tried separately, what next is to be done? Try them all together.

Here we come into broad, open smooth water. Here the daylight of discovery breaks in upon us as the first glimpse of the great Salt Lake broke upon the Mormons. Here we unbuckle our traps, and go straight to work in shovelling up the gold dust. The old Syracuse engineer jumped up in his nether garment, and shouted "Eureka,"[9] and Grubby Greeley answers Abby Kelly at Worcester, with "Eureka."[9] We have got it. Got what? The philosopher's stone—the key to the millennium—the one thing needful—the schedule of the final reformation. The Lord be praised.

It is the philosopher's omnibus bill—it is the putting all in a lump the several experiments of reform of the *Tribune* reformers, with a good deal of new matter, new principles, and fundamental ideas, as put forth on the platform of the Woman's Rights Convention, recently held in Worcester. Let the world rejoice. Lucretia Mott, Abby Kelly, Garrison, Philips, Mrs. Rose, Fred. Douglas, Sojourner Truth, and the Widow Mercy, sitting in council day and night, backed up, heart and soul, by our glorious Greeley, have solved the problem of the age. They have squared the circle of society, and resolved the arcana of its perpetual motion. From our published reports of the proceedings, the speeches, the declarations, and the resolutions of the Worcester Convention, it will be seen that their platform is made up of all the timbers of all the philosophers and spiritual advisers of the Tribune, founded upon the strong pillars of abolition, socialism, amalgamation and infidelity, compassing all the discoveries in heaven and earth. The new dispensation of Lucretia Mott and the philosophers, proposes:

I. To dispense with Christianity and the Bible. After an experiment of nineteen centuries, they declare the system to be a humbug.

---

[5] Hyponotism, named after Franz Mesmer (1734–1815).

[6] Orson Squire Fowler, author of such works as *The Illustrated Self Instructor in Phrenology and Physiology* (New York, 1855) and *Love and Parentage* (New York, 1844). He wrote a letter to the Convention.

[7] Robert Colyer, a British mesmerist, who made an American tour in 1839.

[8] The Rev. Andrew Jackson Davis, one of the leaders of the new spiritualism movement, and author of many books, including *Great Harmonia*, 2 volumes, 4th ed. (Boston, 1850).

[9] Archimedes, the ancient Greek mathematician who discovered the principle of the lever, supposedly proclaimed "Eureka!" and leapt from his bath to tell of his discovery without bothering to dress.

2. To abolish the existing political and social system of society as part of the false machinery of the age.
3. To put all races, sexes and colors upon a footing of perfect equality. The convention having proved by phrenology and biology that, the sexes are equal in point of intellect, and that color is a mere difference of complexion, it is proposed to abolish the only distinction of sex by a universal adoption of breeches.

Most assuredly, this grand reformation involves, as incidentals, the abolition of slavery, black and white, the doctrine of amalgamation to its fullest extent, fun and refinement, as was never dreamed of, even by Davis, in his revelations, or by Graham, from the inspiration of bran bread and turnips.[10]

The philosophers of the Tribune have, therefore, published the Worcester platform in the capacity of the official organ of this tremendous reformation. Old things are to be done away with, and all things are to become new. Seward is to be sustained, and [President Millard] Fillmore is only to be tolerated till the advent of the new dispensation, when Lucretia Mott, Abby Kelly, Douglas, Greeley and Sojourner Truth are to rule the roost. Then, and not till then, shall we realise the jubilee of the Devil and his angels.

Reform papers, such as William Lloyd Garrison's *The Liberator* and Adin Ballou's *Practical Christian*, were as enthusiastic as Bennett's *Herald* was harsh: ". . . may all those who were present at the Convention and sympathizing with it, cherish the holy and sublime aspirations and purposes awakened within them," Ballou wrote in an editorial Garrison reprinted as expressing his own views exactly—"The kingdom of God draweth near!"

Garrison had signed the "Call" and given a major speech at the Convention at which he noted that he had long been a "woman's rights man." Ballou's support was equally predictable. He was the founder of the utopian community of Hopedale, Massachusetts, as well as one of the chief theologians of the Universalist movement in American Protestantism. Only Quakers were as supportive of woman's rights as Universalists. One of Hopedale's residents, Abby Price, gave a major address at the convention.

---

[10] A reference to the Rev. Sylvester Graham, a health and food reformer, who urged the importance of eating bran bread.

The Liberator,
November 1, 1850

THE WOMAN'S RIGHTS CONVENTION

This Convention was held in Worcester on the 23d and 24th inst., and we regret to say that we have barely time and room, this week, hastily to say, that in point of numbers, spirit and ability, it far exceeded our most sanguine hope and expectations, and was really the noblest series of meetings that we ever attended. Days and evenings, Brinley Hall was crowded with as intelligent, orderly, and interested a class of people as we ever saw assembled; and the speaking was uniformly the best we ever heard from such a large number of speakers. Lucretia Mott, Paulina Davis, Mrs. [Sarah] Tyndale, Wm. H. Channing, Wendell Phillips, Lucy Stone, Stephen S. and A. K. Foster, Abby H. Price, Miss [Antoinette] Brown, Frederick Douglass, Miss Morey [Mercy?], Mrs. [Ernestine] Rose—these, that come crowding upon our mind, with others whose names we do not remember, and have not room to record, all spoke with a clearness, an earnestness, a directness, an eloquence, a philanthropy, an impressiveness, and a power, that inspired us with a fresh hope of humanity, and a new purpose to consecrate ourself to a physical, intellectual and moral redemption of the whole race. We should like exceedingly to speak of the address and remarks of each, but must reluctantly fobear [sic]. God bless all these noble men and women, and raise up more like them to labor in the great work of universal reformation, unity and happiness! Meanwhile, may all those who were present at the Convention and sympathizing with it, cherish the holy and sublime aspirations and purposes awakened within them, and unitedly and continually labor for the realization of what they long for! by and by, those who mean to be the doers of the word, as well as hearers and speakers of it, will organize Communities on the principles of justice and equality, in harmony with the law of celestial love. Let us hope on and ever. There is "a good time coming." The kingdom of God draweth near!

• • •

We copy the foregoing notice of the Worcester Convention from the *Practical Christian*, as an exact transcript of our own feelings and sentiments in regard to the proceedings of that highly intellectual and moral assembly. Our readers shall hereafter be furnished with the letters, addresses and speeches read or made on the occasion, as far as practicable.

Other responses were less predictable than Bennett's scorn and Garrison's enthusiasm. Horace Greeley, despite Bennett's fulminations, proved something less than an ardent champion of the new movement. He had opened the pages of the *Daily Tribune* to sympathetic coverage of the convention. He had not, as the author of the letter to the editor reprinted below pointed out, expressed his own views on the subject. When he did, he waffled. Women were entitled to equal rights, the *Tribune* editor wrote. And the world as we know it would not come to an end were they to gain them. Even so, he doubted the expediency of women claiming an equal and active place in public life. He was a believer in democracy, he concluded, and therefore had no choice but to choose principle over expediency. It is noteworthy in this context that he did not choose principle in his discussion of wages for women. They were too low, he maintained. And they should be much higher, but still less than those of men. The letter which prompted Greeley's editorial is also of interest. It combines conventional pieties about women's redemptive qualities and "higher nature" with a frank expression of male self-interest. Someone has to cook the dinners!

New York Daily *Tribune*, Saturday, November 2, 1850 (p. 6)

WOMEN'S RIGHTS AND DUTIES—THE WORCESTER CONVENTION [LETTER TO THE EDITOR]

H. Greeley, Esq.
Dear Sir: I notice that in publishing the proceedings of "the Mothers of our Republic," you refrain from all comment or remarks. I enjoy hearing your opinion, and am particularly anxious to know what you really think of this late [i.e., recent] movement in favor of "Woman's Rights."

Now, I am at a loss to what the Women of the Worcester Convention are aiming at. It is clear that, if we are going to live, or have any private comforts, there must be dinners cooked, children's faces must be washed, and there must be a home—a home to which the mind of the weary husband will turn to bear him up and urge him on in his toils for the inmates of that sanctuary—a home where he can for a time forget, in his wife's and children's society, the toils and troubles of this weary world—a home which he can never leave without carrying with him a new grace, a new strength, drawn from Woman's influence,

to enable him victoriously and manfully to withstand the trials and temptations of the world. Now, if Women are given the right to vote, to electioneer, to become stateswomen, why it is an incontrovertible fact (that is, if they attend properly to politics) that the dinners must go *uncooked*, the children's faces *unwashed*, and home be forgotten—unless, indeed, the men exchange duties with them, as was proposed at the Convention [by C. C. Burleigh], and stay at home and help their wives cook and wash the dishes.

So far from thinking Women "slaves," I do not see how it can appear in such a light to any thinking mind, any true-hearted woman. There is something so superior about Woman that would make one shrink as from profanation at the idea of her mingling in public with "the sterner and *worser* sex"—a spiritualization that raises her far above the intrigues of politicians and the vulgarity of rowdies—a superiority which, if not acknowledged in words, is confessed in actions, even by men who, however degraded they may be, refrain from the slightest word or action that could be commented upon, in the presence of a woman.

The Women of the Worcester Convention seem to have entirely overlooked the immense power given to women in the form of Home Influence. What power can be greater than a mother's holy and elevated example, which has given to the world so many shining lights? than a mother's gentle but impressive remonstrance to a straying son, or a wife's earnest pleadings to a wayward husband? all of which would be of no avail the moment a woman condescended to become a rowdy Senator or intriguing Politician. For my part, I look on Women as missionary angels, sent among men to remind them of their high calling and high duties. It is not because men think that women have no intellect, et cetera that they consider it inexpedient for them to vote. No, it is common sense directs them to this judgment. They know that there are two great duties to be performed in the world, *public* and *domestic* duties; and as no one can deny but that men are stronger than women, the former generally choose the more laborious and inferior duties.

We must also remember, that if women gained these absurd "rights," they would be obliged to maintain them; and this they have not the strength to do; for which of the women at the Worcester Convention could knock a man down if he chose to stand up? and what man would come forward to protect a woman as long as she claimed to herself the right of self-protection? It would be well enough for the ladies to endeavor to protect themselves, if it were practicable; but what rowdy, if he met Miss Dr. So & So out on a sick call at 12 o'clock at night, would stand to listen to her explanations of "Woman's Rights"?

I acknowledge there are some gross injustices done to Women in regard to property and their very low wages; and if it were to reform such abuses as these that Women held conventions, it would be laudable; but such injustices seem to take up but a small share of their attention, and, strange as it many appear, their ambition seems to aim principally at gaining the right to be just as uninteresting and bad as men. One of the ladies [Lucretia Mott] outdid even the Nineteenth Century, when she thought the inspired Apostles, the companions of our blessed Savior, "might have imbibed some of the ignorance of the age." Truly, we of the Nineteenth Century are wondrous wise, or either, I fear, *we* are imbibing some of the infidelity and self conceit of this same wonderful age. There can be no fault found with Miss Lucy Stone's desire not to have it placed on her grave-stone that she was "relict of somebody," as she can easily avoid being the "relict" [widow] of anybody.

I am sorry, dear Sir, to have trespassed so long upon your valuable time, but as I knew that on any subject you are always willing to give both sides a chance, as we Yankees say, I could not refrain from the above remarks. Yours sincerely, A.

Remarks. [Greeley's Editorial Response]

That there is great injustice and evil in the present circumscriptions of Woman's sphere, we firmly believe: that the Worcester Convention indicated precisely the right *remedies* therefor, we are not sure. That the full and equal enjoyment of Political Franchises would improve the lot of Woman, may be doubtful; but we are willing to give the Democratic theory a full and fair trial. Whenever so many Women shall petition for the Right of Suffrage as to indicate that a majority of the sex virtually concur in the demand, then we shall insist that the Franchise shall be extented to them. Being a disciple of the faith which holds that "all just government is founded on the *consent* of the *governed*," we could do not less, even though we knew that the Women would make a bad use of the power thus accorded them. Right first; Expediency afterward.

As to our correspondent's fear that buttered toast will run short, and children's faces get crusted over, in case the Political Rights of Women are recognized as equal to and identical with those of Men, we do not share it. We know people who supposed that, when Slavery was abolished, there could be no more boots blacked, no wood chopped, bacon fried, et cetera. But we see that all needful operations go on, though Slavery *is* abolished throughout this region. We see not why it may not be so in case the slavery of Woman should in like manner be abolished. We do not see how an enlargement of her liberties and duties is to make a mother neglect her children or her household. She now performs her maternal duties because she delights in so doing, and not because man requires it.

Our friend's delightful picture of the home presided over by an exemplary wife and mother we appreciate, but all women are not wives and mothers. Marriage is indeed "honorable in all," when it is marriage; but accepting a husband for the sake of a position, a home and a support, is not marriage. (We must be excused from stating what it *is*.) Now one radical vice of our present system is that it morally *constrains* women to take husbands (not to say, fish for them) without the least impulse of genuine affection. Ninety-nine of every hundred young women are destitute of an independent income adequate to their comfortable support; they must work or marry for a living. But in Industry, Woman's sphere is exceedingly circumscribed, and her reward, as compared with the recompense of masculine effort, very inadequate. Except as household drudges, it is very difficult for seven single women out of eight to earn a comfortable, reputable, independent livelihood in this country, and it is generally much worse in others. Hence false marriages and degradations more scandalous if not more intrinsically vicious.

What Woman imminently needs is a far wider sphere of action, larger opportunities for the employment of her faculties, and a juster reward for her labor. It is a shame, for example, that there should be several thousand male Clerks in our City dealing out dry goods mainly to women; these Clerks should have more masculine employments, and their places should be filled by women. The teachers in our schools should nearly all be women; the number should be doubled and the compensation largely increased. Watchmaking, tailoring, and many other branches of manufacturing industry, should in good part be relinquished to women. Women's work should command in the average two-thirds to three-fourths that of men; the present rates range from one-third to one-half.

Political franchises are but means to an end, which end is the securing of social and personal rights. Other classes have found the Elective Franchise serviceable toward the attainment of these rights, and we see not why it would lose its efficacy in the hands of Women. And as to the exposure of Women to insult and outrage in the Town or Ward Meeting, or at the Election, we trust the effect would be just opposite to that anticipated— namely, that men would be constrained by the presence of ladies to keep sober and behave themselves. The presence of Woman has this effect ever in those public assemblages honored by her presence; and we trust its virtue is far from having been exhausted.

As to Woman having to fight and knock down to maintain their Rights if once conceded, we don't believe a word of it. Knock down whom? Certainly not those who cheerfully concede them all they ask; and if there are any of the other sort, such brutes as choose to commence the game of knocking down, [they] would be very sure to get enough of it before coming to the Women. But there would be no knocking down in the premises.

We heartily rejoice that the Women's Rights Convention was held, and trust it will be followed by others. Our correspondent admits that Woman endures great wrongs which cry aloud for redress, but thinks the Worcester Convention misunderstood both the disease and the remedy. Very well; let the discussion go on, until wiser heads shall be interested and safer counsels prevail. For our part, we are well satisfied with the general scope and bearing of the Worcester discussions, and trust they will be followed up. [Ed.]

ON THE 1850 WOMAN'S RIGHTS CONVENTION

Elizabeth Blackwell's reaction was even more tepid than Horace Greeley's. In 1849 Blackwell became the first woman to gain a medical degree in the United States, a fact which led the organizers of the Worcester Convention to appoint her to one of the committees they established to carry on its work. She felt the new movement had to be respected, she wrote in a letter to her sister, but that its "anti-man" approach was to be deplored. Her view is particularly significant because opening educational opportunities to women, especially in medicine, was one of the central topics of the 1850 convention. In 1850 Blackwell was studying with Dr. James Paget in London, but her sister and mother both attended the Worcester gathering. So her deep misgivings about the convention's overall approach must have come as a surprise and suggest something of the difficulties the early woman's rights activists faced in winning support.

A LETTER TO HER SISTER

Elizabeth Blackwell

December 24, 1850
... Your letter alludes to many topics of interest. First of all this 'Woman's Rights Convention,' held at Worcester, Mass. I have read through all the proceedings carefully. They show great energy, much right feeling, but not, to my judgment, a great amount of strong, clear thought. This last, of course, one ought not to expect in the beginning; but in my own mind I have settled it as a society to respect, to feel sympathy for, to help incidentally, but not—for me—to work with body and soul. I cannot sympathize fully with an anti-man movement.

From *Pioneering Work in Opening the Medical Profession to Women: Autobiographical Sketches* by Dr. Elizabeth Blackwell (London and New York: Longman, Green, 1895.

I have had too much kindness, aid, and just recognition from men to make such attitude of women otherwise than painful; and I think the true end of freedom may be gained better in another way. I was touched by the kind remembrance of W. H. C. [William H. Channing], which [sic] placed my name on the Industrial Committee; and if I were in America and called upon to attend I should certainly send them a note full of respect and sympathy; but I must keep my energy for what seems to me a deeper movement. But I think you did perfectly right to act on the Education Committee, and if I can send you any information I will gladly do so. But I feel a little perplexed by the main object of the Convention—Woman's Rights. The great object of education has nothing to do with a woman's rights, or man's rights, but with the development of the human soul and body. But let me know how you mean to treat the subject, and I will render you what aid I can. . . . My head is full of the idea of organisation, but not the organisation of women in opposition to men. I have been lately meditating constantly on this idea, and seeking some principle of organisation which should be a constantly growing one, until it became adequate to meet the wants of the time. . . .

THE TRUE REMEDY

Catharine E. Beecher

Catharine Beecher, another the convention organizers had hoped would champion the cause, instead became an important critic. Beecher (1800–1878) had long campaigned for women's right to enter the teaching profession—she had organized the Hartford Seminary in large measure to train women as teachers—and for the professionalization of "Domestic Economy," an emerging field of study in which she had written

Catharine E. Beecher, *The True Remedy for the Wrongs of Woman; with a History of an Enterprise Having That for its Object* (Boston: Phillips, Sampson, & Co., 1851), pp. 21–34, 38–43 [written as a series of letters to her sister, Harriet Beecher Stowe].

a classic textbook, *A Treatise on Domestic Economy* (Boston, 1843). Several speakers at the 1850 Convention, including Lucretia Mott, referred to her respectfully as a pioneer. Further, she fully shared the central idea of the reformers of the day, that a perfect society was within their reach. But, as the excerpts below indicate, Beecher was convinced that the woman's rights movement was not the "true remedy for the wrongs of woman." Her own solution emphasized the training of women for their "true" professions, the rearing and educating of children and the keeping of households. This indeed is exactly what she had devoted her entire career to seeking to bring about. What the delegates to the Convention could not have anticipated was her insistence that women should pursue only these "professions" and that they should stay entirely out of the political realm. Beecher's opposition to the woman's rights movement, like Blackwell's characterization of it as "anti-man" and Greeley's tepid endorsement, shows just how difficult a task Paulina Wright Davis, Lucretia Mott, Lucy Stone, and the other pioneers had undertaken.

. . . What is our duty as intelligent and Christian women? It can not be disputed that, even in our own most favored country, our sex, *as a whole*, are in many ways sufferers from unjust laws, opinions, and customs. At the same time, a very large number of women are helpless victims of such misery and wrong as, if fully portrayed, would overwhelm us with indignation and horror.

In the meantime, an organization is effected among our own sex, thought not confined to it, which is earnestly and perserveringly employed in exposing these wrongs, and in awakening the attention and sympathy of all just and generous minds. They are, many of them at least, persons of intelligence, honesty, and benevolence. They are aiming at a noble end, and all we can object to is the *method* they adopt. If we join in the vituperation and ridicule by which they are assailed, we shall only add to the sympathy and respect with which all just and dispassionate minds regard their efforts; and all the interest awakened for their cause by their arguments, their eloquence, and their brave and self-denying course of action, will turn into the only channel which now is opened by them for its outflow.

In a case like this, where a noble object is sought by *wrong* methods, the only way to stop the mischief is, to set about accomplishing the same thing by *right* methods.

• • •

This, then, presents the object at which I would aim in these letters: to set forth *a better way,* and to show some *practical* results, that will tend, as I hope, to convince all whose sympathies are awakened in this direction, that what is now sought by the Woman's Rights party in this country and abroad, can be secured by far safer, less objectionable, and more efficient methods, than those they are now pursuing.

LETTER III

My Dear Sister:

The only true method of estimating the wrongs to which such multitudes of our sex are victims, is to bring before our minds their future condition in that perfected state of society toward which, we believe, humanity, under the guidance of Christianity, is steadily tending.

When this state is fully attained, every man and every woman will *practically* love their neighbors as themselves, and all the institutions of society will emanate from this spirit. And then all men will employ their time, and wealth, and influence, as heartily for the good of others as for themselves and their own families. Of course, all land-monopolies, and all abuse of capital, and every institution that gives undue advantages to any one class, will be known no more.

When this period arrives, every healthful, mature, man will be able to sustain a family; and, saving some few exceptions, every man will have a wife. Of course, as the sexes are about equal in numbers, with these few exceptions, all matured women will be wives, mothers, and housekeepers.

• • •

No doubt, too, there will be many wise methods, in each community, for the *division of labor,* so that those who have a taste and talent for physical employment will have such duties to perform, while gifts that indicate the nurse or the educator will be employed mainly in their appropriate sphere. Still, even then, there will be all the routine of housekeeping, nursing children, the care of the sick, and the education of the young, to be carried forward by the mothers and daughters of each family.

• • •

Whenever this golden period arrives, *all women will be educated*, and, what is more, they will all be educated *for their profession*, as the conservators of the domestic state, the nurses of the sick, the guardians and developers of the human body in infancy, and the educators of the human mind. In addition to all that discipline and knowledge which tends to enlarge and develop the mental faculties, the science and practice of Domestic Economy will be thoroughly taught to every woman. And all that science which is now confined to the profession of a physician will be confided, in a certain extent, to all women; and, to the full extent, to all who are to act professionally as nurses.

And, above all, everything which tends to perfect a woman for the discharge of her grand office as the educator of mind, will be abundantly bestowed. And in that day every woman will be so profitably and so honorably employed in the appropriate duties of her peculiar profession, that the folly of enticing her into masculine employments will be deemed far more ridiculous than we now regard the bright buttons, buff vest, and light small-clothes, of the lady [Helena Maria Weber, of Belgium, who dressed as a man] whose history graced my first letter.

With this view of the matter, we are prepared to understand *what are the real wrongs of woman*. they may all be regarded as involved under these general heads: that her profession is dishonored; that she is not educated for her profession; that in a vast majority of cases she is cut off from all employ in her true vocation; and that where it is open to her, she is drawn to it by few of those motives of honor and advantage that stimulate the other sex.

I will briefly illustrate the operation of these general causes. First, in regard to the dishonor which is awarded to a woman's true profession. In the most cultivated and influential class of society, to live so as not to perform any family work, and to be totally ignorant of both the science and practice of Domestic Economy, is not only very general, but often is boasted of as the particular claim to the character of "a lady."

Meantime, those who really are rendering the most service to society by performing these labors, are despised as the lowest class. Even the teachers of young children, as the general rule, receive poorer wages than are paid to the higher class of domestics, and are regarded as an inferior caste by those who consider themselves the nobility of society.

This estimate of domestic and educational labor operates disastrously on all other portions of society. Each class is striving to rise still higher, and the highest position is deemed to be that in which the occupant renders little or no service to society, but lives solely on the earnings of others.

In respect to the *education of woman for her profession*—in the most intelligent and wealthy classes, it is little regarded. That great class of young ladies, who receive the benefits of our highest schools and seminaries, spend their whole childhood and youth in receiving what is called an education, and then the vast majority come forth profoundly ignorant of all they most need to know. As to the science and practice of Domestic Economy, they are far better instructed in Political Economy, or even in Navigation or Surveying, for these sciences are often a regular part of the course of study in our female institutions.

And as to the knowledge that would qualify them to take charge of a young infant, the cat or the sheep would be altogether their superiors in the care of the young of their own species. And in regard to the still more arduous duty of training the mind of infancy and childhood, our highly-educated young ladies would be far more wisely set to work in constructing and regulating delicate chronometers, or in superintending the working of steam-engines, than in physical, intellectual, and moral education.

When this is true of the most cultivated class, nothing better is to be expected of those less favored, except so far as necessity drives them to learn certain things by practice which they would shun if fortune would but elevate their social position.

Meantime, to acquire a little smattering of some foreign tongue, or to learn to play a few tunes on some instrument which soon are to be forgotten, is a matter to which parents devote care, and effort, and large expense, and which children are trained to regard as the most creditable acquisitions of an education.

But the grand source of the heaviest wrong that oppresses our sex is found in the fact that they are so extensively cut off from honorable and remunerative employ. This is owing in part to the disgrace which is attached to the performance of the most important services of the family, and in part to the fact that, to a wide extent, men have usurped the most important department of woman's profession, and thus she has been driven to take up the relinquished employments of man.

The *training of the human mind* in the years of *infancy and childhood*—this, it is claimed, is the appropriate and highest vocation of woman. And in all those states and cities of our country where education prospers the most, it has flourished just exactly in proportion to the extent in which men have forsaken and women have been restored to this employ.

There are now more than *two million* children in this country *without any schools!* There are probably as many more in schools taught by men, who could be far more appropriately employed in shops or mills, or other masculine pursuits. Were all these children placed in schools at the ordinary rate of apportionment of pupils to teachers, it would require two hundred thousand women to meet the demand. Where are these women? They are living in indolent ease, or they are toiling in shops and mills, or in some other employments, which yield a pittance scarcely sufficient to sustain life. I have no doubt that, in this country, there is that number of women already so far qualified, that a few weeks of additional training would fit them to become teachers.

• • •

I have made the situation of our sex in shops and mills a distinct subject of inquiry and of *personal* investigation; and it is my solemn conviction that if there is no other way to relieve our sex but to remove them from their appropriate vocations to labor in manufactories and shops, it would be far better for woman, and for *the coming generation,* that she follow the example of the Germans at the West, and toil in the open air in horticulture and farming. It would be better for her health, better for her morals, and better for her children.

If I should state all I can *prove* on this subject, and that, too, in reference to our best-conducted manufacturing establishments, it, probably, would make a great hue-and-cry among capitalists; yet nothing is needed but to go to these places and converse with the most intelligent and candid female operatives, to learn what would abundantly establish my position—that, as the general rule, it would be far better for women to be employed on farms and gardens than in shops and manufactories.

• • •

... [T]he wrong resulting from excluding woman so extensively from the true and highest vocation of her sex, I do not regard as bearing exclusively on the poverty-stricken class. I regard the women who are highest as to social position, in large numbers, as almost equal sufferers. To exhibit clearly my meaning I will quote a few sentences from Dr. Coombs:

Inactivity of intellect and feeling is a very frequent predisposing cause of *every form of nervous disease.* For evidence of this, we have only to look at the numerous victims to be found, who have no call to exertion in gaining the means of subsistence, and no objects of interest on which to exercise their mental faculties. The intellect and feelings, not being provided with interests external to themselves, must either become *inactive and weak*, or *work upon themselves, and thus become diseased.*

The most frequent victims of this kind of predisposition are females of the middle and higher classes, especially those of a nervous constitution and *good natural abilities.* The liability of such persons to melancholy, hysteria, hypochondriasis, and other varieties of mental distress, really depends on a state of *irritability of the brain occasioned by imperfect exercise.*

Now, we know by experience, that there is no other avocation that so effectively and so healthfully exercises every intellectual faculty as that of a teacher, while, in this service, all the social, moral, and benevolent emotions, are kept in full play. I think the most truly happy persons I have ever known—those who would claim to be fully content with their lot, and as happy as they wish to be on earth (and I have seen such)—were successful teachers.

• • •

Indeed, the most painful drawback to my enjoyment in the pursuit of this profession has been, the results of high cultivation on the character and happiness of young ladies of the higher classes during those periods when, after completing their school education, they find no appropriate employment for their developed energies and affections. That restless longing for excitement, that craving for unattainable good, that morbid action of the imagination, that dissatisfaction with the world, that factitious interest in trifles, and those alternations of high excitement and brooding apathy—these are the secret history of many a gifted and highly-cultivated female mind.

Many a young woman of fine genius and elevated sentiment finds a charm in Byron's misanthropic repinings, because they so exactly picture her own experience—the experience, to a greater or less degree, of every well-developed mind which has no nobler object in life than that which ordinarily occupies the thoughts of most of our highly-educated young ladies.

JANE GRAY SWISSHELM VS. PARKER PILLSBURY

The following exchange between Jane Gray Swisshelm and Parker Pillsbury illustrates further the difficulties women activists encountered in building a coalition. Swisshelm, editor and publisher of one of the most influential anti-slavery newspapers, the *Saturday Visiter,* signed the "Call" to the convention and printed extensive excerpts from its proceedings, including the resolutions. Her initial editorial reaction, reprinted below, was positive, if not enthusiastic, but she did criticize the convention for tying together woman's rights with those of people of color. This called forth a defense of the convention from Parker Pillsbury, like Swisshelm a longtime abolitionist. Their dispute, in turn, led Swisshelm to a more detailed critique of mid-century reform in general and the woman's movement in particular.

Swisshelm disliked what she saw as the universalizing approach of her fellow reformers, their tendency to attempt to do everything at once rather than patiently take one step at a time. Pillsbury did not address this point, arguing instead the need for civil rights for persons of color. Parker Pillsbury was a prominent supporter of both abolition and woman's rights. In her 1870 History Paulina Wright Davis singled him out as a:

> name that well deserves not one page but many, for his good deeds and unselfish work. A man with a strong, vigorous mind, a quick conception of principle, and perfectly fearless in his advocacy of them, holding always his personality so in reserve as sometimes to be overlooked among the many more forthputting. Parker Pillsbury was for some time editor of the *National Anti-Slavery Standard,* and co-editor of the *Revolution.* His pen, wherever found, has always been sharpened against wrong and injustice, and has done for the Woman cause an incalculable amount of good. His editorials have been marked by an almost prophetic spirit; and the profoundness of their thought will be more justly appreciated as there is a larger development and a higher demand for unqualified justice.

Pillsbury's letter exemplifies the link many supporters of woman's rights saw between their cause and that of African Americans. In it he eloquently itemized the extent of segregation in the North in the years before the Civil War. The simple fact that Pillsbury had to defend the resolution from the criticisms of one as prominent and as devoted to both woman's rights and abolition as Swisshelm highlights the splits within the ranks of "Reformers" [the capitalization is Swisshelm's] and, more especially, within the ranks of feminists. Swisshelm maintained that she too supported that cause, but her insistence that the woman's movement should not be expected to confront the "American prejudice against color" foreshadowed the split in the movement in 1869 over the inclusion of the word "male" in the federal constitution.

The Saturday Visiter, November 2, 1850

THE WORCESTER CONVENTION.

We regret that the proceedings did not arrive in time for us to give them entire. The able address of the President, Mrs. Davis, is postponed [i.e., will be published in a subsequent issue], and also the last day's reports. As will be seen we copy from the New-York Tribune, and Mr. Greeley's general candor leads us to suppose this is as correct a report as will be likely to appear. This is a matter of some moment, as we learn some of the press employed reporters to report and caricature the proceedings. This bit of spleen is too silly to excite anger; and we could not help smiling at the following extract of a telegraphic report sent to our city [Pittsburgh]. We cut it from the Commercial Journal.

> Miss Elizabeth Wilson, of Ohio, put in a protest against the despotism of man, especially that despotism which makes the female sex inferior in point of intellect, when it is no such thing. She thought that Jenny Lind, in consenting to sing for the pleasure of these male tyrants, was violating every principle of female delicacy and propriety!
>
> Speeches and resolutions of a similar character were made and passed, and at 10 1/2 o'clock the convention adjourned to the following day.

This *Miss* Wilson is a married woman past the maredian [sic] of life, and of the most matronly appearance—a woman who has shown herself a match in logic for some of our able Bible commentators—the author of "A Scriptural view of Woman's rights and Duties." What a pretty *Miss* she must have appeared to our sage reporter! The report that speeches and resolutions were made or passed condemning Jenny Lind, is evidently a falsehood cut out of the whole cloth—the manufacture of some ninny who mistakes lying for wit.

We rejoice that Lucretia Mott was there. She is a woman, take her for all and all who has not her equal *as a woman* in this country. A wife, a mother and grandmother—a lady who moves in the first circles of the aristocratic city of brotherly love [Philadelphia]. She has ever been a *pattern* of the domestic virtues—her children have arisen to call her blessed, and her husband also he doth praise her, as well as the poor and needy, the trodden and oppressed to whom she has ever been an active and steadfast friend. It speaks well for the respect which gentlemen editors feel for women, and the domestic virtues of women, when they permit a *squirt* of a telegraphic reporter to bedabble with small wit and large impudence—to interlard with falsehoods and misrepresentations, the reports of any meeting dignified by the presence and active participation of such women.

• • •

At the time of writing we have only seen the first day's proceedings. These are all we could have wished except the introduction of the color question. The convention was not called to discuss the rights of color; and we think it was altogether irrelevant and unwise to introduce the question. We dislike very much the omnibus plan of action, and like Col. Benton we would contend to the last possible moment against any bundle of measures, even though we were in favor of every one taken separately and singly.[1] In a woman's rights convention the question of color had no right to a hearing. One thing at a time! Always do one thing at a time, and you will get along much faster than by attempting to do a dozen. The question of the

---

[1] A reference to Thomas Hart Benton, Senator from Missouri, who opposed the Compromise of 1850. The Compromise was an "omnibus" measure, one of whose provisions, the Fugitive Slave Law, was especially hateful to abolitionists like Swisshelm.

rights of colored men is already before the people. Let it work out its own salvation in its own strength. Many a man is in favor of emancipating every Southern slave, and granting the rights of citizenship to every free negro, who is by no means agreed that his wife or mother should stand on a political equality with himself. Many a man believes his wife and mother to be inferior to his boot-black, and many a woman ranks herself in the same scale. Then there are many of both sexes who are, or would be, anxious for the elevation of woman as such, who neverthe-less hate "the niggers" most sovereignly. Why mingle the two questions? For our part we would say no resolution should be passed at that convention that would not have been as acceptable to the citizens of Georgia as to those of Massachusetts.

We are pretty nearly out of patience with the dogged perseverance with which so many of our reformers persist in their at-tempts to do every thing at once. They re-mind us of the little fellow who bought a bunch of carrots to feed his pet rabbit. When he took them to the cage he found the bunch would not go through the aperture, but he pushed and struggled and crushed and thrust, then cried out in vexation, "I cannot get the carrots into the cage, father!"

"Of course not all at once, my son! Untie the string and put in one at a time!"

"But I want to put them all in, father!"

"Well, so you can if you do as I bid you."

Sammy sat and studied a moment! It was very clear that one carrot could pass the barrier, and that in time all might go through, but that was not his plan; so he continued:

"But while I put in one, the rest will be left out!"

"Very true; but if you do not put in one, all will be left out!"

"But I want them all in!" says Sammy, making a rather desparate [sic] thrust, "and none of 'em's got any right to be foremost!"

So Mr. Clay[2] was determined to thrust a bundle of bills through Congress, and for months he resisted, with desparation[sic], every effort to untie the string—he wanted 'em all in, and none of 'em had any right to be foremost; and now the Worcester Conven-tion is walking in the footsteps of this illustri-ous example. They, too, have made up a bundle, and we would advise them with all possible speed to untie the string. The sub-ject of woman's admission to the rights of citizenship is of sufficient importance to claim consideration as a separate measure. "One at a time! One at a time!" called Billy Smith when he was a Court-crier, and bidden to "call John Brown and Mary Brown" into court, and to call one at a time. We always liked Billy's plan of obeying orders, and very often follow his example, and call for one at a time. Then let us have the one that's called for. This convention was called to discuss Woman's rights, and if it had paid right good attention to its own business, it would have had work plenty.

---

[2] Henry Clay, Senator from Kentucky and original author of the Compromise of 1850.

WOMAN'S RIGHTS CONVENTION AND PEOPLE OF *COLOR*.

⟡⟡⟡

The North Star, December 5, 1850
[reprinted from the *Pittsburgh Visitor*]

Dear Mrs. Swisshelm: In the last *Visiter*, you say of a resolution relating to people of color, offered by Mr. Wendell Phillips in the late Convention of Women, at Worcester, Mass.

> "We are pretty nearly out of patience with the dogged perseverance with which so many of our Reformers persist in their attempt to do everything at once."

And again:

> "In a Woman's Rights Convention, the question of color had no right to a hearing."

It seemed as though the usually kindly spirit and good judgment of the *Visiter* were a little wanting in these two utterances. I should not have noticed it at all in most of the public journals—indeed, I neither know nor care what but a few of them do say; for I should no more think of having them in my house, political or religious, than I would of inoculating the family with the foulest leprosy that ever unjointed the bones of a son of Abraham. But your *Visiter* finds ready entrance and cheerful greeting, so that we are a little solicitous about its bearing. . . .

"*Dogged and perseverance*" are two ugly words standing together, and Mr. Phillips has ever been very watchful to prevent any other topic from creeping to whatever platform he occupied, devoted to any particular reform. And those two words look strange indeed to some of us, standing in connection with his name and the resolutions to which you have taken exception.

But by way of explanation, (or if you please, apology,) permit me to say that colored persons are held in such estimation in this country, that you must specify them whenever or wherever you mean to include them.

Lyceums, circuses, menageries, ball-rooms, billiard-rooms, conventions, everything, "the Public are respectfully invited to attend." But who ever dreamed that "the public" meant anything colored? From church and theatre; from stage-coach, steam-ship and creeping canal-boat; from the infant school, law school and theological seminary; from museum, athenæum and public garden, the colored race are either excluded altogether, or are admitted only by sufferance, or some very special arrangement, and under disadvantages to which no white person would or should submit for a moment.

Free Masons must be white—both face and apron. Odd Fellows, too, must be constitutionally light of skin; and even the Sons of Temperance, and Daughters likewise, must be bleached to the popular complexional standard, or they are beyond the reach of salvation.

The Methodist Discipline provides for "separate Colored Conferences." The Episcopal church shuts out some of its own most worthy ministers from clerical recognition, on account of their color. Nearly all denominations of religionists have either a written or unwritten law to the same effect. In Boston, even, there are Evangelical churches whose pews are positively forbidden by corporate mandate from being sold to any but "respectable white persons." Our incorporated cemeteries are often, if not always, deeded in the same manner. Even our humblest village grave yards generally have either a "negro corner," or refuse colored corpses altogether; and did our power extend to heaven or hell, we should have complexional salvation and colored damnation, unless we could first blot the unfortunate, unfashionable race altogether and forever out of existence.

We have striven to separate the Ethiopian from all claim to human recognition and human sympathy. Nobody but abolitionists ever mean colored people, no matter how often they speak of "the public," or of their "fellow citizens" or "fellow-sinners."

We have proscribed our colored brethren every way—everywhere; and under the late [recent] Fugitive Slave Law, every colored man is to be presumed a slave, unless there is proof positive to the contrary; and if any one is only claimed and sworn to as a slave, such proof is at once made impossible. Before this law was enacted, his life was a lingering torture—before, we were killing him by exclusion and oppression; now we are murdering him with fear. We have barbed the iron arrows that pierced him. We have poisoned the fangs which were already tearing him in pieces—we have heated red hot the chains that bound him as in adamant before. We have separated him from us by a gulf which has neither shore nor bottom. So far as human sympathy and regard are concerned, almost everywhere the horse and hound are as human as he.

And his race know it and feel it, as we cannot. Even the women's Convention demonstrated this, for scarcely a colored person, man or woman, appeared in it.

On the large committees appointed to carry out the plans of the Convention, embracing many persons in all, not a single colored member was placed. It is to be presumed that nobody thought of it, for we are not expected to think of colored people at all.

Under such circumstances, is it strange, is it an unpardonable sin, is it "dogged perseverance," to declare in a Convention called to demand and extend the rights of women, that we mean women of sable as well as sallow complexion? of the carved in ebony as well as the chisseled [sic] in ivory? If we did not thus mean, the Convention should not have been held, or being held, it would only deserve the scorn and contempt of every friend of God and his children. Color was not discussed there—it need not have been. But it was needed that the declaration be made in regard to it. That ANY women have rights, will scarcely be believed; but that colored women have rights, would never have been thought of, without a specific declaration.

Most truly yours,
Parker Pillsbury.
Concord, N.H., Nov. 18

The Saturday Visiter,
Nov. 23, 1850

"WOMAN'S RIGHTS" AND THE COLOR QUESTION.

We give [print] Mr. Pillsbury's article on this subject, and if we failed to prove the bad policy of linking these two questions, Mr. Pillsbury will surely succeed. Every thing he says about the exclusion of colored people from places and positions they have a right to occupy, is so much against uniting their cause to that of woman. The women of this glorious Republic are sufficiently oppressed without linking their cause to that of the slave. The slave is sufficiently oppressed without binding him to the stake which has ever held woman in a state of bondage. There is no kind of reason why the American prejudice against color should be invoked to sink woman into a lower degradation than that she already enjoys—no kind of reason why the car of emancipation, for the slave, should have been clogged by tying to its wheels the most unpopular reform that ever was broached, by having all the women in the world fastened to its axle as a drag.

• • •

... As to our applying the words "dogged perseverance" to any one in particular, we did not even notice by whom the objectionable resolution had been offered. We meant the Convention, and nearly all the reformers with whom we are acquainted; but if a personal application be thought necessary, we freely make it to Mr. Pillsbury himself. You, sir, show dogged perseverance in insisting that our starving seamstresses shall not strike for higher wages unless they put in a protest in favor of the boot-blacks—that woman shall not strike off her shackles until she can liberate every man that wears one—that she shall take no step forward until she overcomes a prejudice which oppresses another branch of humanity. You, Mr. Pillsbury, and the rest of your male coadjutors, enjoying all the rights for which women contend, have not been able to conquer the American prejudice against color, and now you expect that woman, crippled, helpless, bound, shall do what you have failed to perform with the free use of all your powers and faculties!

• • •

The question of woman's right to equal privileges with the other sex, is like a little boat launched upon a tempestuous river. It *may* carry woman into a safe harbor, but it is not strong enough to bear the additional weight of all the colored men in creation. True, they may get on board, if they covet the honor of the company already there; but the chance [risk] is the whole concern sinks. As an individual we have done all we felt able to aid the colored man. We would still lend him an oar or show him how to make one; but we do not want him in our boat. Let him row his own craft! He is as large and strong as a woman; and if we judge him rightly, he would prefer the exercise, and separate quarters, to getting into such very bad company. If he would not—if he is either so lazy or so selfish that he would peril the life of others for a poor chance of saving his own, he is not worth saving, and we would very colly [sic] cut the fingers off such a loafer, throw him back into the water and see him drown.

As for colored women, all the interest they have in this reform is *as women*. All it can do for them is to raise them to the level of men of their own class. Then as that class rises let them rise with it. We only claim for a white wood-sawyer's wife that she is as good as a white wood-sawyer—a blacksmith's mother is a good as a blacksmith—a lawyer's sister is a good as a lawyer; at least this is our way of understanding this question. . . . The call [to the Convention] was explicit. It was to discuss the rights of Sex. We signed that call . . . and had no thought it was to be converted into an abolition meeting. With quite as much propriety it might have been turned into a Temperance or Law-Reform meeting, or a meeting to express sympathy with the Hungarian refugees. . . . We feel as if our name had been used for a purpose for which we did not give it, and we know of other signers of that call who are in the same predicament. It was a breach of trust, and one we shall remember when our name is asked for to another call.

Harriet Taylor

When this essay first appeared in the *Westminster and Foreign Quarterly Review,* one of England's premier journals of political opinion, virtually everyone attributed it to John Stuart Mill. Mill, widely recognized as one of the most eminent British economists and philosophers, later credited the essay to his wife, Harriet Taylor. (See his letter to Paulina Wright Davis included in her *History*.) Similarly, he wrote that the views expressed in his subsequent book, *The Subjection of Women*, also derived from Taylor. In his *Autobiography* he went even further, claiming that Taylor was responsible for the key ideas in most of his work. Biographers and historians have long sought to trace the parameters of Taylor's influence upon Mill which clearly was both profound and exceedingly difficult to pin down. Most scholars, however, accept Mill's claim that Taylor wrote "Enfranchisement of Women."

The essay itself had a profound effect on both sides of the Atlantic, not least of all because of the attribution of its authorship to Mill. It gave the woman's rights movement a claim to intellectual respectability at a time when most commentators, when they deigned notice the arguments of movement spokespeople, only scoffed. It also directly affected the debate over woman's rights within the fledgling movement. The resolutions adopted at the 1851 national woman's rights convention, according to Wendell Phillips who introduced them, sought to embody the essay's central contentions.

"Enfranchisement of Women" also anticipated some of the arguments that would continue to divide advocates of woman's rights down to the present such as that between so-called "difference" feminists and "equality" feminists as the following quotation demonstrates:

> Like other popular movements . . . this may be seriously retarded by the blunders of its adherents. Tried by the ordinary standard of public meetings, the speeches at the [1850 Worcester] Convention are remarkable for the preponderance of the rational over the declamatory element; but there are some exceptions; and things to which it is impossible to attach any rational meaning, have found their way into the resolutions. Thus, the resolution which sets forth the claims made in behalf of women, after claiming equality in education, in industrial pursuits, and in political rights, enumerates as a fourth head of demand something under the name of "social and spiritual union," and "a medium of expressing the highest moral and spiritual views of justice," with other similar verbiage, serving only to mar the simplicity and rationality of the other demands: resembling those who would weakly attempt to combine nominal equality between men and women with enforced distinctions in their privileges and functions. What is wanted for women is equal rights, equal admission to all social privileges; not a position apart, a sort of sentimental priesthood. . . . The strength of the cause lies in the support of those who are influenced by reason and principle; and to attempt to recommend it by sentimentalities, absurd in reason, and inconsistent

with the principle on which the movement is founded, is to place a good cause on a level with a bad one.

At the 1870 "Twentieth Anniversary Convention," Elizabeth Cady Stanton, Lucretia Mott, Susan B. Anthony and others hailed this essay for establishing the intellectual credibility of their crusade.

[HARRIET TAYLOR],

"ENFRANCHISEMENT OF

WOMEN," REPRINTED FROM

THE WESTMINSTER AND

FOREIGN QUARTERLY REVIEW

FOR JULY 1851.

Most of our readers will probably learn from these pages [New-York Tribune, For Europe, October 29, 1850], for the first time, that there has arisen in the United States, and in the most enlightened and civilized portion of them, an organized agitation on a new question—new, not to thinkers, nor to any one by whom the principles of free and popular government are felt as well as acknowledged, but new, and even unheard of, as a subject for public meetings and practical political action. This question is, the enfranchisement of women; their admission, in law and in fact, to equality in all rights, political, civil and social, with the male citizens of the community.

It will add to the surprise with which many will receive this intelligence, that the agitation which has commenced is not a pleading by male writers and orators for women, those who are professedly to be benefitted remaining either indifferent or ostensibly hostile; it is a political movement, practical in its objects, carried on in a form which denotes an intention to preserve. And it is a movement not merely for women, but by them. Its first public manifestation appears to have been a Convention of Women, held in the State of Ohio, in the Spring of 1850. Of this meeting we have seen no report. On the 23rd and 24th of October last, a succession of public meetings was held at Worcester, in Massachusetts, under the name of a

"Women's [sic] Rights Convention, of which the President was a woman [Paulina Wright Davis], and nearly all the chief speakers women; numerously reinforced, however, by men among whom were some of the most distinguished leaders in the kindred cause of negro emancipation. A general, and four special committees were nominated, for the purpose of carrying on the undertaking until the next annual meeting.

• • •

. . . In regard to the quality of the speaking, the proceedings bear an advantageous comparison with those of any popular movement with which we are acquainted, either in this country or in America. Very rarely, in the oratory of public meetings, is the part of verbiage and declamation so small, that of calm good sense and reason so considerable. The result of the Convention was, in every respect, encouraging to those by whom it was summoned; and it is probably destined to inaugurate one of the most important of the movements towards political and social reform, which are the best characteristics of the present age.

That the promoters of this new agitation take their stand on principles, and do not fear to declare these in their widest extent, without time serving or compromise, will be seen from the resolutions adopted by the Convention. . . .

It would be difficult to put so much true, just, and reasonable meaning into a style so little calculated to recommend it as that of some of the resolutions. But whatever objection may be made to some of the expressions, none, in our opinion, can be made to the demands themselves. As a question of justice, the case seems to us too clear for dispute. As one of expediency, the more thoroughly it is examined the stronger it will appear.

• • •

. . . After a struggle which, by many of its incidents, deserves the name heroic, the abolitionists are now so strong in numbers and influence, that they hold the balance of parties in the United States. It was fitting that the men whose names will remain associated with the extirpation, from the democratic soil of America, of the aristocracy of color, should be among the originators, for America and for the rest of the world, of the first collective protest against the aristocracy of sex; a distinction as accidental as that of color, and fully as irrelevant to all questions of government.

• • •

. . . While, far from being expedient, we are firmly convinced that the division of mankind into two castes, one born to rule over the other, is in this case, as in all cases, an unqualified mischief; a source of perversion and demoralization, both to the favored class, and to those at whose expense they are favored; producing none of the good which it is the custom to ascribe to it, and forming a bar, almost insuperable while it lasts, to any really vital improvement, either in the character or in the social condition of the human race.

• • •

. . . Throughout history, the nations, races, classes, which found themselves the strongest, either in muscles, in riches, or in military discipline, have conquered and held in subjection the rest. If, even in the most improved nations, the law of the sword is at last discountenanced as unworthy, it is only since the calumniated eighteenth century.[1] Wars of conquest have only ceased since democratic revolutions began. The world is very young, and has only just begun to cast off injustice.

It is only now getting rid of negro slavery. It is only now getting rid of monarchial despotism. It is only now getting rid of hereditary feudal nobility. It is only now getting rid of disabilities on the grounds of religion.[2] It is only beginning to treat any *men* as citizens, except the rich and a favored portion of the middle class.[3] Can we wonder that it has not yet done as much for women? As society was constituted until the last few generations, inequality was its very basis; association grounded on equal rights scarcely existed; to be equals was to be enemies; two persons could hardly cooperate in anything, or meet in any amicable relation, without the law's appointing that one of them should be the superior of the other. Mankind have outgrown this state, and all things now tend to substitute, as the general principle of human relations, a just equality, instead of the dominion of the strongest. But of all relations, that between men and women being the nearest and most intimate, and connected with the greatest number of strong emotions, was sure to be the last to throw off the old rule and receive the new; for in proportion to the strength of a feeling, is the tenacity with which it clings to the forms and circumstances with which it has even accidentally become associated.

When a prejudice, which has any hold on the feelings, finds itself reduced to the unpleasant necessity of assigning reasons, it thinks it has done enough when it has reasserted the very point in dispute, in phrases with appeal to the pre-existing feeling. Thus, many persons think they have sufficiently justified the restrictions on women's field of action, when they have said that the pursuits from which women are excluded are *unfeminine*, and that the *proper sphere* of women is not politics or publicity, but private and domestic life.

• • •

---

[1] The reference is to the American and French Revolutions.
[2] A reference to the Catholic Emancipation Act of 1832 by which Parliament extended limited freedom of religion to Catholics and repealed the provisions barring them from holding public office.
[3] In 1833 Parliament passed a Reform Bill which extended the franchise to males who met a specified property qualification.

Concerning the fitness, then, of women for politics, there can be no question: but the dispute is more likely to turn upon the fitness of politics for women. When the reasons alleged for excluding women from active life in all its higher departments, are stripped of their garb of declamatory phrases, and reduced to the simple expression of meaning, they seem to be mainly three: the incompatibility of active life with maternity, and the cares of a household; secondly, its alleged hardening effect on the character; and thirdly, the inexpediency of making an addition to the already excessive pressure of competition in every kind of professional or lucrative employment.

The first, the maternity argument, is usually laid most stress upon: although (it needs hardly be said) this reason, if it be one, can apply only to mothers. It is neither necessary nor just to make imperative on women that they shall be either mothers or nothing; or that if they have been mothers once, they shall be nothing else during the whole remainder of their lives.

● ● ●

... There is no inherent reason or necessity that all women should voluntarily choose to devote their lives to one animal function and its consequences. Numbers of women are wives and mothers only because there is no other career open to them, no other occupation for their feelings or their activities. Every improvement in their education and enlargement of their faculties— everything which renders them more qualified for any other mode of life, increases the number of those to whom it is an injury and an oppression to be denied the choice.

● ● ●

But secondly, it is urged, that to give the same freedom of occupation to women as to men, would be an injurious addition to the crowd of competitors, by whom the avenues to almost all kinds of employment are choked up, and its remuneration depressed. This argument, it is to be observed, does not reach the political question. It gives no excuse for withholding from women the rights of citizenship. ... Even if every woman, as matters now stand, had a claim on some man for support, how infinitely preferable is it that part of the income should be of the woman's earning, even if the aggregate sum were but little increased by it, rather than that she should be compelled to stand aside in order that men may be the sole earners, and the sole dispensers of what is earned.

● ● ●

The third objection to the admission of women to political or professional life, its alleged hardening tendency, belongs to an age now past, and is scarcely to be comprehended by people of the present time. There are still, however, persons who say that the world and its avocations render men selfish and unfeeling; that the struggles, rivalries and collisions of business and of politics make them harsh and unamiable; that if half the species must unavoidably be given up to these things, it is the more necessary that the other half should be kept free from them; that to preserve women from the bad influences of the world, is the only chance of preventing men from being wholly given up to them.

● ● ●

... In the present condition of human life, we do not know where those hardening influences are to be found, to which men are subject, and from which women are at present exempt. Individuals now-a-days are seldom called upon to fight hand to hand, even with peaceful weapons; personal enmities and rivalries count for little in worldly transactions; the general pressure of circumstances, not the adverse will of individuals, is the obstacle men now have to make head against. That pressure, when excessive, breaks the spirit, and cramps and sours the feelings, but not less of women than of men, since they suffer certainly not less from its evils.

● ● ●

But, in truth, none of these arguments and considerations touch the foundations of the subject. The real question is, whether it is right and expedient that one-half of the human race should pass through life in a state of forced subordination to the other half. ...

When, however, we ask why the existence of one-half the species should be merely ancillary to that of the other—why each woman should be a mere appendage to a man, allowed to have no interests of her own, that there may be nothing to compete in her mind with his interests and his pleasure; the only reason which can be given is, that men like it. It is agreeable to them that men should live for their own sake, women for the sake of men; and the qualities and conduct in subjects which are agreeable to rulers, they succeed for a long time in making the subjects themselves consider as their appropriate virtues.

• • •

... Our argument here brings us into collision with what may be termed the moderate reformers of the education of women; a sort of persons who cross the path of improvement on all great questions; those who would maintain the old bad principles, mitigating their consequences. These say, that women should be, not slaves, nor servants, but companions; and educated for that office; (they do not say that men should be educated to be the companions of women). But since uncultivated women are not suitable companions for cultivated men, and a man who feels interest in things above and beyond the family circle, wishes that his companion should sympathize with him in that interest; they therefore say, let women improve their understanding and taste, acquire general knowledge, cultivate poetry, art, even coquet with science, and some stretch their liberality so far as to say, inform themselves on politics; not as pursuits, but sufficiently to feel an interest in the subjects, and to be capable of holding a conversation on them with the husband, or at least of understanding and imbibing his wisdom. Very agreeable to him, no doubt, but unfortunately the reverse of improving. . . . The modern, and what are regarded as the improved and enlightened modes of education of women, abjure, as far as words go, an education of mere show, and profess to aim at solid instruction, but mean by that expression, superficial information on

solid subjects. Except accomplishments,[4] which are now generally regarded as to be taught well, if taught at all, nothing is taught to women thoroughly. Small portions only of what is attempted to teach thoroughly to boys, are the whole of what it is intended or desired to teach to women. What makes intelligent beings is the power of thought; the stimuli which call forth that power are the interest and dignity of thought itself, and a field for its practical application. Both motives are cut off from those who are told from infancy that thought, and all its greater applications, are other people's business, while theirs is to make themselves agreeable to other people. High mental powers in women will be but an exceptional accident, until every career is open to them, and until they, as well as men, are educated for themselves and for the world—not one sex for the other.

• • •

The common opinion is, that whatever may be the case with the intellectual, the moral influence of women over men is almost always salutary. It is, we are often told, the great counteractive of selfishness. However the case may be as to personal influence, the influence of the position tends eminently to selfishness. The most insignificant of men, the man who can obtain influence or consideration nowhere else, finds one place where he is chief and head. There is one person, often greatly his superior in understanding, who is obliged to consult him, and whom he is not obliged to consult. He is judge, magistrate, ruler, over their joint concerns; arbiter of all differences between them. . . . The generous mind, in such a situation, makes the balance incline against his own side. . . . But how is it when average men are invested with this power, without reciprocity and without responsibility? Give such a man the idea that he is first in law and in opinion—that to will is his part, and hers to submit; it is absurd to suppose that this idea merely glides over his mind, without sinking in, or having any effect on his feelings and practice. . . . If there is any self-will in the man, he becomes either the conscious or

---

[4] A reference to the teaching of subjects such as drawing and music in schools for women.

unconscious despot of his household. The wife, indeed, often succeeds in gaining her objects, but it is by some of the many various forms of indirectness and management.

Thus the position is corrupting equally to both; in the one it produces the vices of power, in the other those of artifice. Women, in their present physical and moral state, having stronger impulses, would naturally be franker and more direct than men; yet all the old saws and traditions represent them as artful and dissembling. Why? Because their only way to their objects is by indirect paths. In all countries where women have strong wishes and active minds, this consequence is inevitable; and if it is less conspicuous in England than in some other places, it is because English women, saving occasional exceptions, have ceased to have either strong wishes or active minds.

• • •

... In the United States at least, there are women, seemingly numerous, and now organized for action on the public mind, who demand equality in the fullest acceptation [sic] of that word, and demand it by a straight-forward appeal to men's sense of justice, not plead for it with a timid deprecation of their displeasure.

Like other popular movements, however, this may be seriously retarded by the blunders of its adherents. Tried by the ordinary standard of public meetings, the speeches at the Convention are remarkable for the preponderance of the rational over the declamatory element; but there are some exceptions; and things to which it is impossible to attach any rational meaning, have found their way into the resolutions. Thus, the resolution which sets forth the claims made in behalf of women, after claiming equality in education, in industrial pursuits, and in political rights, enumerates as a fourth head of demand something under the name of "social and spiritual union," and "a medium of expressing the highest moral and spiritual views of justice," with other similar verbiage, serving only to mar the simplicity and rationality of the other demands: resembling those who would weakly attempt to combine nominal equality between men and women with enforced distinctions in their privileges and functions. What is wanted for women is equal rights, equal admission to all social privileges; not a position apart, a sort of sentimental priesthood.... The strength of the cause lies in the support of those who are influenced by reason and principle; and to attempt to recommend it by sentimentalities, absurd in reason, and inconsistent with the principle on which the movement is founded, is to place a good cause on a level with a bad one.

There are indications that the example of America will be followed on this side of the Atlantic; and the first step has been taken in that part of England where every serious movement in the direction of political progress has its commencement—the manufacturing districts of the North. On the 13 of February, 1851, a petition of women, agreed to by a public meeting at Sheffield, and claiming the elective franchise, was presented to the House of Lords by the Earl of Carlisle.

Woman's Rights Tracts, ... No. 4 (Syracuse, 1852 or 1853) as excerpted.

Commonwealth of Massachusetts

One of the immediate outcomes of the 1850 and 1851 conventions was a petition campaign to strike the word "male" from the Massachusetts state constitution. The legislative committee charged with investigating the issue turned to the alleged indifference of the majority of women to justify their refusal. It was an argument anticipated in the convention by Abby Kelley Foster, among others. Ask one of Henry Clay's slaves, in his master's presence, if he had any desire for freedom, she objected when Wendell Phillips tried to argue that the greatest obstacle to the reform would prove to be the opposition of women. The slave will profess the greatest contentment with his situation. But who would believe him? The legislative committee explicitly rejected her reasoning. The fact that only a minority of women were demanding suffrage did prove, they contended, that the majority were content with existing arrangements. Silence was consent.

In Convention, July 1, 1853.

The Committee on Qualifications of Voters, to whom was referred the petitions of Francis Jackson and others, that the word "male" may be stricken from the Constitution, and also of Abby B. Alcott and other women of Massachusetts, that they may be allowed to vote on the amendments that may be made to the Constitution, Report:

That the petitioners have leave to withdraw.

The Committee feel that in making this report, they should not do justice to themselves or to the intelligent and respectable petitioners, if they did not frankly state the reasons on which their conclusion is founded.

The petitioners ask that women may be allowed the right of suffrage, in matters pertaining to political affairs. The request is a novel one, and so far as known to the Committee, the first ever presented to any government or other political organization.

At the request of the petitioners, a hearing was granted them at two different sittings of the Committee, and patient attention given to the arguments presented by persons of learning and ability of both sexes, who appeared in their behalf. These persons maintained the following propositions:

1. That women are human beings, and therefore have human rights, one of which, is, that of having a voice in the government under which they live, and in the enactment of laws they are bound to obey.

2. That women have interests and rights, which are not, in fact, and never will be, sufficiently guarded by governments in which they are not allowed any political influence.
3. That they are taxed, and therefore, since taxation and the right of representation are admitted to be inseparable, they have a right to be represented.
4. That so far as education and general intelligence are concerned, they are as well qualified to exercise the elective franchise, as many who now enjoy that right.
5. That in mental capacity and moral endowments, they are not inferior to many who now participate in the affairs of government.
6. That there is nothing in their peculiar position, or appropriate duties, which prevents them from taking a part in political affairs.

Of the truth or fallacy of these several positions, the Committee do not feel called upon to decide.

All questions involving the rights and interests of any part of the human family, should ever be determined by some well established and generally recognized principle or fundamental maxim of government; otherwise it cannot be expected that such decision will be regarded as reasonable or satisfactory.

Upon what principle, then, shall the present question be decided?

The Declaration of Independence asserts, that "all governments derive their just powers from the consent of the governed." By the "consent of the governed," the Committee understand the consent, either express or implied, of the persons concerned. At the present time, there are, within the State of Massachusetts, not far from 200,000 women, over twenty-one years of age. Of these, less than 2,000 have asked to be admitted to the right of suffrage. From this fact, the Committee have a right to infer, and also from their personal knowledge of the views and feelings of the class of persons referred to, that a great majority of the women of Massachusetts, do willingly consent that the government of the State should be, as it hitherto has been, in the hands of their fathers, husbands, brothers and sons. Of the correctness of this conclusion, the Committee entertain no doubts.

It may be said, in reply to this, that it cannot be justly inferred from the silence of the women of Massachusetts, that they do consent to the present limitations of the right of suffrage. But the Committee do so infer, because they know that the women aforesaid, do now, and always have, enjoyed the right of petition, to the fullest extent, and have often exercised that right in behalf of the unfortunate and oppressed, and in aid of many noble and philanthropic objects of legislation. In one case, it is believed, that more than 50,000 women petitioned the General Court, for the enactment of a law for the suppression of the sale of intoxicating drinks.

It may be further urged, that by the same course of reasoning, it might be shown that those who are held in bondage, consent to the laws under which they live. But this is not true. Slaves have no right of petition. They cannot make known their wants to the government. They are speechless and helpless. Their whole existence is a stern and living protest against the wrongs they suffer, and they are kept in subjection only by the strong arm of power.

In view of these indisputable facts in relation to the right of petition, in this Commonwealth, enjoyed by all its inhabitants of both sexes, the Committee feel justified in deciding that a vast proportion of the women of Massachusetts do consent to their political condition, and therefore, that the powers exercised by the government of this Commonwealth, over that class of its population, are "just powers," and it is inexpedient for this Convention to take any action in relation thereto.

Amasa Walker, *Chairman.*

EPILOGUE

However slow the progress of the woman's rights movement proved, the issues its proponents raised rapidly moved into the mainstream of American popular culture. Nowhere is this more evident, or more fraught with consequence, than in the way Northerners used images associated with the movement to portray secession and, later, the Reconstruction of the South. The anonymous poem, "A Fast Lady of State," is a good example. Many southern states, like Virginia, Georgia, and the Carolinas, had women's names; others, like Louisiana or Flo(rida), were easily transposed or, in the cases of Mississippi and Missouri, abbreviated to Miss. So it was a small step to use the rhetoric of the woman's rights movement to picture South Carolina as a rebellious young woman throwing off the authority of that patriarch, Uncle Sam or, in a slightly earlier incarnation, Brother Jonathan, as in "Brother Jonathan's Lament for Sister Caroline" by Oliver Wendell Holmes, Sr.

An early and imaginative appropriation of this trope was a cartoon showing Abraham Lincoln as an exasperated schoolmistress trying to make Caroline spell "constitution" correctly. "Se-con-ces-sti-consti-si-tu-constitu-on-constitution" she replies. "Caroline, you are the worst brat in the whole school," Lincoln snaps, adding, "if you don't mend your ways, I'll try what effect stripes will have." "Don't spell it any other way," a second pupil interjects, promising that "Miss Sippy, Miss Souri, Louisa Anna and all of us will back you up."

Reconstruction lent itself to a similar iconography. In "A Precious Fix for a Boss," President Andrew Johnson informs Miss Alabama and her sisters that she will have to take up the matter of finding accommodations in the U.S. Hotel with the clerks, that is, with the Republican Congress which had wrested control of policy from him. "Naughty Andy" shows the president as a bad boy urging the South, his "Sis," to refuse to take her medicine. This particular cartoon is especially interesting since it also employs "Columbia," a traditional female symbol of the United States. "Don't be a bad boy, Andy," she informs Johnson. "Dr. Congress knows what is best for Sissy." In "May Be, or May Not Be" the North is Uncle Sam and the South his now contrite wife. He will consent to a "reunion," he tells her, but only if she breaks all contact with her "mother," slavery.

"The Great Event of the Age. The Union of North and South," a pro-Johnson cartoon, offers a fascinating variant on this theme. Here the bride is the North and the groom, his presidential pardon resting in his hat, the South. Parson Johnson pronounces the blessing as Democratic party editors James Gordon Bennett of the New York *Herald* and Henry Raymond of the New York *Times* warn off "foreign rowdies" and Uncle Sam urges the southern "gals" still outside the union to have a little patience. "I'll let you in directly," he promises. Republican cartoons favored Congress in its struggles with Johnson. In them the South is invariably female. And the message is always the necessity for her, as daughter, sister, or wife, to learn obedience.

If the use of woman's rights imagery to portray the South reinforced the view of those who thought women's independence would rend the basic fabric of society, the exigencies of war led to more positive appropriations of the woman's rights agenda. Consider the cartoon series

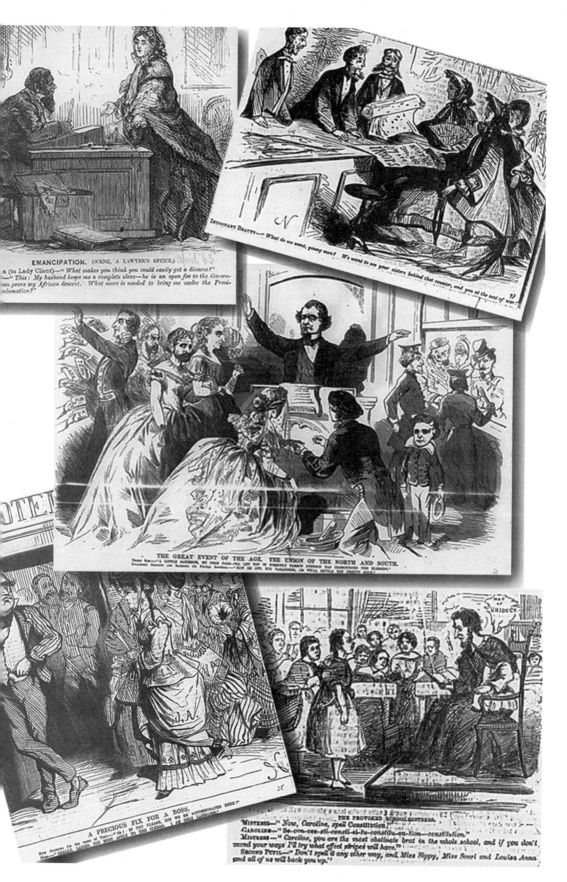

EMANCIPATION. (SCENE, A LAWYER'S OFFICE.)

R (to Lady Client)—"*What makes you think you could easily get a divorce?*"

—"*This: My husband keeps me a complete slave—he is an open foe to the Government—prove my African descent. What more is needed to bring me under the Presidential Proclamation?*"

INDIGNANT BEAUTY—"*What do we want, young man? We want to see your sisters behind that counter, and you at the seat of war——*"

THE GREAT EVENT OF THE AGE, THE UNION OF THE NORTH AND SOUTH.

A PRECIOUS FIX FOR A BOSS.

THE PROVOKED SCHOOLMISTRESS.

MISTRESS—"*Now, Caroline, spell Constitution!*"

CAROLINE—"*So-con-cee-sti-consti-si-tu-consti-tu-tion—constitution.*"

MISTRESS—"*Caroline, you are the most obstinate brat in the whole school, and if you don't mend your ways I'll try what effect stripes will have.*"

SECOND PUPIL—"*Don't spell it any other way, and Miss Sippy, Miss Souri and Louisa Anna and all of us will back you up.*"

prompted by the first draft law. Women could take care of the sick, thus enabling physicians to enlist in the Union Army. Just as speakers at the Worcester Convention had demanded, women could certainly hold down positions as clerks in stores. That way, as the "indignant beauty" tells the "young men" who inquire what she wants, they can go off to the front and their sisters can wait on customers.

"Emancipation" shows the extent to which the analogy between the situation of women and slaves, long insisted upon by woman's rights advocates, had entered into the popular culture. "What makes you think you can easily get a divorce?" the lawyer asks. "This," his client replies: "My husband keeps me as a complete slave—he is an open foe of the government—I can prove my African descent. What more is needed to bring me under the Presidential Proclamation?"

Not all of the uses of female imagery comported so well with the demands of the new movement, as one cartoon, "How to Get Recruits," with its protrayal of young women offering a kiss to each volunteer, demonstrates. And what are we to make of the "Patriotic Young Lady" whose devotion to the soldiers at the front causes her to shorten her skirts? Or of the "Resistless Breastworks—Forelorn Hope" with its suggestion that Southern belles would, Circe-like, seek to seduce the Union troops and thus stave off the inevitable defeat? Much Civil War iconography employed precisely the sorts of stereotypes of women as "dolls" that Ernestine Rose and other early woman's rights activists sought to discredit.

The overall impact of secession, war, and reconstruction on the prospects of the woman's movement was clearly mixed. Labor shortages enabled women to play new roles, some of which—particularly nursing—would remain open to them once the sectional crisis was over. The use of imagery associated with woman's rights to describe secession, on the other hand, had a powerfully negative impact.

A FAST LADY OF STATE*

I will not live with Uncle Sam!
I'll give the door behind a slam,
And let the world know who I am!

I've always felt a palsying shame,
That I, a bold imperial dame,
Should be compelled to live so tame.

He tells me that I can't secede,
Nor revolutionize. Indeed!
I trample under foot the creed!

A clement queen he knows I am;
I bore the crimes of Uncle Sam,
Until he proved a hopeless sham.

But now his stubborn bearing calls
For blows convincing, till he bawls,
And cries "Enough!" and overhauls

His hateful acts of forty years;
And then, with penitential tears,
Admits my right to box his ears.

My Uncle stares and calls me "fast"
And let him stare! He finds, at last,
My days of compromise are past.

The Yankees said I would not dare
To consummate the "dreadful scare;"
But now they whisper, "Oh, forbear!"

Their hair, affrighted, stands on end,
To see me bristle and defend
My rights, without a single bend.

But I will grant no peace until
Myself and *boys*—By Congress Bill—
Can go just when and where we will.

---

*Unidentified clipping in Civil War Caricatures folder, American Antiquarian Society.

I'm out of patience!—that I am!
I'll give the door a stunning slam,
And smash the face of Uncle Sam!

BROTHER JONATHAN'S LAMENT FOR SISTER CAROLINE (MARCH 25, 1861)

Oliver Wendell Holmes, Sr.

She has gone—she has left us in passion and pride,—
Our stormy-browed sister, so long at our side!
She has torn her own star from our firmament's glow,
And turned on her brother the face of a foe!

O Caroline, Caroline, child of the sun,
We can never forget that our hearts have been one,—
Our foreheads both sprinkled in Liberty's name,
From the fountain of blood with the finger of flame!

You were always too ready to fire at a touch;
But we said: "She is hasty,—she does not mean much."
We have scowled when you uttered some turbulent threat;
But Friendship still whispered: "Forgive and forget!"

Has our love all died out? Have its altars grown cold?
Has the curse come at last which the fathers foretold?
Then Nature must teach us the strength of the chain
That her petulant children would sever in vain.

They may fight till the buzzards are gorged with their spoil,—
Till the harvest grows black as it rots in the soil,
Till the wolves and the catamounts troop from their caves,
And the shark tracks the pirate, the lord of the waves:

In vain is the strife! When its fury is past,
Their fortunes must flow in one channel at last,
As the torrents that rush from the mountains of snow
Roll mingled in peace through the valleys below.

BROTHER JONATHAN'S LAMENT FOR SISTER CAROLINE (MARCH 25, 1861)

Our Union is river, lake, ocean, and sky;
Man breaks not the medal when God cuts the die!
Though darkened with sulfur, though cloven with steel,
The blue arch will brighten, the waters will heal!

O Caroline, Caroline, child of the sun,
There are battles with Fate that can never be won!
The star-flowering banner must never be furled.
For its blossoms of light are the hope of the world!

Go, then, our rash sister! afar and aloof,—
Run wild in the sunshine away from our roof;
But when your heart aches and your feet have grown sore,
Remember the pathway that leads to our door!

Guide to Further Research

Overviews

For overviews of the culture of antebellum America, several works are especially helpful. The first is Alice Felt Tyler's classic *Freedom's Ferment* (Minneapolis, MN, 1944). A second is Robert H. Wiebe's underappreciated *The Opening of American Society: From the Adoption of the Constitution to the Eve of Disunion* (New York, 1985). Most useful of all, perhaps, are Robert H. Abzug, *Cosmos Crumbling: American Reform and the Religious Imagination* (New York, 1994), and David S. Reynolds, *Walt Whitman's America: A Cultural Biography* (New York, 1995).

The Woman's Rights Movement

Serious scholarship on the woman's rights movement began with Eleanor Flexner's *Century of Struggle: The Women's Rights Movement in the United States* (Cambridge, MA, 1959). A useful analysis of Flexner's influence upon subsequent studies is Ellen Carol DuBois, "Eleanor Flexner and the History of American Feminism," *Gender & History* (1991) 3: 81–90. DuBois has written several standard accounts of the origins of the movement, including *Feminism and Suffrage: The Emergence of an Independent Women's Movement in America, 1848–1869* (Ithaca, NY, 1978, 1993) and *Woman Suffrage and Women's Rights* (New York, 1998). A recent brief survey is Sylvia D. Hoffert, *When Hens Crow: The Woman's Rights Movement in Antebellum America* (Bloomington, IN, 1995).

Like Flexner, DuBois generally follows the paradigm established by Elizabeth Cady Stanton and Susan B. Anthony in their *History of Woman Suffrage* (co-edited by Mathilda Josyln Gage and Ida Husted Harper), initially published in New York, 1881–1922. Stanton, Anthony, and their collaborators relied chiefly upon their own records and memories. So their account naturally emphasized those events in which they were personally involved. It is an emphasis subsequent historians of the movement have followed. As a result, one can find studies such as Joseph E. Ryan, "Prelude to Seneca Falls: An Analysis of Elizabeth Cady Stanton Prior to the Convention," *New England Journal of History* (1995) 52: 21–27 or Jeanne Stevenson-Moessner, "Elizabeth Cady Stanton, Reformer to Revolutionary: A Theological Trajectory," *Journal of the American Academy of Religion* (1994), 62: 673–697 or Judith Wellman, "The Seneca Falls Women's Rights Convention: A Study of Social Networks," *Journal of Women's History* (1991) 3: 9–37. Perhaps the most useful of all of these, because of its comparative perspective and sophisticated use of the notion of "political culture," is Kathryn Kish Sklar, "'Women Who Speak for an Entire Nation': American and British Women at the World Anti-Slavery Convention, London, 1840," in Jean Fagan Yellin and John C. Van Horne, eds., *Abolitionist Sisterhood: Women's Political Culture in Antebellum America* (Ithaca and London, 1994). It is impossible to find comparable studies of Paulina Wright Davis or Lucy Stone.

Since Anthony did not become active until 1852 or so and since Stanton spent much of the 1850s mothering her large family, scholars who follow the lead of their *History* pay little heed to the early conventions, of which the one in Worcester in 1850 is the most significant. This has meant that, even though it was a commonplace among the first generation of woman's rights activists that their movement began with the 1850 gathering, historians have not studied it or the other early conventions. Instead, those who have looked beyond Stanton and Anthony's *History* for the beginnings of the movement have looked to women's roles in benevolent or charitable associations and other reforms, especially temperance and anti-prostitution. An important work in this historiographical tradition is Keith Melder, *Beginnings of Sisterhood: The American Women's Rights Movement, 1800–1850* (New York, 1977). Also important is Barbara J. Berg, *The Remembered Gate: Origins of American Feminism, The Woman and the City, 1800–1860* (New York, 1978). Ann M. Boylan, "Women in Groups: An Analysis of Women's Benevolent Organizations in New York and Boston, 1797–1840," *Journal of American History* (1984), 71: 497–523, and "Timid Girls, Venerable Widows, and Dignified Matrons: Life Cycle Patterns Among Organized Women in New York and Boston, 1797–1840," *American Quarterly* (1986), 38: 779–797, are important case studies.

Biographical Studies of Individuals

The most conspicuous exception to the rule that early leaders of the woman's rights movement receive scholarly attention roughly in proportion to their prominence in Stanton and Anthony's *History* is Sojourner Truth. There are several editions of her autobiography (written by Olive Gilbert—Truth could neither read nor write) in print, including Penguin's *Narrative of Sojourner Truth: A Bondswoman of Olden Time, with a History of Her Labors and Correspondence Drawn from her Book of Life; also, A Memorial Chapter* (New York, 1998). There is also Nell Painter's heralded biography, *Sojourner Truth: A Life, a Symbol* (New York, 1996). Painter discusses the challenges of writing Truth's life in "Sojourner Truth in Life and Memory: Writing the Biography of an American Exotic," *Gender & History* (1990), 2:3–16.

Another important exception is Margaret Fuller whom, had she lived, Paulina Wright Davis intended to ask to preside over the Worcester Convention. An excellent recent study is Eve Kornfeld, *Margaret Fuller: A Brief Biography with Documents* (Boston, 1997). A fuller treatment is Charles Capper, *Margaret Fuller: An American Romantic Life* (New York, 1992), vol. 1: *The Private Years*. One can also consult Capper, "Margaret Fuller as a Cultural Reformer: The Conversations in Boston," *American Quarterly* (1987), 39:509–528. Also interesting is Sandra M. Gustafson, "Choosing a Medium: Margaret Fuller and the Forms of Sentiment," *American Quarterly* (1995), 47:34–65. On the general subject of the links between the woman's rights movement and spiritualism, see Ann Braude, *Radical Spirits: Spiritualism and Women's Rights in Nineteenth-Century America* (Boston, 1989).

Sklar's work (see above, under The Woman's Rights Movement) helps reclaim Lucretia Mott as the most important early leader of the woman's rights movement, a position that Stanton, for one, always insisted she held. Also helpful in this regard is Nancy A. Hewitt, "Feminist Friends: Agrarian Quakers and the Emergence of Woman's Rights in America," *Feminist Studies* (1986) 12:27–50. Hewitt highlights the key roles Quaker women, like Mott, played in the early movement. An earlier essay is Dana Greene, "Quaker Feminism: The Case of Lucretia Mott," *Pennsylvania History* (1981) 48:143–154. Quakers also provided much of the leadership, and rank and file, of the abolitionist movement. And, as Eleanor Flexner long ago pointed out, the connections between the woman's rights movement and abolitionism were many and profound. A helpful study is Kristin Hoganson, "Garrisonian Abolitionists and the Rhetoric of Gender, 1850–1860," *American Quarterly* (1993) 45:558–595. For an earlier period, see Lori D. Ginzberg, "'The Hearts of Your Readers Will Shudder': Fanny Wright, Infidelity, and American Freethought," *American Quarterly* (1994), 46:195–226.

Connections with Other Reform Movements

Garrisonian abolitionists broke with the more moderate wing of the antislavery movement on the eve of the World Anti-Slavery Convention in London in 1840 over the issue of what roles women might take in the crusade. The Garrisonians encouraged women like Abby Kelley Foster to become itinerant lecturers in the cause, even when this involved speaking before audiences of both men and women. Men willing to support this kind of female activism risked having their own masculinity challenged in the popular press, as Stacey M. Robertson notes in "'Aunt Nancy Men': Parker Pillsbury, Masculinity, and Women's Rights in the Nineteenth-Century United States," *American Studies* (1996), 37:33–60. Susan Zaeske looks at "The 'Promiscuous Audience' Controversy and the Emergence of the Early Woman's Rights Movement," *Quarterly Journal of Speech* (1995) 81:191 207. Dorothy Sterling's *Ahead of Her Time: Abby Kelley and the Politics of Anti-Slavery* (New York, 1991, 1994) stresses the importance of "women find[ing] their voices." Also helpful is Joel Bernard, "Authority, Autonomy, and Radical Commitment: Stephen and Abby Kelley Foster," *Proceedings of the American Antiquarian Society* (1980), 90:347–386.

Another important link is between woman's rights and temperance. A good introduction is Ian R. Tyrrell, "Women and Temperance in Antebellum America, 1830–1860," *Civil War History* (1982), 28:128–152. Many temperance reformers were NOT woman's rights activists, but it would be virtually impossible to find a woman's rights advocate who was not in favor of temperance reform in the nineteenth century. This was so for several reasons but the most important, perhaps, was the connection women saw between drinking and domestic abuse. Women, as the early advocates of woman's rights kept insisting, had virtually no legal protection against an abusive spouse or parent. So the campaign for woman's rights and for temperance ran along parallel tracks right up to the passage of the Eighteenth (women's suffrage) and Nineteenth (prohibition) Amendments after World War I.

Legal Reform and Other Woman's Rights Struggles

A good place to begin an analysis of the campaign for legal reform is Ellen Carol DuBois, "Outgrowing the Compact of the Fathers: Equal Rights, Woman Suffrage, and the United States Constitution, 1820–1878," *Journal of American History* (1987), 74:836–862. Some of the most important of these rights involved holding property independently of husbands or fathers. Several useful overviews are: Marylynn Salmon, "The Legal Status of Women in Early America: A Reappraisal," *Law and History Review* (1983), 1:129–151; Emily F. VanTassel, "Women, Property, and Politics in Nineteenth-Century Law," *Reviews in American History* (1983), 11:374–380; Carole Shammas, "Re-Assessing the Married Women's Property Acts," *Journal of Women's History* (1994), 6:9–30; and Zorina B. Khan, "Married Women's Property Laws and Female Commercial Activity: Evidence from United States Patent Records, 1790–1895," *Journal of Economic History* (1996), 56:356–388.

Another key area for reform was education. This has received far less scholarly attention than it merits. One place to begin is Patricia Smith Butcher, *Education for Equality: Women's Rights Periodicals and Higher Education, 1849–1920* (Westport, CT, 1989), although the focus here is upon the press and not education per se. For a broader study of how the press treated the question of woman's rights, see Sylvia D. Hoffert, "New York City's Penny Press and the Issue of Woman's Rights, 1848–1860" *Journalism Quarterly* (1993), 70:656–665.

Popular Notions of Womanhood and Sisterhood

The penny press is but one point of entry into the larger issue of women's place in society. A pioneering essay here is Barbara Welter's "The Cult of True Womanhood," reprinted in her *Dimity Convictions: The American Woman in the Nineteenth Century* (Athens, OH, 1976). Another extremely influential collection of essays is Carroll Smith-Rosenberg, *Disorderly Conduct: Visions of Gender in Victorian America* (New York, 1985). A review of some recent scholarship is Kathy Peiss, "Going Public: Women in Nineteenth-Century Cultural History," *American Literary History* (1991), 3:817–828. Also useful as a review is Peter W. Bardaglio, "Separate Spheres and Sisterhood in Victorian America," *Reviews in American History* (1990), 18:202–207. In addition, one should consult Linda Eisenmann, "Sisterhood and the Family Claim in Nineteenth-Century America," *History of Education Quarterly* (1989), 29:465–473.

Index